THE RAPE OF THE SABINE WOMEN

EVE SUSSMAN & THE RUFUS CORPORATION

LOUISIANA MUSEUM OF MODERN ART

PREFACE

BY DIRECTOR POUL ERIK TØJNER

With its series of small exhibitions under the overall heading Louisiana Contemporary, the museum is working to give its visitors regular presentations of some of the best works from the younger artists who are contributing to a renewal of the present art scene.

This is the eighth exhibition in the series over a three-year period, and characteristically it presents yet another work type and a form of artistic collaboration that has not been shown earlier at the Louisiana Museum. Eve Sussman's cooperation with the loosely associated group of actors, musicians, dancers etc. who call themselves The Rufus Corporation has led in their most recent co-productions to works that move beyond the now well-established form of the video installation towards the fields of film, documentary, theatre and Gesamtkunstwerk – or perhaps we should rather speak of the incorporation of elements from all these traditional and well known forms in an entirely new idiom that is none of them, but which still feels patently 'right'. Sussman herself tentatively suggests she is "a sculptor who works with film".

At present the cinematic repertoire is playing a substantial role in contemporary art. For a generation that has grown up with film as the clearest shared reference, the narrative style of film forms a background against which artists can act and react. The American artist Eve Sussman uses the medium in her expeditions into the realms of phenomenology, myth and microsociology. With her point of departure in some of the icons of art history she shoots and edits her way into situations and images that have a stylized clarity all their own. In so doing she spies out new frontiers for both film-makers and visual artists. First and foremost, her combination of improvisation and professional rigour in the execution of the finished work demonstrates the original, assured hand of the fully mature artist.

No exhibition would be possible without help from a number of people. We would like to take this opportunity to thank lenders and gallery-owners. Thanks to Galleri Bo Bjerggaard, lender, and the artist's gallery in Copenhagen (with special thanks to Britt Bjerggaard, who has also given us invaluable support for the exhibition and the catalogue. Thanks to Torben Solgaard and the Richard J. Massey Collection for their loans to the exhibition. Thanks to Hetland Nordic for sponsoring the Fatboy cushions for the exhibition. And of course, above all, thanks to Eve Sussman & The Rufus Corporation for their support and cooperation, and not least to Catherine Mahoney, Eve Sussman's Production Manager. Finally, thanks to those who continue to make these exhibitions possible – Louisiana's principal sponsor DONG, and Nykredit, whoa supports the Louisiana Contemporary series.

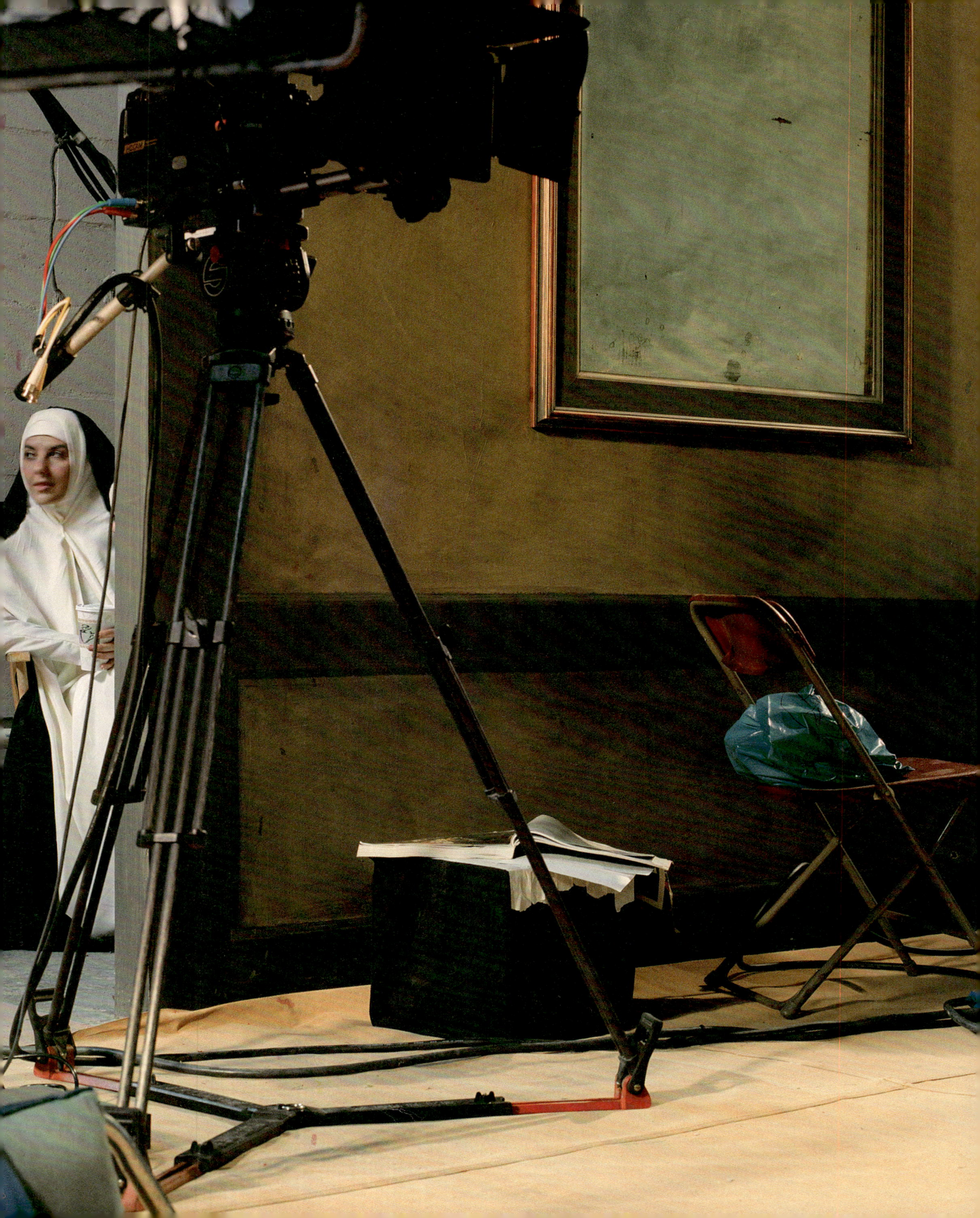

INTO ART HISTORY WITH EVE SUSSMAN ...

BY HELLE CRENZIEN

Eve Sussman literally gets into works of art. Not content to look, she has to appropriate and penetrate the history of art – to the great pleasure of the rest of us, the viewers. The history of art takes on a new dimension with Sussman: the past is aroused from its centuries of sleep and becomes living tableaux that make us look with more than ordinary interest at the works of the great masters.

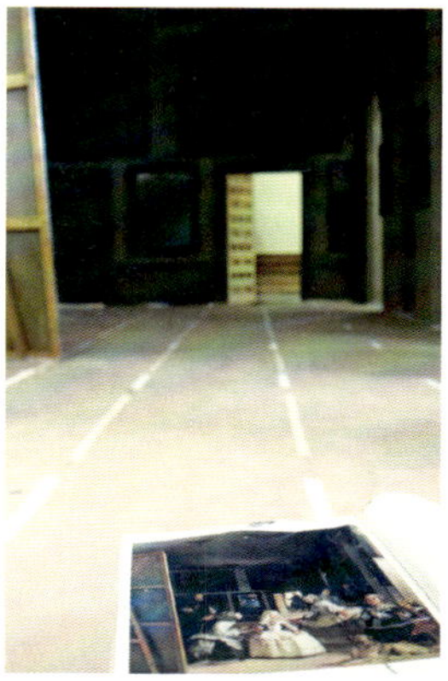

Empty Set
Production Still from
89 Seconds at Alcázar
Photo: Benedikt Partenheimer

In 2004 Eve Sussman had her big breakthrough at the Whitney Biennale in New York with the critically acclaimed *89 Seconds at Alcázar*, but there is every reason also to take a closer look at her earlier works, since throughout her career she has been moving in a direction that has so far seen high points like her recent works *89 Seconds at Alcázar* and *The Rape of the Sabine Women*. Eve Sussman's works have always focused on the visual interaction of image, viewer and surroundings, with a keen sense of suspense or expectations that was emphasized by the critics in 2004.[1] Several of the early works are site-specific and thus decidedly rooted in the surroundings. At first glance her two most recent works may not seem site-specific; and yet they are, in the sense that when they are shown, their size and staging are carefully adapted to the architectural context and the specific target group in question.

In 1997 Eve Sussman showed the installation *Ornithology* at a gallery in New York. It consisted of 12 outdoor surveillance cameras in a 2 m. wide airshaft between converted factory buildings in downtown Manhattan and recorded the life of pigeons, projected on the gallery walls. The cameras running constant live-feed produced a surveillance situation where the viewer was on guard, expectant, waiting for a 'moment' that might be missed. After a long session of cooing and flapping one might suddenly see a bird's-eye as large as the gallery wall; a pigeon had assumed a position suitably close to the camera, and the effect was monstrous, even grotesque and hilariously surprising, as our voyeurism of these vilified creatures made us and them more human.

In the same year, Sussman was invited to participate in the Istanbul Biennale curated by Rosa Martinez, where she created the site-specific installation *How to Tell the Future From the Past*. She chose the Sirkeci Train Station as her site; the

Opposite page:
Widow on the Set
Production Still from
89 Seconds at Alcázar
Photo: Benedikt Partenheimer

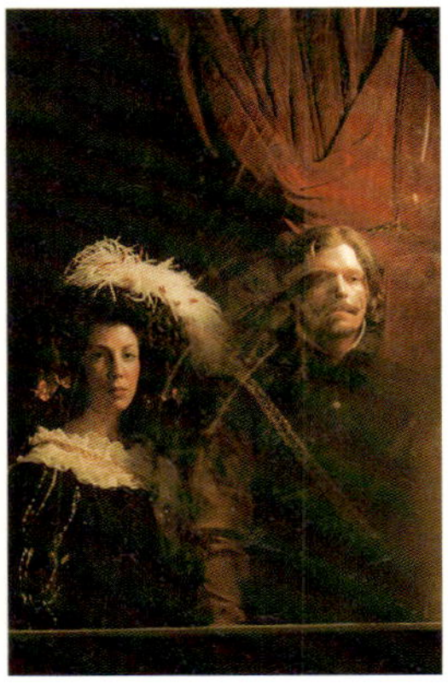

Philip & Mariana Reflected
Photographic Still from
89 Seconds at Alcázar
Photo: Benedikt Partenheimer

last stop on the Orient Express – its Orientalist architecture was a place full of history and desire. Once more she built something interactive, wiring the entire station with her own cameras. The projections mixed the live-feed with Super-8 footage and conflated these images with four stories projected in both Turkish and English. Although Sussman had made previous forays into experimental narrative this was the first in which images, text and surroundings were fused into stories where the narrative was sustained by the interaction of the viewer and one's intuitive reflex to synthesize the text we read with the pictures that pass us by.

Sussman followed *How to Tell the Future...* with another foray into experimental narrative and three-screen panoramic projection in the piece *Scenes from an Exile*. It was the first work in which she chose not to find enigmatic gestures in the cinema verité of the everyday, but to direct performers in a cinematic context.

In 2001 Sussman made a 20-minute short film titled *Solace* about everyday life during the days immediately following September 11. From her studio overlooking the Manhattan skyline she used her signature surveillance gaze and verité cinematographic style not merely to document the mood of the moment but to create metaphors for the event. Food becomes paramount. A mop hangs from a window, its strings blowing in the breeze as if it were human hair. Mixing verité with fiction, in a scripted moment, a soprano appears – performed by Kati Agocs – to sing Henry Purcell's *Music for Awhile* in the kitchen. The inhabitants, unaware of the singer's presence, continue their breakfast.

Eve Sussman was born in 1961 in London, UK. She is an American citizen, based in Brooklyn, NY. She formed the Rufus Corporation in 2004, its name inspired by a computer and an infamous evil think tank. The company's places of participation, like the participants, are always changing. Independent actors, dancers, musicians and artists have worked with the Rufus Corporation since its inception, during pre-production of *89 seconds at Alcázar*.

In *89 Seconds at Alcázar* Sussman quotes Diego Velázquez' painting as precisely and accurately as possible. *The Rape of the Sabine Women*, on the other hand, is a free interpretation of the myth, initially inspired by the painting *The Intervention of the Sabine Women* by Jacques-Louis David. Eve Sussman has been described as a "sculptor/installation artist" – and more recently sculptor turned filmmaker.

89 SECONDS AT ALCÁZAR

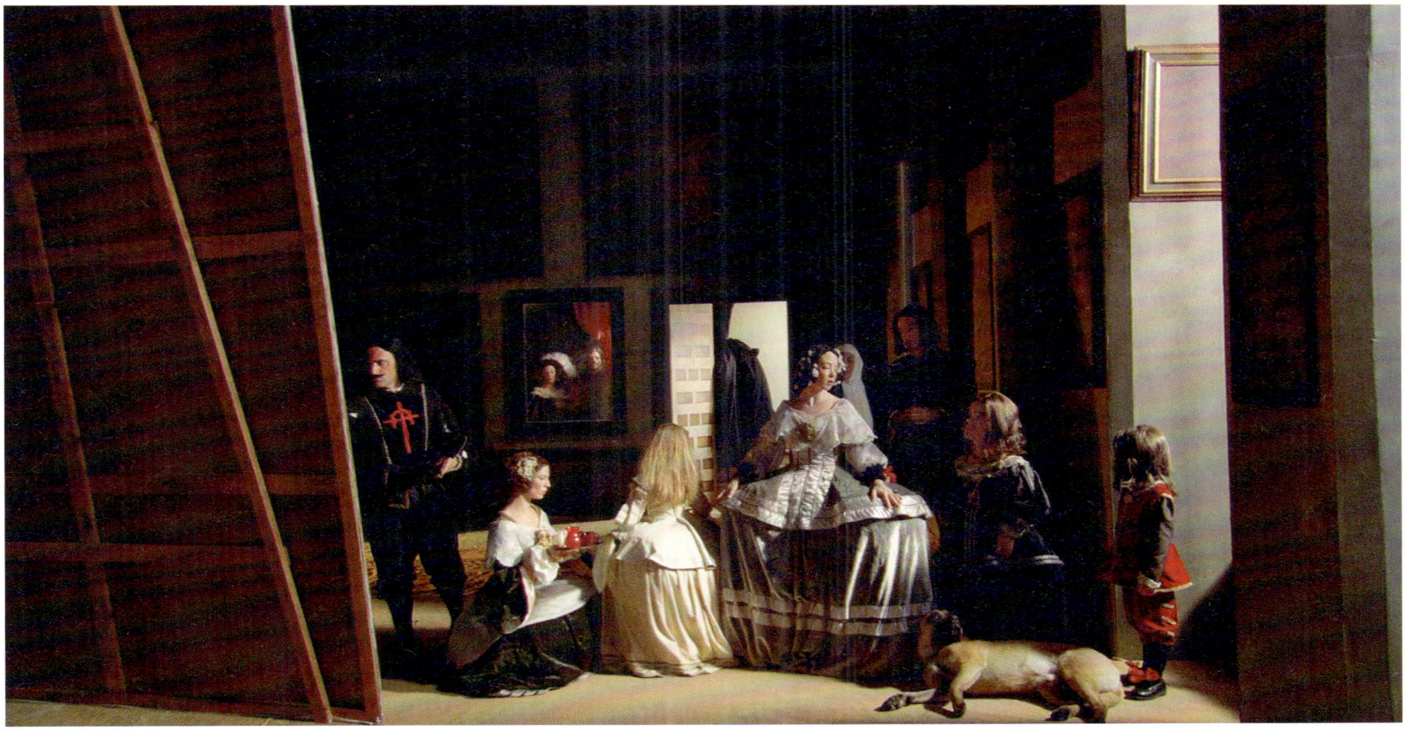

Her Back to the Camera

Video Still from *89 Seconds at Alcázar*

In 1656 the Spanish court painter Diego Velázquez (1599-1660) painted an unconventional portrait of the Spanish Royal Family. The work surprises you by looking as if an episode that took place at the palace has been 'frozen'. It is as if time stands still and the clock is stopped forever at a quite specific moment. The whole group on the canvas appears as in a snapshot. It is a virtuoso picture and a showpiece for the potential of painting – besides being a highly 'alternative' portrait of the Royal Family for that age, it is also a painting about painting, where the artist plays illusionism off against reality and conjures up a quite special relationship between the viewer and the figures depicted.

The painting shows a large room in the palace of King Philip IV of Spain in Madrid.[2] In the room are nine people from the court. Five of them are gazing out of the picture-space, towards the Royal couple or the viewer. The centre of attention is the young *infanta* (princess) Margarita, surrounded by her entourage of maids-in-waiting, bodyguards, two dwarves and a sleeping mastiff. Diagonally behind this ensemble of people, Diego Velázquez has

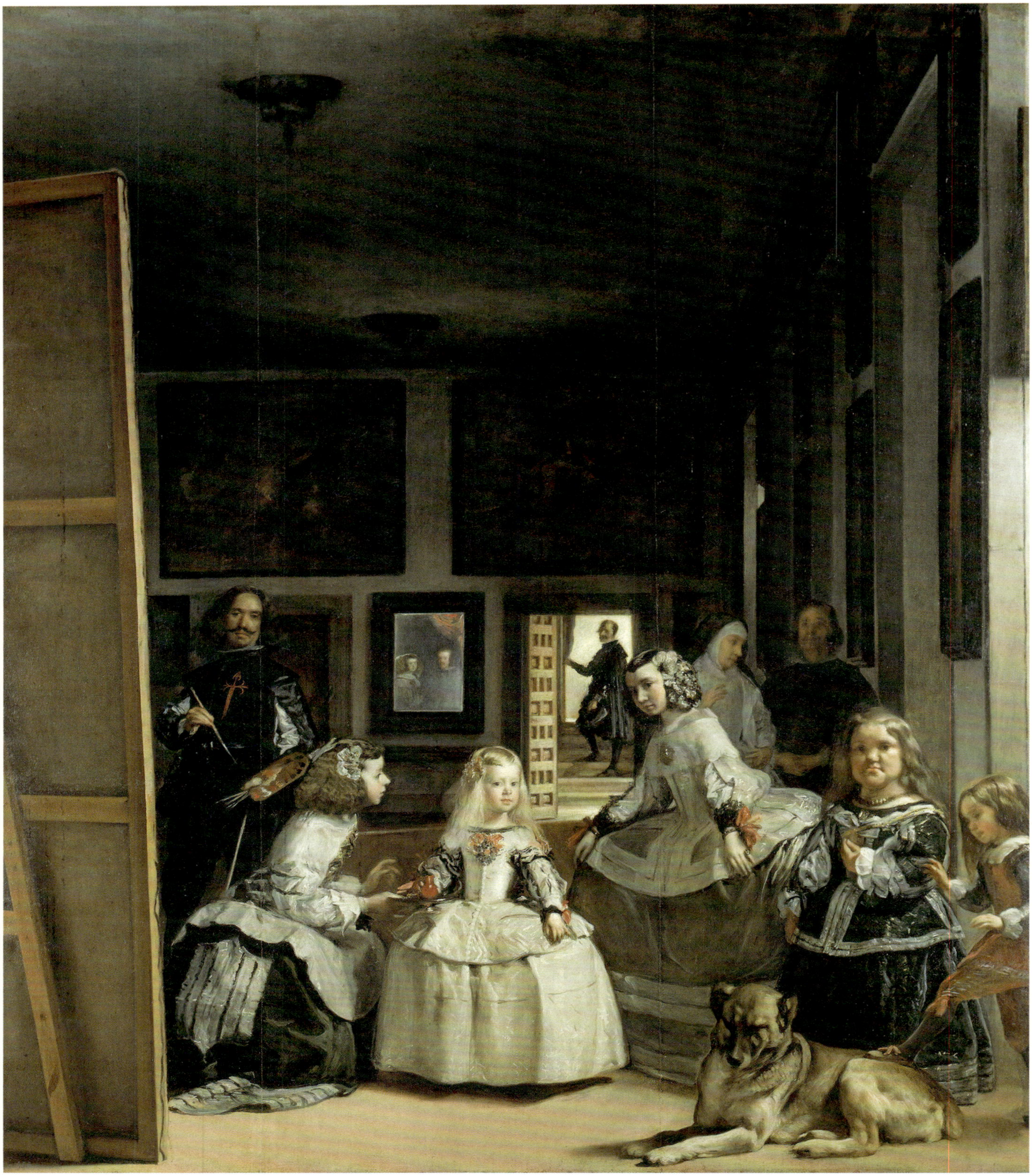

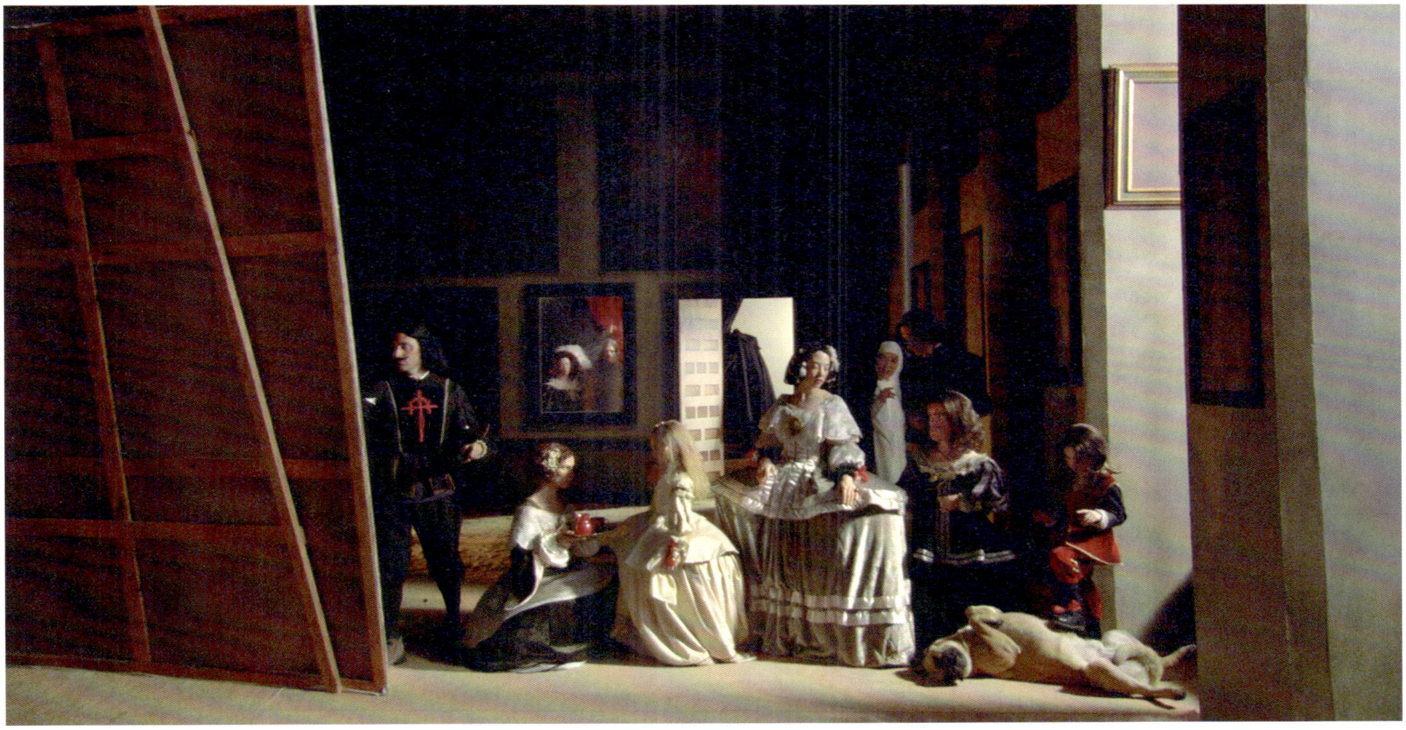

portrayed himself painting on a large canvas. The artist's gaze too extends beyond the picture-space to the point where the Royal couple – or the viewer – has been placed. In the background of the room hangs a mirror that reflects a portrait of the Royal couple. They may in fact be standing in the room, at the point from which the viewer sees the picture – or they may be a reflection of the artist's canvas.

In other words, the viewer is in the same place as the King and Queen, and in this way becomes part of the totality. One is drawn into the picture as was Eve Sussman when she saw the work at the Prado Museum in Madrid in the winter of 2000.

The title *89 Seconds at Alcázar* refers to the moments that precede – and follow – the setting-up of the gallery of characters as it looks in Velázquez' group portrait. Sussman is more interested in psychological states than in the history of art. History is only a point of departure for an investigation of how people in a group react to and with one another in a situation where apparently banal movements build up a narrative picture.

Dog Rolls
Video Still from *89 Seconds at Alcázar*

Opposite page:
Diego Velázquez
Las Meninas, 1656
Oil on canvas
318 x 276 cm
Museo Nacional del Prado, Madrid

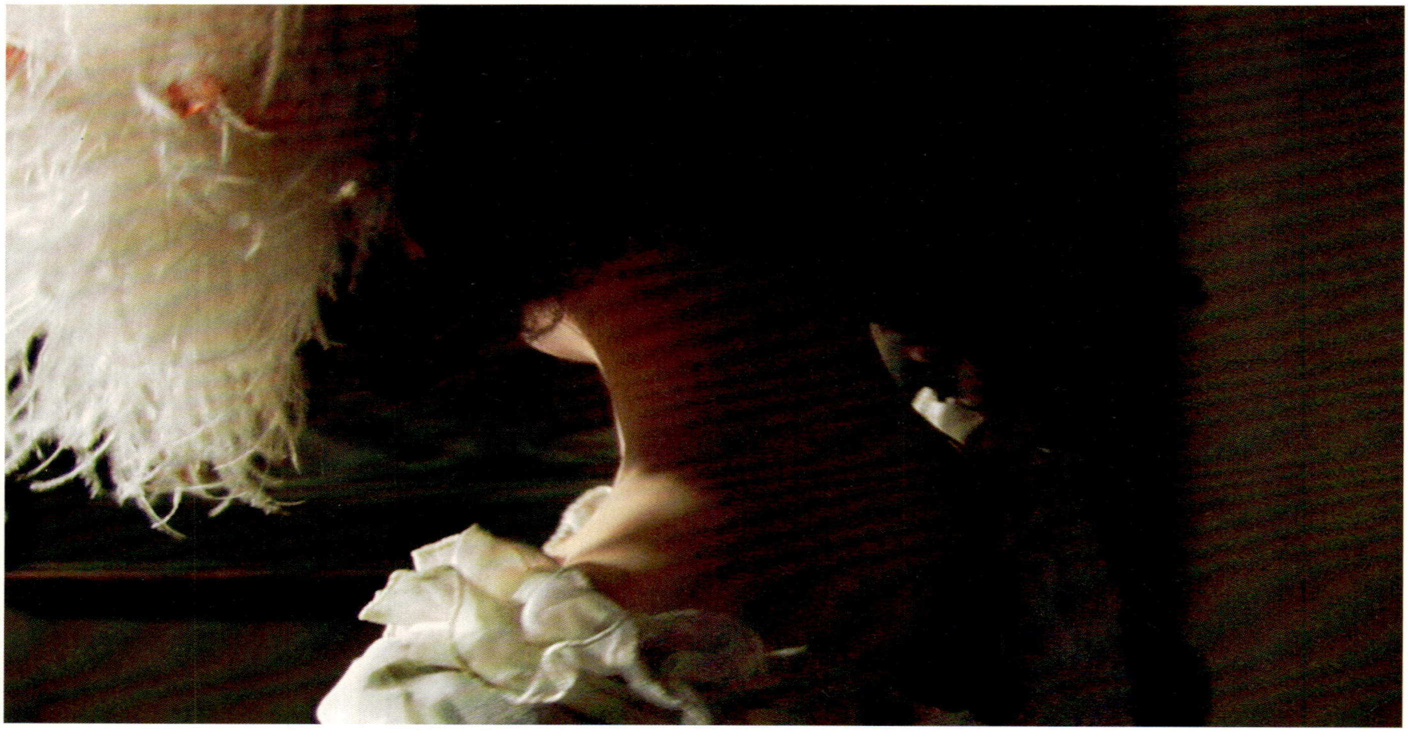

Light on Her Neck

Video Still from *89 Seconds at Alcázar*

Along with The Rufus Corporation she has choreographed, draped and staged her performance, which builds on and mimes Diego Velázquez' painting – but without showing the painting itself. It is as if Eve Sussman continues the illusionism that Velazquez already demonstrated for us in 1656.

In a 10-minute loop the viewer follows the whole episode in sound, images and movements: looks are exchanged, murmuring is heard, fire sputters, the dog growls and we hear the swishing of the drapes. The whole session was shot in a room in Brooklyn which Eve Sussman had recreated almost to the millimetre as a copy of the room in the Alcázar, and the scenes were shot at eye-level with a steadicam mounted on the shoulder of a cameraman, giving the viewer the feeling of being there in the room.

The viewer's expectations are high – when will that so-familiar picture

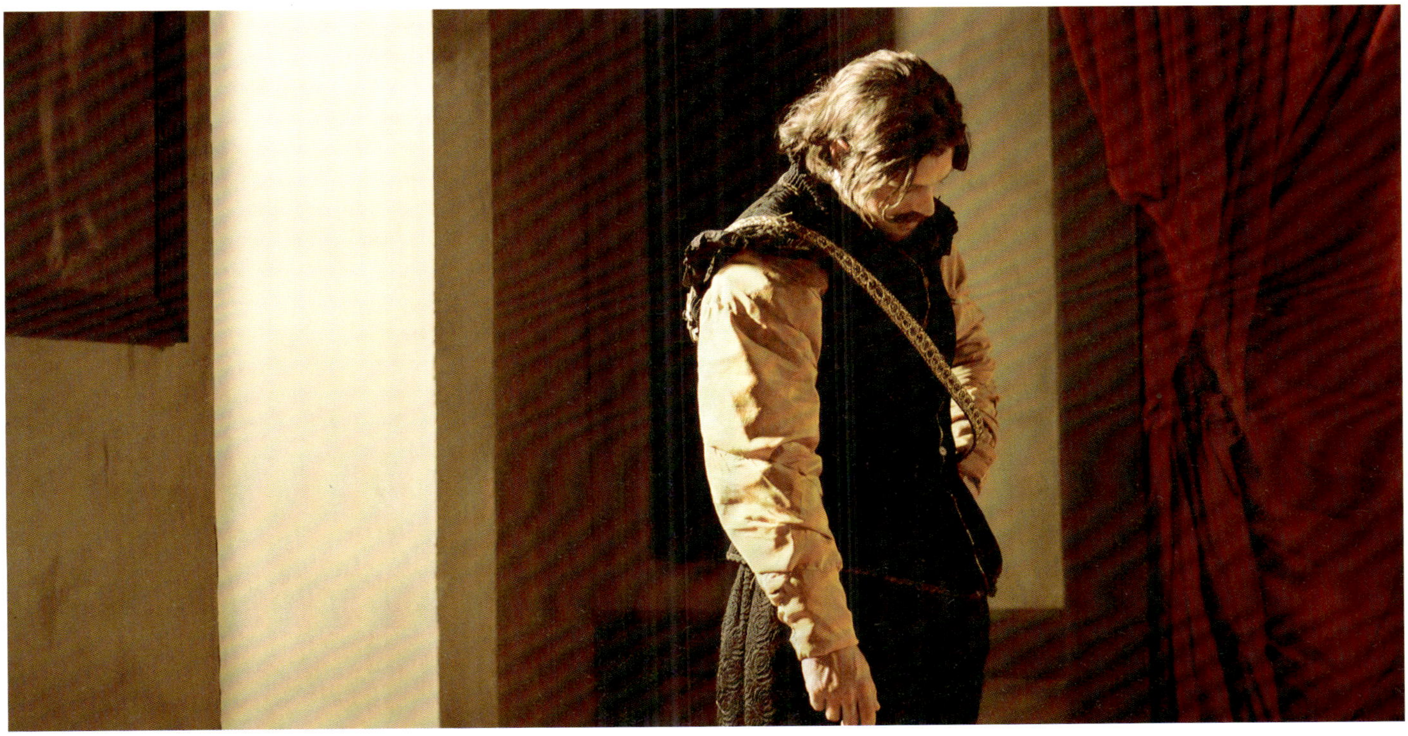

King Sleeps

Photographic Still from *89 Seconds at Alcázar*

Photo: Benedikt Partenheimer

come together, when will the ensemble be done with exchanging gazes, shifting around ... when will the little princess be quite ready? Fascinated by the whole scenario, attentively listening and visually satiated by the sumptuousness of the dresses and materials, our expectations reach a climax. But just as it seems that the picture will now freeze, it becomes blurred and the whole ensemble continues as if the 'photographing' is over. Eve Sussman teases the viewer's expectations and imagination by stressing the absence of the familiar, since she does not show Velázquez' subject in its entirety, as a frozen object, but dissolves the work and instead lets the viewer witness the process, the becoming. She turns the painting into a performance, and characteristically she gives *89 Seconds at Alcázar* an open ending. Eve Sussman is not so interested in conveying what the picture represents, but rather in clarifying how it represents.[3]

THE RAPE OF THE SABINE WOMEN

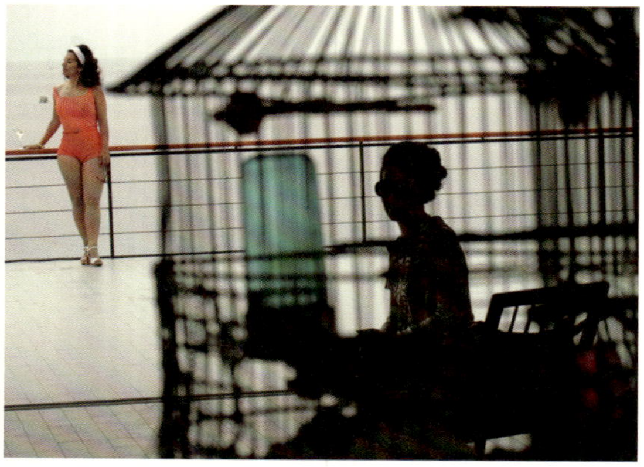

Themis in the Birdcage
Photographic Still from *The Rape of the Sabine Women*
Photo: Ricoh Gerbl

The Rape of the Sabine Women is Eve Sussman's most recent work, created in collaboration with The Rufus Corporation. It is a giant projection and sound installation, and also takes as its point of departure one of the striking works of art history, Jacques-Louis David's *The Intervention of the Sabine Women* from 1796-99. Other artists, including Nicolas Poussin, have also painted the Sabine women. But whereas Poussin paints the shameless abduction, David chooses to show the myth at a slightly later stage, when the Sabine women intervene to prevent their fathers from forcibly removing them. The story of the Sabine women is one of the myths of the foundation of the city of Rome. Once Romulus has murdered his brother Remus, and Rome is well on its way to developing into a society, it becomes clear that the town suffers from a shortage of women. Romulus invites the inhabitants of the neighbouring towns to a banquet, and in the course of the feast the Romans abduct the women who are present. The neighbouring people were known as the *Sabines,* so the event became known as *The Rape of the Sabine Women.* After years of disputes, the Sabines gathered to do battle to free the women or steal them back, but the women intervened between the battling men, and when it became clear that the women in fact did not want to return, the conclusion of the whole affair was that love won over conflict: the women were allowed to stay with their Romans.

Eve Sussman enters into the work and turns the classical painting into an 83-minute film. She visualizes the myth on which the painting is based, but renews it by transposing the story and its actors to the 1960s and adding several extra psychological layers – layers that cannot be read out of the painting, but are derived from the myth. *The Rape of the Sabine Women* was shot in Berlin at the Pergamon Museum and at the Tempelhof Airport, as well as in Greece – respectively in Athens at the local meat market, on the island of Hydra, and finally in the antique Herodion Theatre.

The inspiration from Jacques-Louis David's painting took Eve Sussman back to the original Roman myth and gave her the idea of creating a modern version of the myth, although that does not mean one can speak of an appropriation. The work was rather created with a basis in improvisation: the actors improvised with movements, cameras, music and sounds. Each location where the work was shot had its own special theme, around which the ensemble improvised before the final shoot on location.

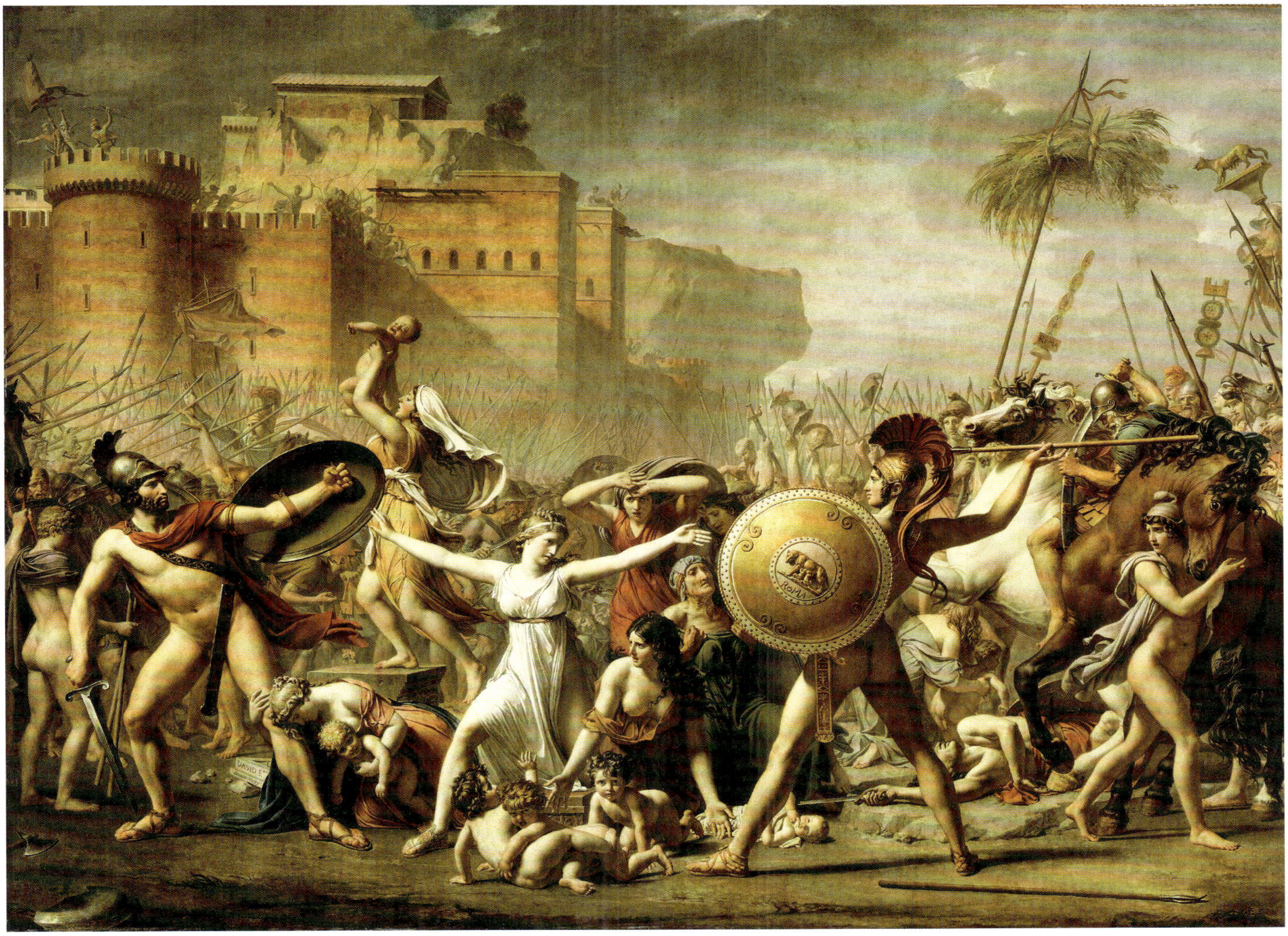

Jacques-Louis David

The Intervention of the Sabine Women, 1796-99

Oil on canvas

385 x 522 cm

Musée du Louvre, Paris

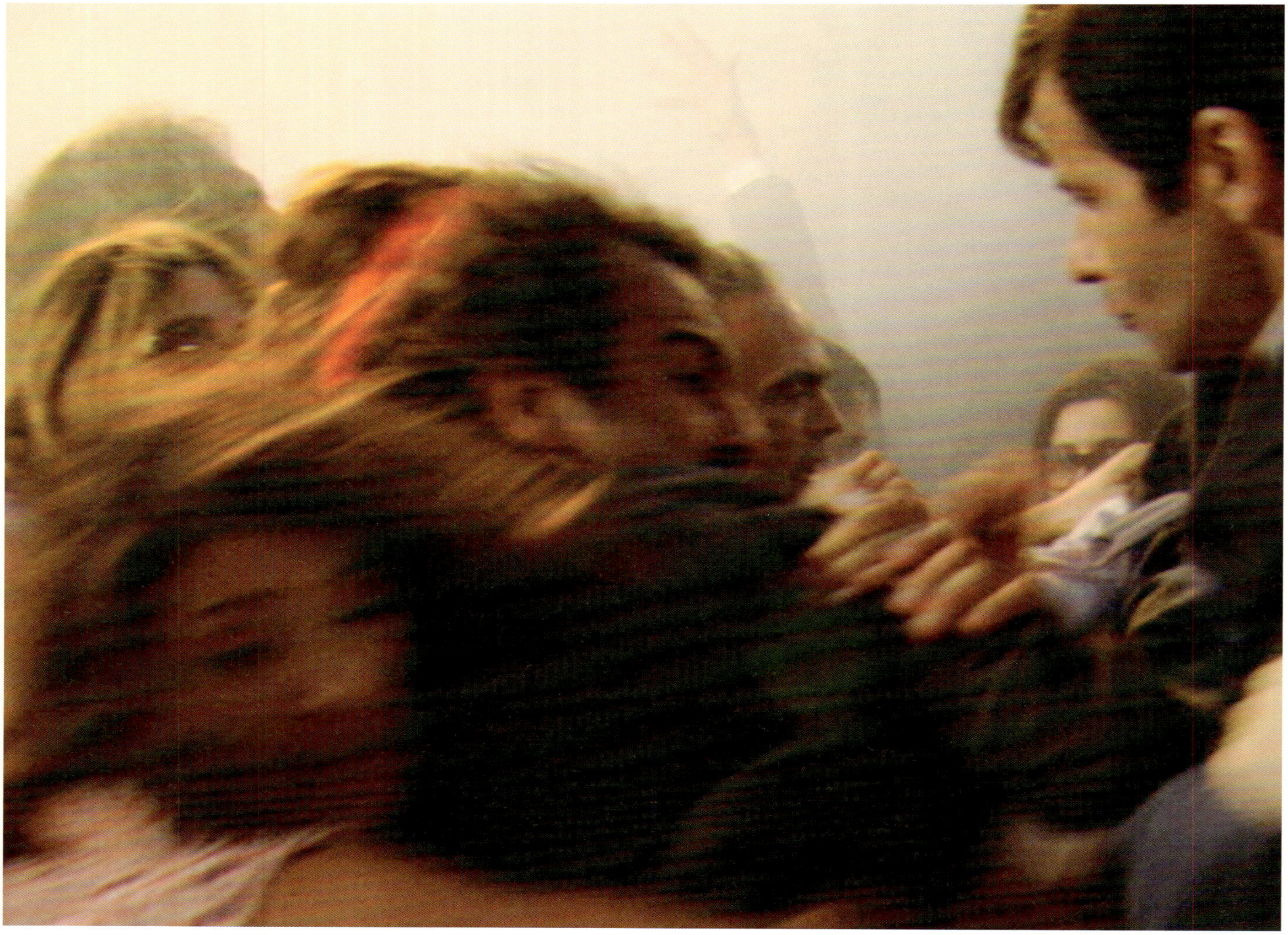

Untitled

Video Still from *The Rape of the Sabine Women*

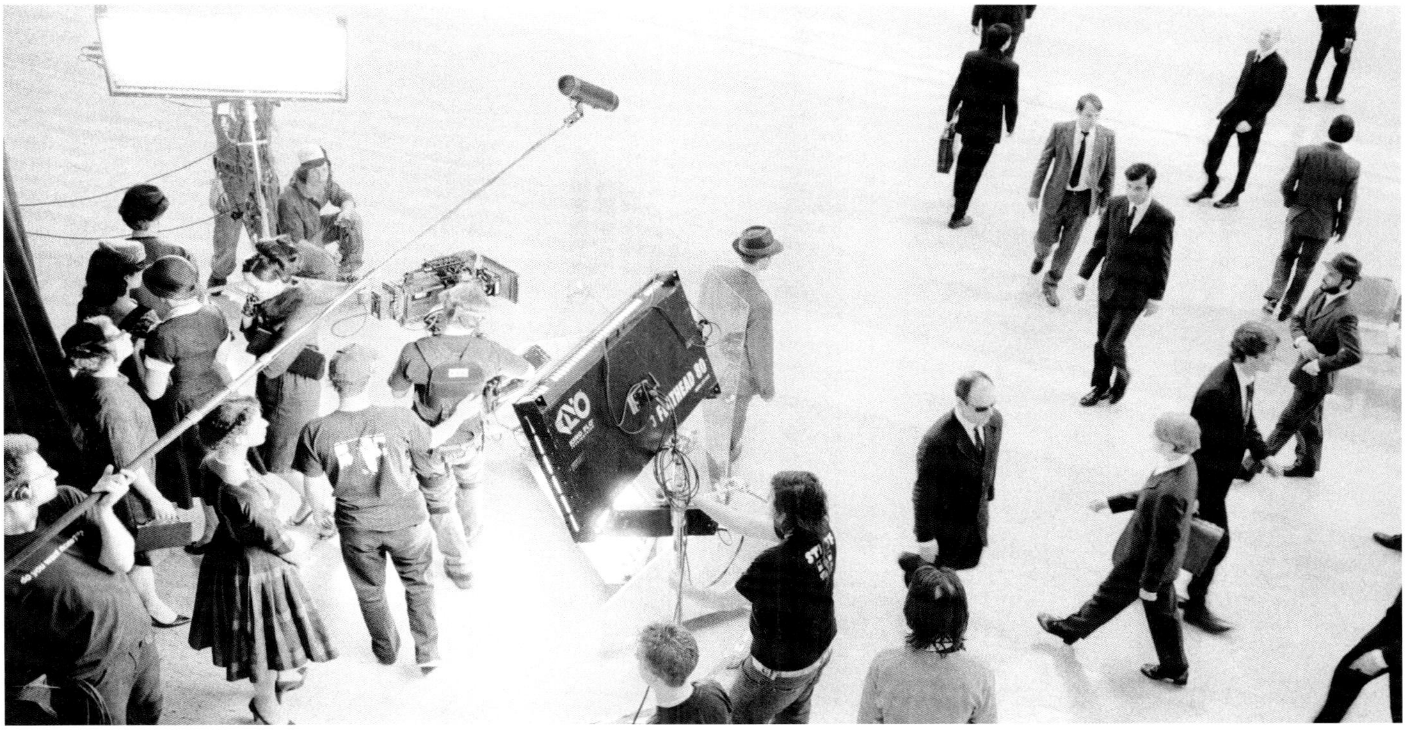

Untitled (Tempelhof)
Production Still from *The Rape of the Sabine Women*
Photo: Bobby Neel Adams

The narrative is based on five scenarios: *A Mission – Museum, A Convention – Airport, Abduction – Meat Market, Better Homes and Gardens – House, The Intervention of the Sabine Women – Theatre.* The work has no real plot, but exhibits strong pictorial or visual narrativity of a symbolic and metaphorical character, based on physical and non-verbal expression. The audio side of the work consists of sound and music recorded on location and improvised by the musicians as the filming progresses. The soundtrack is fully integrated in the work and becomes a texture that supplements the visual aspect in a way that strengthens the overall impression. The soundtrack during the abduction, for example, which takes place in the meat market in Athens, includes the sharpening – of large butchers' knives. At other points in the process there are very simple, monotone sounds performed on various instruments and in other places the sound becomes more melodious with resemblances to traditional Greek bouzouki music. The soundtrack was created by Jonathan Bepler with the musicians using bouzouki, baglamas, drums, electric guitar and bass, Bradford Reed's homemade pencilina, knives,

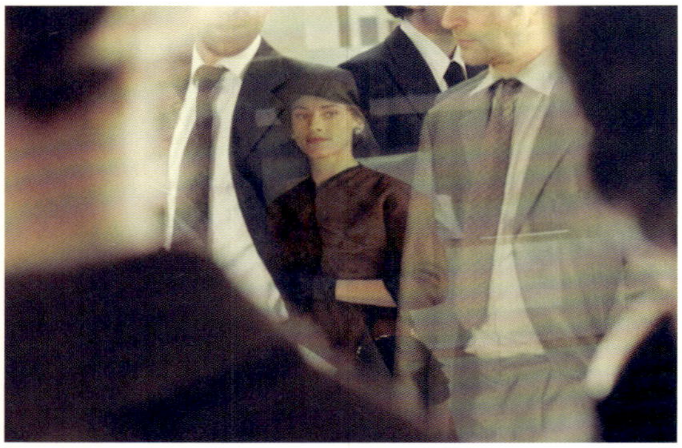

Marilisa Reflected

Production Still from *The Rape of the Sabine Women*

Photo: Ricoh Gerbl

voice and ambient and conducted sounds including the coughing choir at the Pergamon.

In the introductory scene the observer meets a number of men in suits who move around in Berlin's Pergamon Museum. In glimpses one sees the frieze on the Hellenistic altar where the battle between gods and titans is depicted (and points forward to the concluding battle in the work). The predatory nature of the men in suits is signalled by a wolf stealing through the museum (in the myth Romulus and Remus are fostered by a wolf). At the Pergamon Museum we also meet for the first time a recurring character in the form of the old custodian. He is a true mythical figure: viewer and witness, he presents the suited men with their destiny and knows the story even before it has taken place. He is a seer and an observer of the events that are played out. He is present in all the acts of the film – you see him as a custodian, as a security guard at the Tempelhof Airport, as a casual customer in the meat market, as a tourist with a camera by the villa on Hydra. At the end of the film he stands watching – indifferent, resigned to the inexorable chaos being played out in front of him.

The scene changes after the Pergamon Museum and the men go by public transport to the Tempelhof Airport, and the number of men in suits is more than doubled there. At the airport they all open their newspapers and light their cigarettes synchronously. A change of scene transports the viewer from a world of steel, marble and metal to the exact opposite, the meat market in Athens, where the butchers stand offering their wares and wielding their big, sharp butcher's knives. Quickly and efficiently a number of young women are accosted and abducted. Here too there is a single brutal scene with a violent assault in an apartment where dead rabbits and ducks are hung up as hunting trophies heavy with symbolism.

Although the work looks far back in time, with its origins in Jacques-Louis David's painting and the Roman myth, the look of Sussman's film is first and foremost a visualization of the 1950s and 1960s. The idea of having the tale unfold in this particular time frame came to the artist when her attention was drawn to the modernist architecture of Greece, which often goes unnoticed. In the awareness of people interested in cultural history and architecture, 'Greece' tends to remain *ancient* Greece. The 1960s, in Greece as well as in the western European world, was in general a time of new

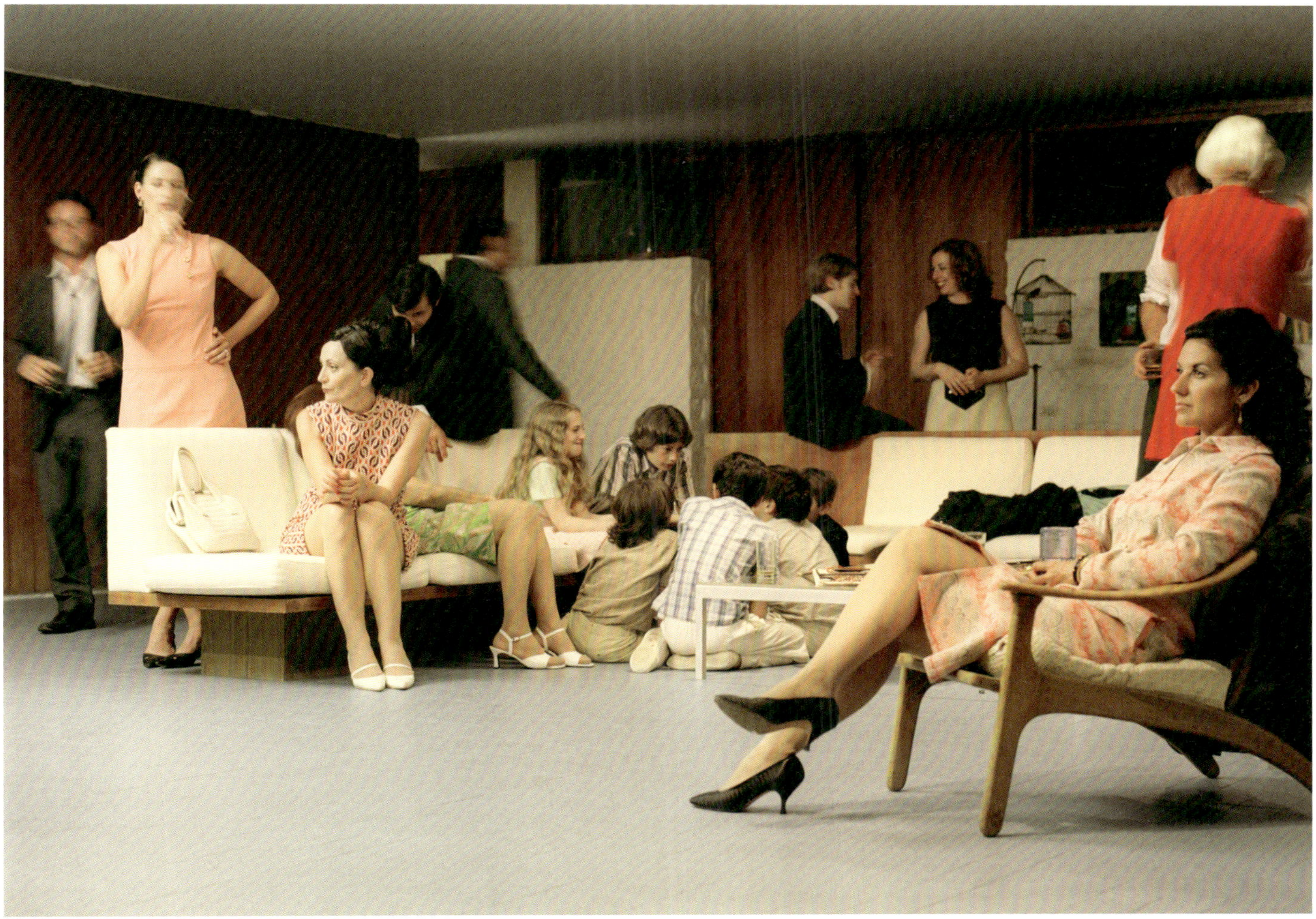

Living Room

Production Still from *The Rape of the Sabine Women*

Photo: Benedikt Partenheimer

departures – a period of pioneering experiments in architecture and design, a time when contemporary culture ranged from David Hockney's pool idylls through the fashion photography of *Vogue* to the Beat Generation and French-Italian experimental films. Eve Sussman is able to integrate all this and more in *The Rape of the Sabine Women.*

After the violent assault the men and the abducted women reappear in an affluent summer residence on the cliffs of the Aegean, time has elapsed, children appear. It is here the theme of *Better Homes and Gardens* is played out. – The house, built by renowned Greek architect Nikos Valsamakis in 1961, retains all of its original exterior and interior design, and is one of the

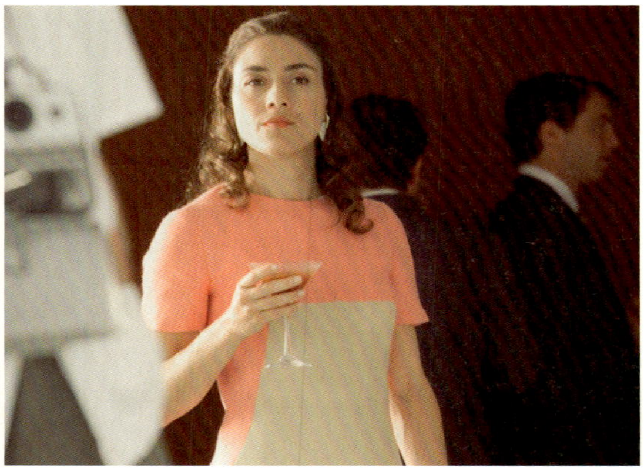

Untitled
Production Still from *The Rape of the Sabine Women*
Photo: Ricoh Gerbl

best examples of Greek-style "case-study" architecture. At first children and adults appear in a harmonious scenario. Years have passed, and the women have had children by the men who abducted them. The women are luxuriously dressed in fashionable clothes and are wearing jewellery; their nails are varnished and their hair styled. The scene is typified by a laidback 'high-society' mood. A singing bird in a cage perhaps symbolizes that the women have now become *trophy wives.* A little later in the session jealousy arises among the men and the fixed role patterns begin to crumble. In the idyll on Hydra there are already pointers to the concluding scene, which is set in the ruins of the ancient Herodion Theatre at the Acropolis. The scene has been moved from Hydra to here and becomes more and more tumultuous. Fathers and brothers who have appeared to fetch their women home confront the men who once abducted them, and the women who intervene do not have the strength and power to keep the confrontational groups apart. Everything becomes chaos, bodies twist and turn in a huge fight where no one is winning. The dust settles and like an image of the dawn of civilization and a perspective on its development, everything ends in a quagmire. No happy ending!

In the work *The Rape of the Sabine Women* the artist examines concepts like gender identity, and she has a lot to say when it comes to describing men's and women's interrelationships. With a basis in the performative strategies that thematicize the body and its various identity parameters such as gender and sexuality, Eve Sussman operates in the work with the filmed performance as a kind of manipulating observer, and in the working process she provokes the actors into interacting. In the various shots she places groups of actors together and notes the hierarchies and status clarifications that arise among people when several are gathered in one place. The interactions of the people are organic and keep developing independently of time, place and each actor's individual perception. In both *89 Seconds at Alcázar and The Rape of the Sabine Women* Eve Sussman makes use of a performative strategy where she allows great scope for improvisation in the scenes. She has her storyboard but allows the individual actors room and freedom to choose the way they act in the given scene: "...in terms of what people are doing in a specific scene the actors improvise a lot, however, there is a structure to many of the improvisations that Claudia (the choreographer) and I have come up with based on rehearsals with the actors".[4] She herself creates and maintains the overall vision that sorts the scenes/ images and composes the whole narrative side of the film project. *The Rape of the Sabine Women* is a large, ambitious project, using among other things surveillance cameras (as in some of the early works) to create a more precise overview of the entire scenario, an overview that cannot be established by the artist and her cameramen in their work behind the lens. As in *89 Seconds at Alcázar* Eve Sussman is the artistic director; she is rarely on-camera herself, and this also goes for the stills that The Rufus Corporation have produced in connection with the shooting. The cameramen and photographers are Bobby Neel Adams, Benedikt Partenheimer and Ricoh Gerbl. *The Rape of the Sabine Women* is an expansive work which in its concluding scenes involves almost 400 actors and Eve herself describes the work with scenes like this as follows: "Usually all of the photographers are shooting. Everybody's shooting. We are running two video cameras plus sometimes a film camera, three still cameras and sound recording ... It's like being in a football game or a war zone or a rock concert".[5] In her studio this very extensive material is edited in a long working process and gathered into one long sequence. To give an idea of the amount of raw material to be dealt with, there are 140 hours of video, 100 hours of music and 6000 photos.

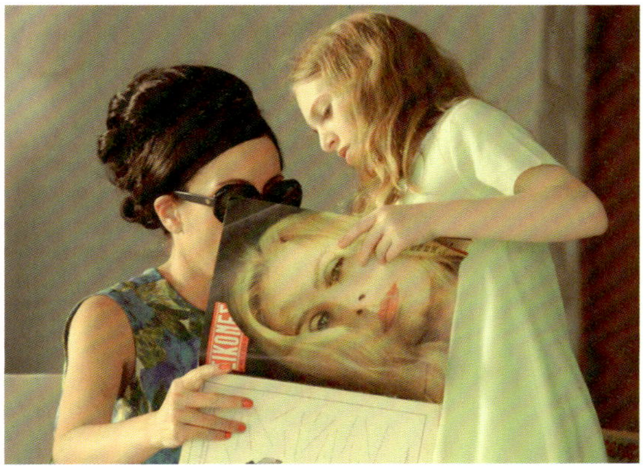

Eikones, April 1964

Production Still from *The Rape of the Sabine Women*

Photo: Ricoh Gerbl

What lies in the future? This exactly is the question that Eve Sussman and longtime Rufus Corporation collaborator Jeff Wood have posed to themselves, in what they are billing as a noir-science fiction project. The Rufus Corporation has once again taken as their starting-point another icon of art history. In 1918 the Russian artist Kasimir Malevich (1878-1935) created a 'Suprematist' composition that shocked classically trained art historians by consisting of a white square on a white ground: *White on White*. The Rufus Corporation is present involved in wide-ranging research that has taken them to undisclosed locations in Central Asia, to develop the next project, *White on White: A film noir.*

Notes:

1. Jerry Saltz, "Being There", *Village Voice*, May 12 – 18, 2004
2. In her title Eve Sussman does not use the name of the King's palace in Madrid but chooses to refer to Alcázar, which is another of the Spanish Royal Family's palaces near Seville.
3. Camilla Jalving, *Værk som handling: Performativitet som kunsthistorisk metode og tema i samtidskunsten.* PhD dissertation, Copenhagen University 2005, forthcoming.
4. Eve Sussman interviewed by Marek Claassen, Artfacts.Net 25.4.2007
5. Eve Sussman interviewed by Marek Claassen, Artfacts.Net 25.4.2007

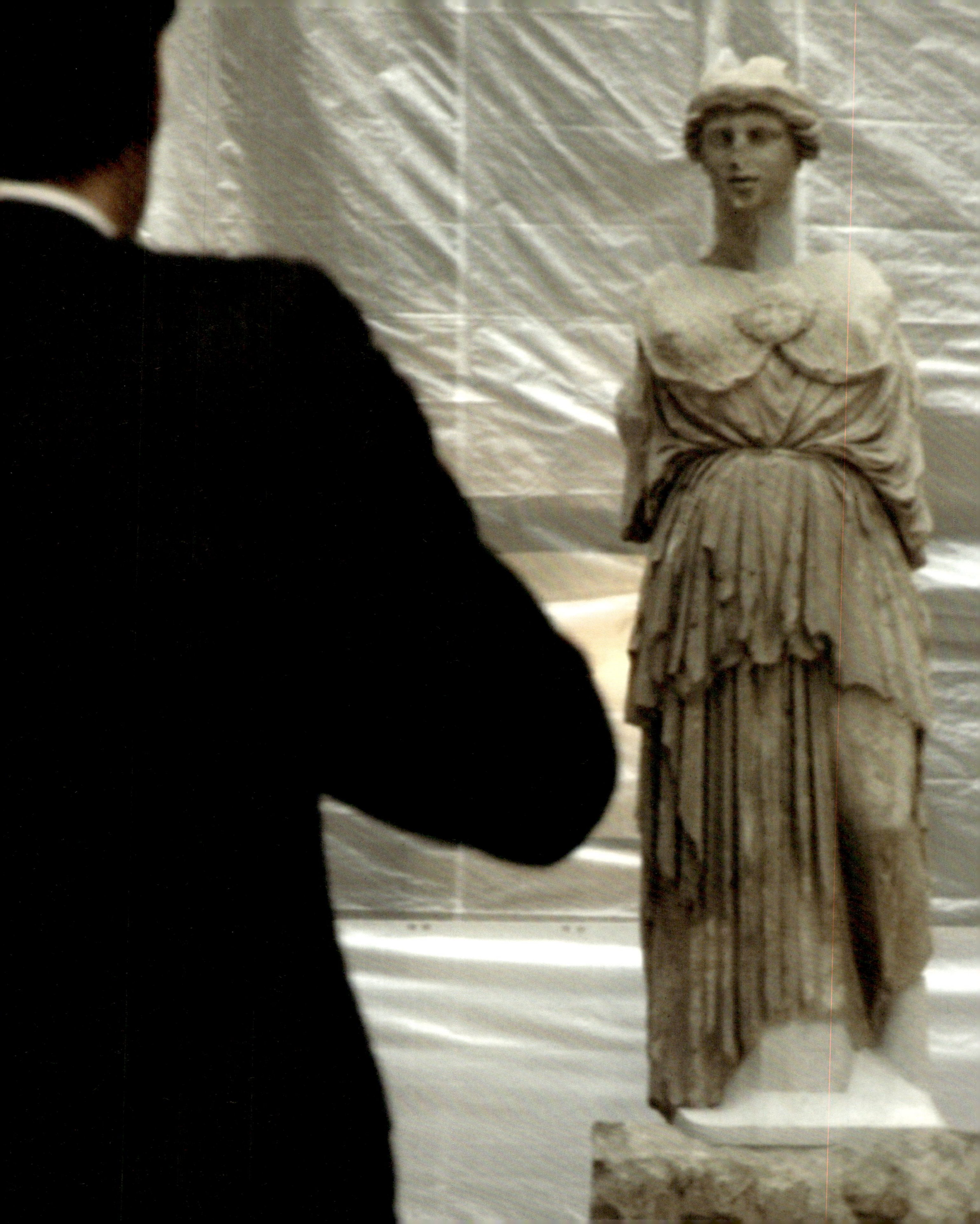

OUT OF ART HISTORY (AND INTO ALL SORTS OF OTHER HISTORIES) WITH EVE SUSSMAN & THE RUFUS CORPORATION ...

BY MICHAEL JUUL HOLM

I summon the supernatural beings / Who first contrived /
The transmogrifications / In the stuff of life. /
You did it for your own amusement. / Descend again, be pleased to reanimate /
This revival of those marvels. / Reveal now, exactly / How they were performed /
From the beginning / Up to this moment.

A lone wolf lies in front of the entrance to the imposing Pergamon Museum in Berlin. Inside, a lone wolf in the form of a youngish man in a suit, with narrowed eyes and a narrow tie, moves slowly through the otherwise almost empty space. In a focusing moment, he seems to glide out in front of, even *out of* a statue of Athene, and fills the frame. Athene, as we know, is the goddess of wisdom, art and war. And first of all we have been reminded – by the quotation above – of Ovid, who in Ted Hughes' award-winning retelling urges us to witness the return of history, to prepare ourselves for a re-enchantment and revival of the deeds and misdeeds of bygone times. Look at the picture here on the left: Athene wears her special attribute, the aegis with the head of the Medusa. Looks are exchanged. According to tradition, anyone who looks Medusa in the eye is turned into stone, but in this case we are to witness the opposite: a life-giving gaze. 'De-petrification', reanimation. And then, finally, there is the title – the key. Perhaps.

So if I note, that Eve Sussman's one-hour, 23-minute long filmic video work *The Rape of the Sabine Women* takes its point of departure in mythological material, I have, at least, not said too much.

In fact, I've said a little too little.

For what does it mean in this context to have a 'point of departure'? It means, figuratively, that you start somewhere: the point of departure is the base from which something develops, unravels or unfolds; the point of departure is a determinant of this unfolding.

But there is also a slightly different way of understanding the phenomenon, 'point of departure' – as a jumping-off point, a place you simply leave or abandon. Jumping off the diving board, a ledge, abandoning ship, are irreversible actions. In

Opposite page:
Untitled
Video Still from
The Rape of the Sabine Women

that sense the point of departure is a transitive figure. The better the take-off the longer the leap or movement, the greater the final distance from the starting-point

The Rufus Corporation's *The Rape of the Sabine Women* (unlike their previous one, which dealt with the famous Velázquez painting *Las Meninas*) is from the outset not only tied to a myth but is completely interwoven with mythology.

And it unfolds as an unravelling of its mythological cocoon. As the yarn unwinds, it accelerates away from its point of departure, whose role has been to determine the direction of the journey, as the booster rocket sets the course of the spaceship into outer space.

Usually we associate myth with a meaning and a moral: myths bear the narratives of cultures. Myths edify, their succinct form communicating a shared experience or explanation of success (or failure – and thus a reversed recipe for success); in this case the story of how the Roman Empire could expand into a world power by integrating the surrounding peoples.

Here is a myth that bears its own dissolution within itself; and that is exactly what is slowly made clear to us, not as a point, but as a method.

The balance of terror

Elsewhere in this catalogue you can read about the Roman foundation myth, the bold mass bride-stealing that enabled Romulus' warriors to procreate and have descendants with women from the surrounding Sabine towns. The myth is familiar – the practice to which it refers – bride-stealing – is also widely known from a long succession of historical cultures and periods.

However, it involves an ambivalence, and is constantly in the process of disintegrating, for right beneath the positive interpretation I gave above, lies another, equally powerful one. According to this narrative a primal act of violence lies at the foundation of civilization; indeed, one could say that the civilized world, in the self-understanding of the Romans, was quite literally and specifically *derived* from this *Ur*-violence (although not, as one might think, from sexual assault; the word 'rape' here is etymologically closer to rob, raptor, rapacious; in other words it means stealing, snatching, or as in rapture, to be carried away – not raping in the modern sense).

Sussman has not only been inspired by the Roman myth; her first entry point to this remarkable tale of the domestication of the alien – the mother of all integration stories, you could say – comes not from the Roman historian Livy's history *Ab Urbe Condita*, but from the French Revolutionary painter Jacques-Louis David. It is from his painting (reproduced on p. 13), that Sussman & The Rufus Corporation's film work has borrowed its fundamental drama. The painting does not exactly show the harmony between peoples reconciled by women; it is rather a snapshot of the balance of terror between opposing powers. The spears are raised, but not yet thrown. The atmosphere is fraught, the violence is only just held in check by the threat of counter-violence.

What's in a name?

While romances, novels, plays and poems, as early as antiquity and at least since the Middle Ages, have had titles that could help to prepare the reader for a point, function as didactic reading instructions, a great number of the titles of allegorical works of visual art that we know today are attached to the works by art historians far later. One exception to this was in fact the history painting, which after all was meant to (also) depict specific events like the Last Day of Pompeii or … the rape of the Sabine women. Only relatively recently (viewed in the longer perspective that this particular title suggests) has the naming of a work grown into an active element among the visual artist's resources.

Sussman's choice of title tells us this much: that there are strands in this story that can be meaningfully followed up with David's painting and Livy's and others' accounts in mind. Certain basic manoeuvres take place between women and men in these neo-, semi- and fully classical settings (besides the Pergamon Museum they are Tempelhof (Temple Courtyard!) Airport in Berlin, the meat market in Athens, a sixties-modernist luxury villa built into the cliffs of Anavissos on the Agean, and finally the classical Herodeon Amphitheatre at the Acropolis in Athens). All these can perhaps be grasped more quickly if one has the original story at the back of one's mind.

This, then, is in part what the work is 'about': the title first points to an outline of the course of events (the myth); and afterwards, given the linkage with the quote from Ovid, the opening scene and the more modern surroundings, more abstractly to a theme we might call 'How can mythical material be brought to life for modern people?' or 'Can we make ourselves contemporaries of the past?'. Any modern work that was given this title would immediately become the object of a gaze of this kind. So what do I mean by saying that the work is *unravelled* from its mythical origin?

Crime scene

It isn't as if we actually lose our bearings at any point. On the contrary … the great thing about The Rufus Corporation's work is precisely that the threads leading back to the point of departure and the myth continue to be there, in the warp and woof. The story is told.

But while the entertaining, suspenseful and visually beautiful dramatization of Livy's and Plutarch's words unfolds as re-enactment and as modern morality from some non-specific 'sixties', a number of smaller, so to speak local (also in the sense that they are actually tied to certain places) histories or simply motifs appear on stage and steal the scene.

For example, let's look a little more closely at the setting that the title already proclaims as the original crime scene. We are in a meat market and some viewers will quickly note that the action has now shifted (by way of the German subway!) to Greece; the labels on the goods are written in the Greek alphabet, and the sound of the butchers sharpening their knives pulsates in a kind of call-and-response with women's voices praising the wares: *Malako! Malako!* (Tender! Tender!), they shout ...

Among the many cuts of meat on the counters and the flayed animal carcasses on hooks, the camera sporadically follows a few young women who are out shopping; they are the ones who are going to be abducted, lightning-fast, in flashes, as stylized violence or as a less hostile takeover when one woman quite literally changes hands. The meat market is already so intensely present that as a scenario it transcends any symbolic coupling, however obvious, of death, flesh and sex: we are simply fascinated by the place and its teeming life of its own, displayed by a sauntering camera at chest height.

In a back room, something much more dramatic is going on. We think it is a back room of the meat market, for hares and ducks are hanging there to mature, but is it possible that it is a quite different place – an outhouse, a shed, a more remote place where no one can come to their aid?

By all appearances it looks as though a woman is being raped, or perhaps one should be content to say violence is part of the game. The situation in the stuffy little place is hard to work out; everything is registered very objectively: the woman is pursued into a corner, grabbed, thrown around on the floor, intercourse is accomplished – (or is it?), she resists but seems to give up and let it happen. There is a kind of mute pathos about the scene, both parties make conventional silent-film-like gestures of sorrow, but not really of unhappiness. What are we witnessing?

Is it a private act, a recurrent game between the two? A playing-through of something eternally human, a hint at the dark side of the myth, a seasoning of the main dish, so to speak? I think we can say that this is where the work prepares to pick apart the myth, which is finally allowed to disintegrate into its possible layers; violence, passion and the new order are compacted together in the smallest, most wretched room of the film – here we have dead animals, dirty dishes and washing, a bricked-up door, domestic, closed and timeless – only to move apart into their separate strands later.

Dismembering the animal

By having the players in The Rufus Corporation act through small sketch-like scenes like this, which *could* be part of a 'modern production' of the drama of the Sabine women – but which by no means has to be – and following them with fixed, handheld and automatic (surveillance) cameras, Sussman takes her leave of the myth by digging down *into* it.

With footage of an overwhelming array of precisely designed, choreographed theatrical material, she edits her way to a mythological toolbox. She uses a well known myth that has already been interpreted by visual art in several variants to show, not so much her own version of an interpretation, as, more basically, what a myth actually is. What we observe is a kind of dissection in which the animal is first cut up anatomically into muscles, organs etc., later physiologically as cross-sections of these parts to see more accurately how they work inside. Myths are verbalizations of fundamental conditions, but the fundamental conditions have their own fundamental elements: building-blocks, cells, molecules, elementary particles.

So one can easily point to themes in the work that only relate vaguely to the model in (art) history. The theme of travel/movement/encounter is struck up before the story begins at all; in a small prelude we see the players – in several meanings of the word – moving towards a meeting-place. It is clear that the meeting of the Romans with the Sabines and the other surrounding peoples (and we must remember that at this point the Romans were in fact not a people, simply a motley crew of warriors from several peoples) represents a kind of 'culture clash'. But the video work's journey back through the history of civilization from Berlin to Athens to the Greek islands, by air, sea and rail, is more of a meta-layer that perhaps has something to do with re-animation: so, precisely so, can we be made contemporary with the past. But that is already out on the fringes of interpretation. What we in fact experience is that something is going on with motion, trade, traffic – perhaps even 'trafficking'. Comings and goings – *Verkehr,* the Germans would say with a suitably comprehensive expression.

Right from the beginning we meet the theme *man* (well, wolf … as man) *versus space* – or *in* space. The architectures chosen, the grand fantastic ones and the one little dirty room we are in, each give rise to a wealth of reflections (not necessarily intellectual ones – sometimes real reflections like echoes etc.) related to mankind's relationship with space: the way we move through space (synchronized, sauntering, adapted to 'the other' with whom we are not actually together in any real sense; shuffling, anticipating, focusing on prey, etc.) or the way we sense places spatially (as fall, volume, plateau, delimitation) and psychologically (shelter, trap, home, anonymous public space).

The interwoven production shots and scenes with players preparing themselves, the grainy focuses that give us the camera's unfiltered 'gaze' at things, the visual stage directions etc., all form an independent layer insisting that what we are experiencing is a construct – they work like Brecht's signboards lowered in front of the audience with words like "Don't stare so romantically!" – and the different lightings and effects make it clear right up on the surface that this is not a 'film' film, but a work of art edited together.

A split second of happiness

So what levels of interest are invested in the work along the way? How much are we shifted up and down in scale? Can we set up a kind of typology, perhaps even a hierarchical syntax? As we have seen, the myth, the basic narrative is there all the time as superstructure. But from this

1) Olympian level we zoom in and out towards

2) another level of myth, that is the 'modern myths' of style, (self)presentation, coolness, organization, monastic isolation between people, designed life. The surveillance gaze and the objectifying shots as a whole – disinterested, clinical, alien – point with great stylistic assurance in the domestic scenes (it is here – that is at the level of the superstructure, the myth, the overarching narrative, that the women are domesticated and become mothers, housewives, passive trophies and thus Roman women, no longer Sabine women) to the whole twentieth century's globalized dream of merging the good life and perfected style in the phenomenon that has become known as 'lifestyle', with all it has to offer of quasi-happiness. The cover of this book shows the only moment in the film when quasi-happiness *can* be seen for a split second (before it is broken by the emergence of the 'triangle') with some good will as (true) happiness.

3) Studies of social and psychological interactions; microsociological 'games' among the actors involved, exchanges of looks worthy of a Bergman film, a kind of pre-verbal lexicon of body-language relations.

4) A level of almost pure aesthetic revival: of Nouveau Vague film, art-histori-

cal, modernist architectural details, for example, from Ernst Sagebiel's Tempelhof; of the sixties with designs by Gio Ponti, Joe Colombo and Jean Prouvé; of the phenomenon 'Balkan' (which we can now hardly pronounce without the appendage 'War'); of the mass grave or the moment just before that, the fall.

5) And not least, a level of purely sensory phenomenology all the way down at the tactile level; the camera's palpation of surfaces, dissolves, the sea viewed from a distance, a sun-drenched wall. How does it look? How close can we get? How near away?

Soundtracks

What are the elements that permit this curious wandering from the narrative superstructure to its nooks and crannies and visual peripheries? Why are we so captivated by what we see *now* that the overall framing of the myth seems to be elevated out of sight, out of mind for a while?

I think it is mostly because of what we cannot see. The invisible hand: the temporality, the overall extent of the work and its sequential division into places, acts, scenes – and not least the sound, the music.

Right from the waking-up soundtrack of the first few minutes, the Mauricio Kagel-inspired coughing, throat-clearing, polyphonic breathing of life into the petrified heroes and gods who slowly glide into semi-cacophonous chanting or modernist Luigi Nono-like mixed choir – and from there to a number of well known cinematographic sound effects such as the chopping sound of a helicopter rotor, the subsonically and submarinely undulating voices from afar and real sounds mixed with acoustic instruments, the soundtrack is a whole work in its own right, and unlike the freehand drawing of the images it is kept strictly within a rule-bound syntax we know by heart, mainly from film. If we do not sense which kind of interest is appropriate to which scenes, it is because the sound hasn't been turned up properly.

What more? Throughout the work we are constantly met by the same spectator – a witness, a narrator, a chronicler or the Angel of History, perhaps. Standing with his back to the future, his face turned to the constantly reanimated history. That is how the last image fades out. Myths are always about good and evil; this one is about both, and this work's treatment of myth illustrates in images and sound that, in the words of Jean Baudrillard, evil is there, everywhere, as an obscure object of desire. But also that "... it is the world itself which resists domination."[1] From the beginning, up to this moment.

1 Jean Baudrillard: *The Spirit of Terrorism*; original **L'esprit du terrorisme**, *Le Monde*, October 11 2001.

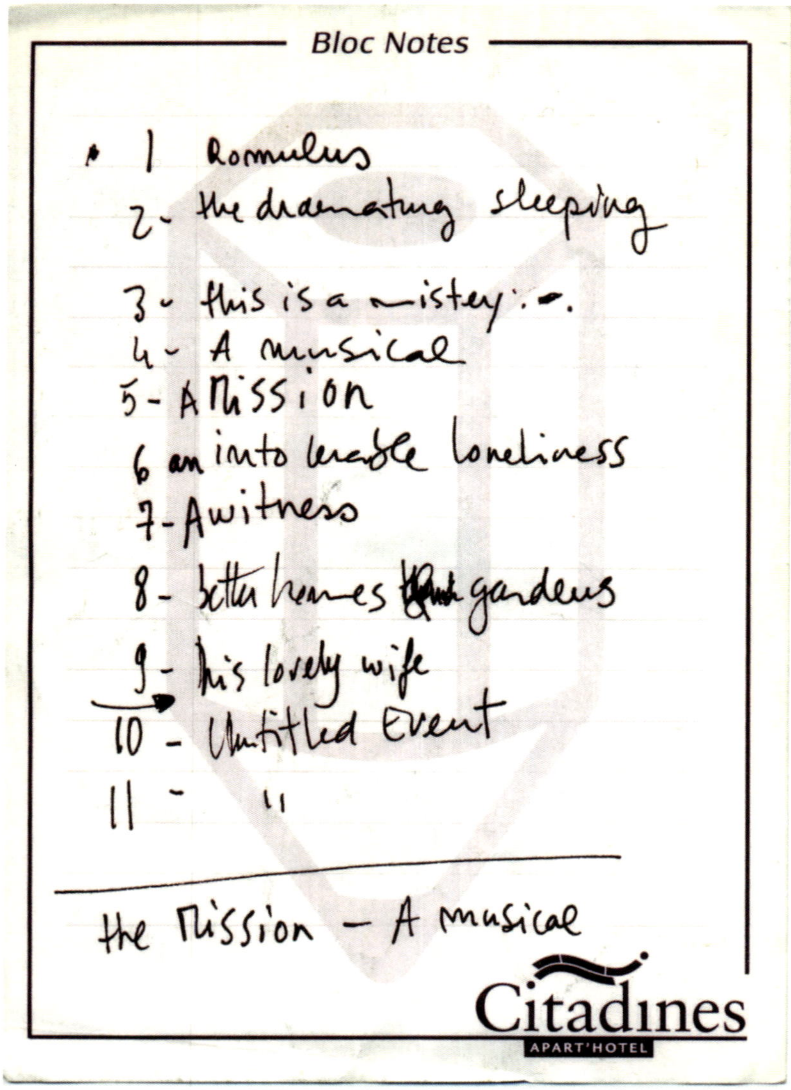
Bloc Notes

1 Romulus
2- the dreaming sleeping
3- this is a mistery.
4- A musical
5- A Mission
6 an intolerable loneliness
7- A witness
8- better homes ~~than~~ gardens
9- his lovely wife
10 - Untitled Event
11 - "

the Mission – A musical

**...You did it for your own amusement.
Descend again, be pleased to reanimate
this revival of those marvels.
Reveal, now, exactly how they were performed
from the beginning
up to this moment.**

Tales from Ovid, Ted Hughes

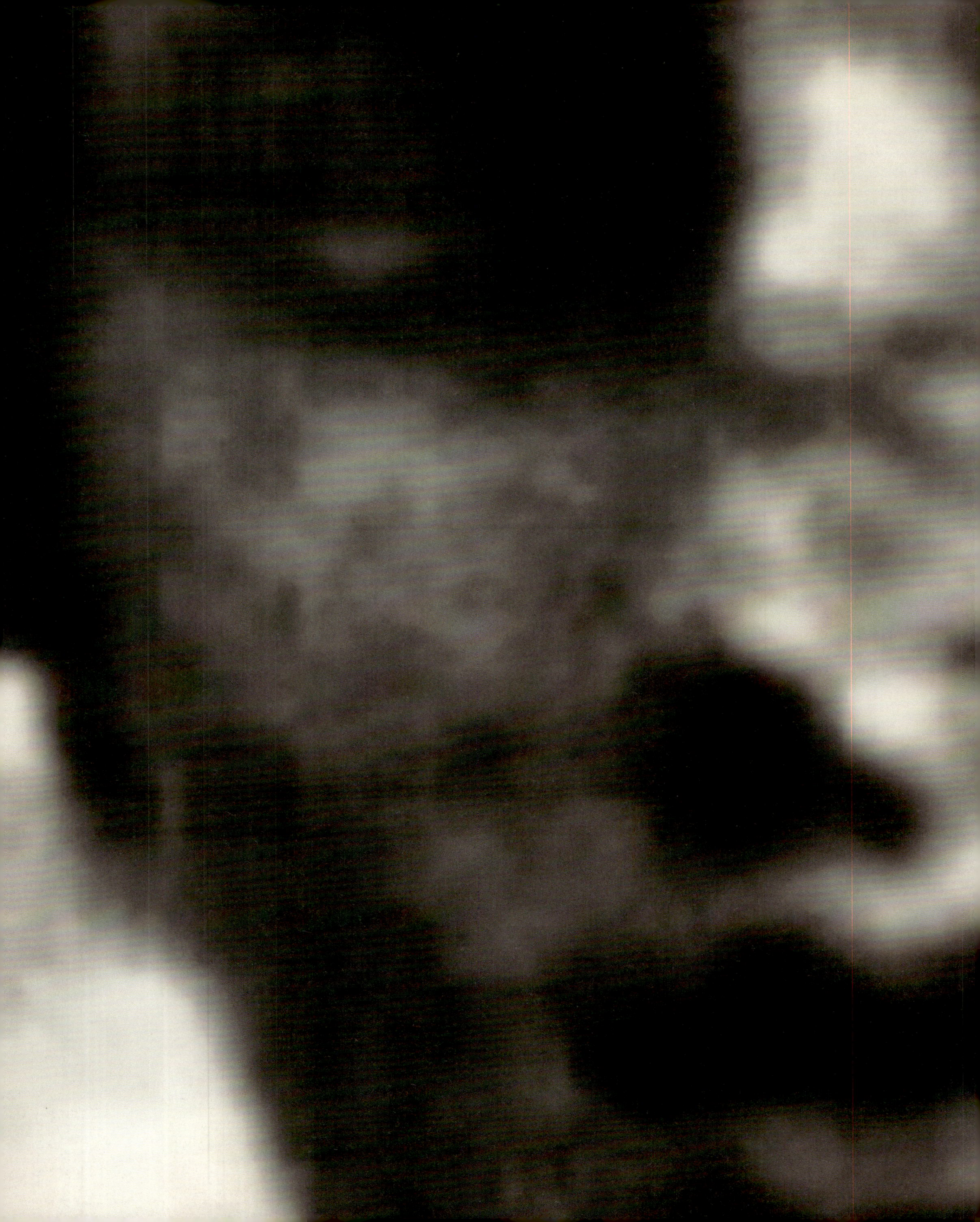

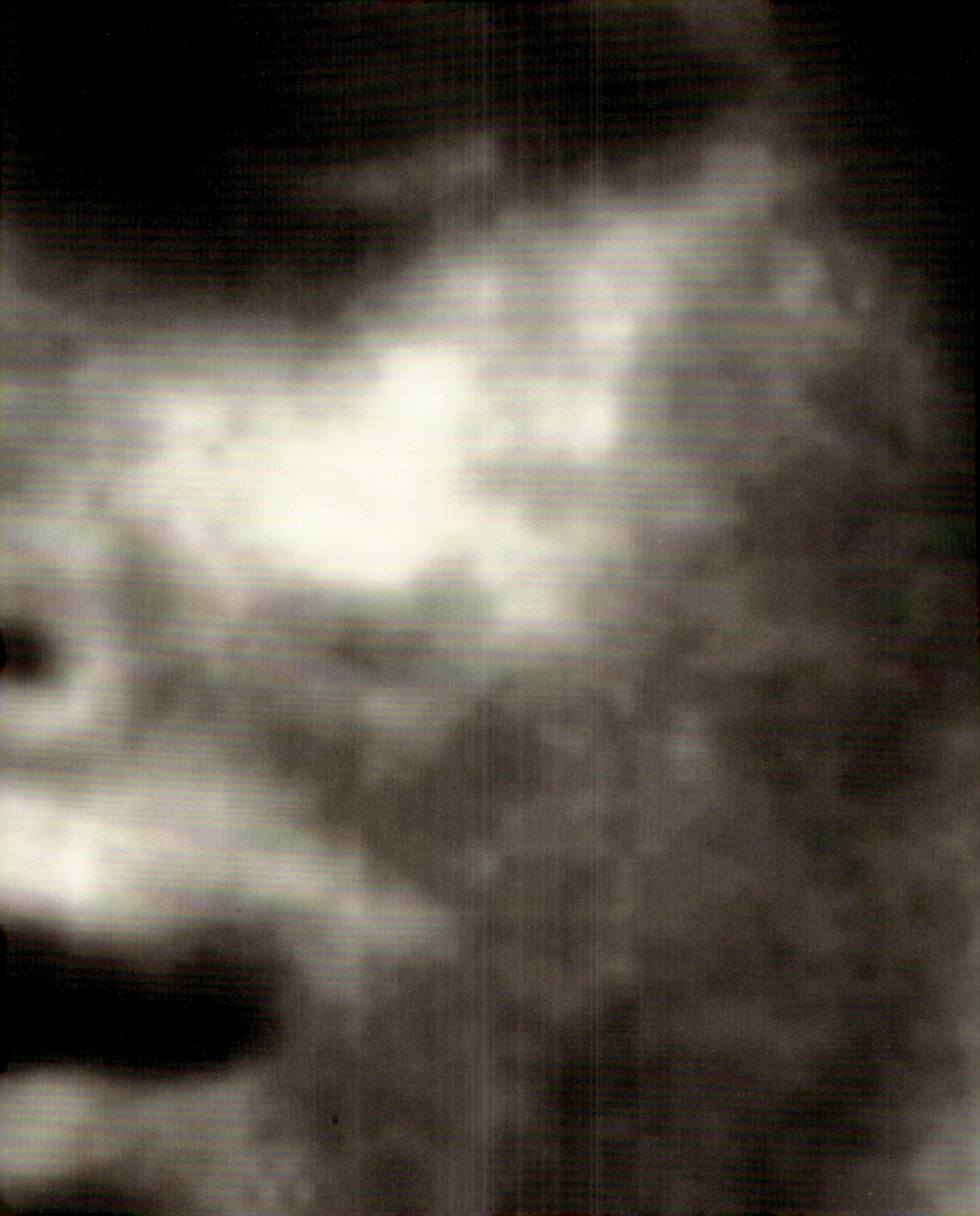

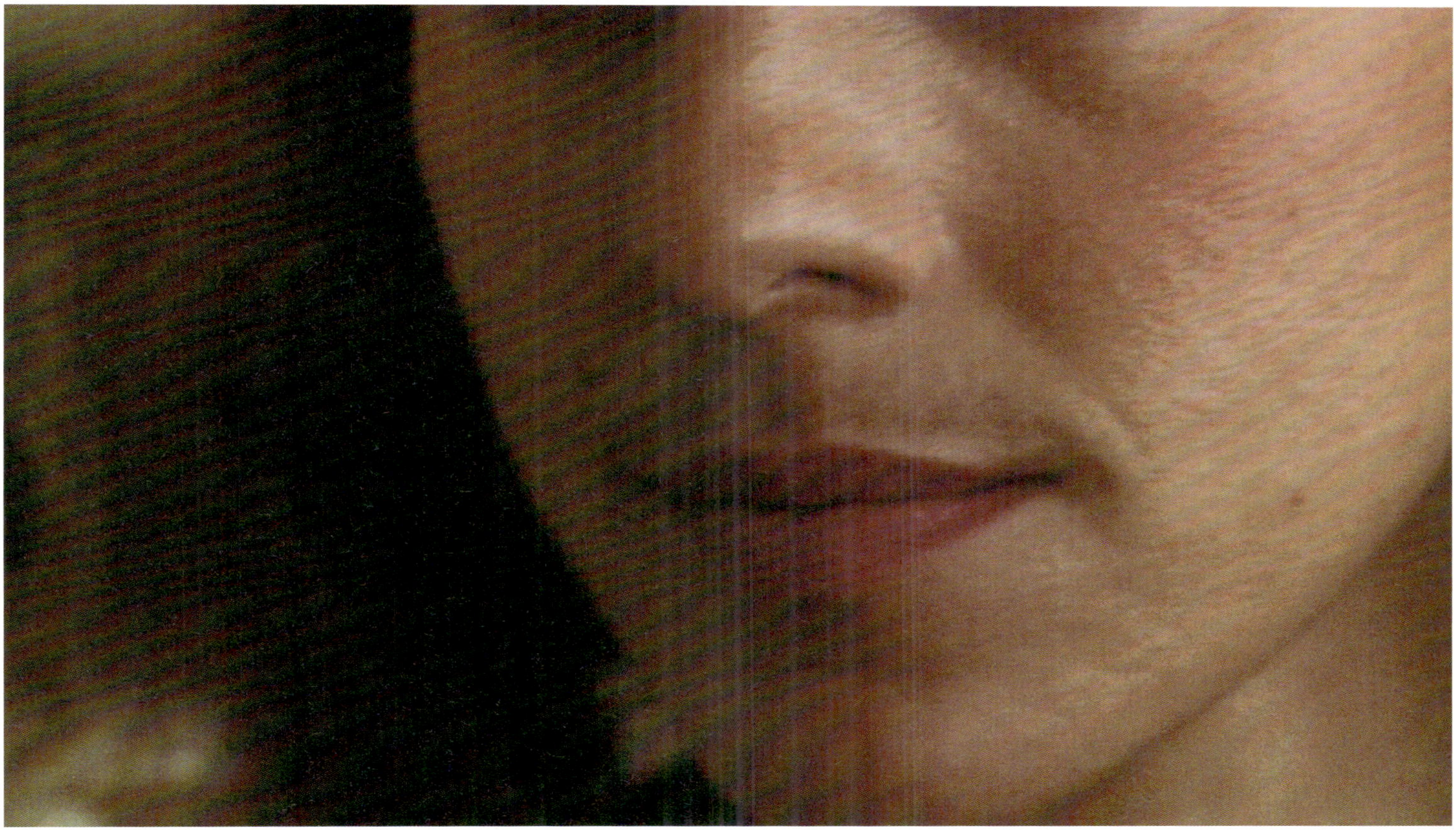

THE RAPE OF THE

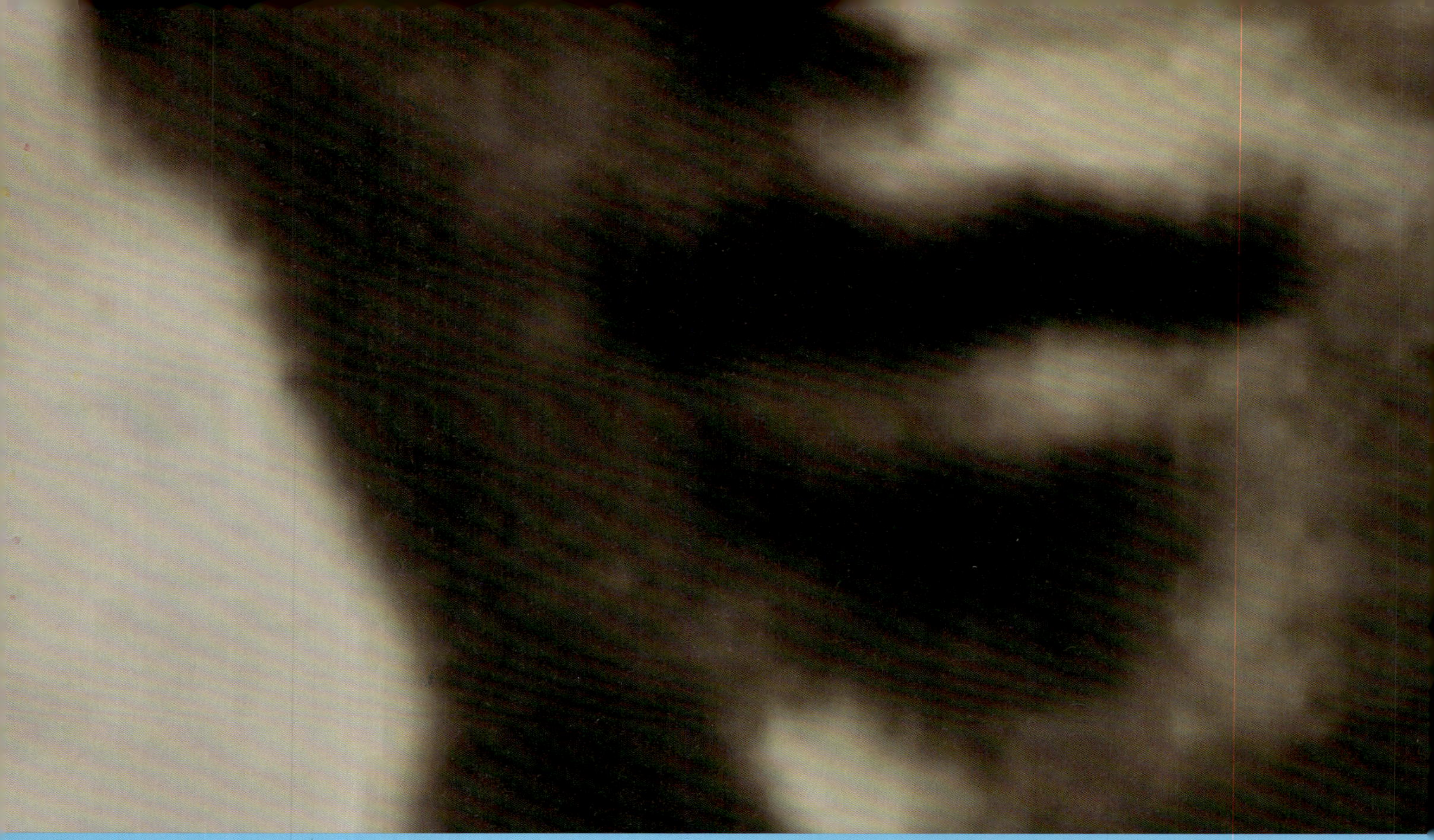

SABINE WOMEN

THE RUFUS CORPORATION

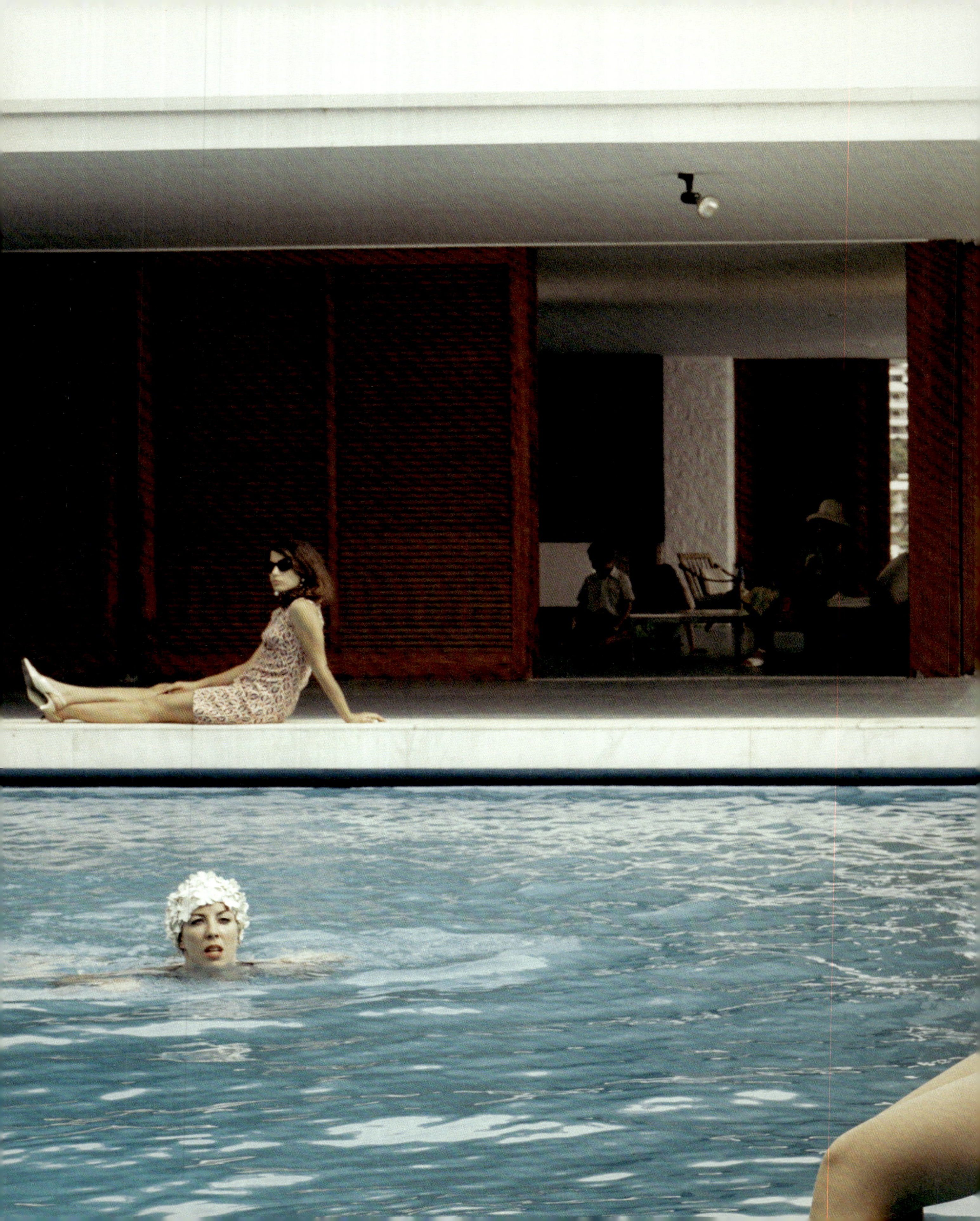

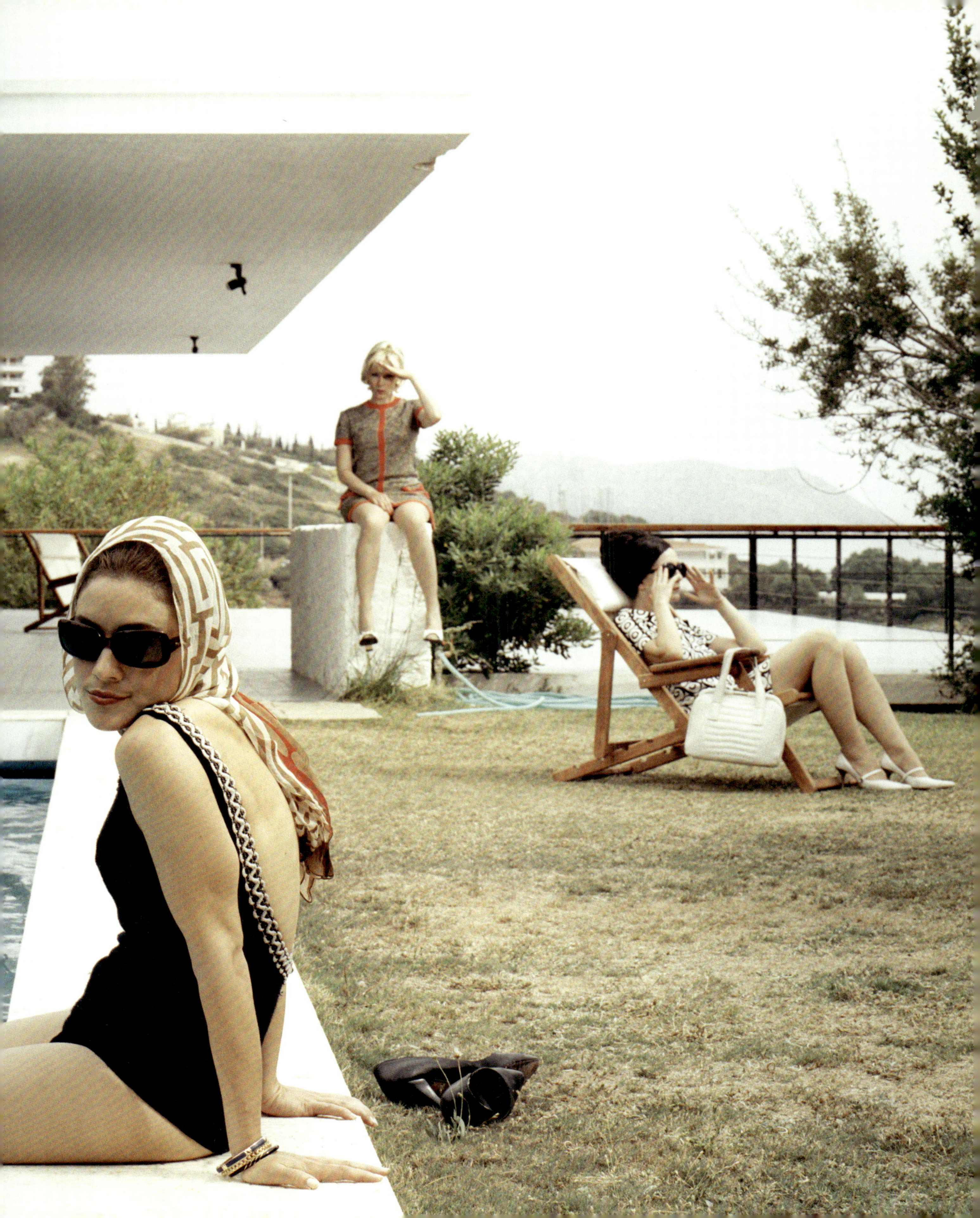

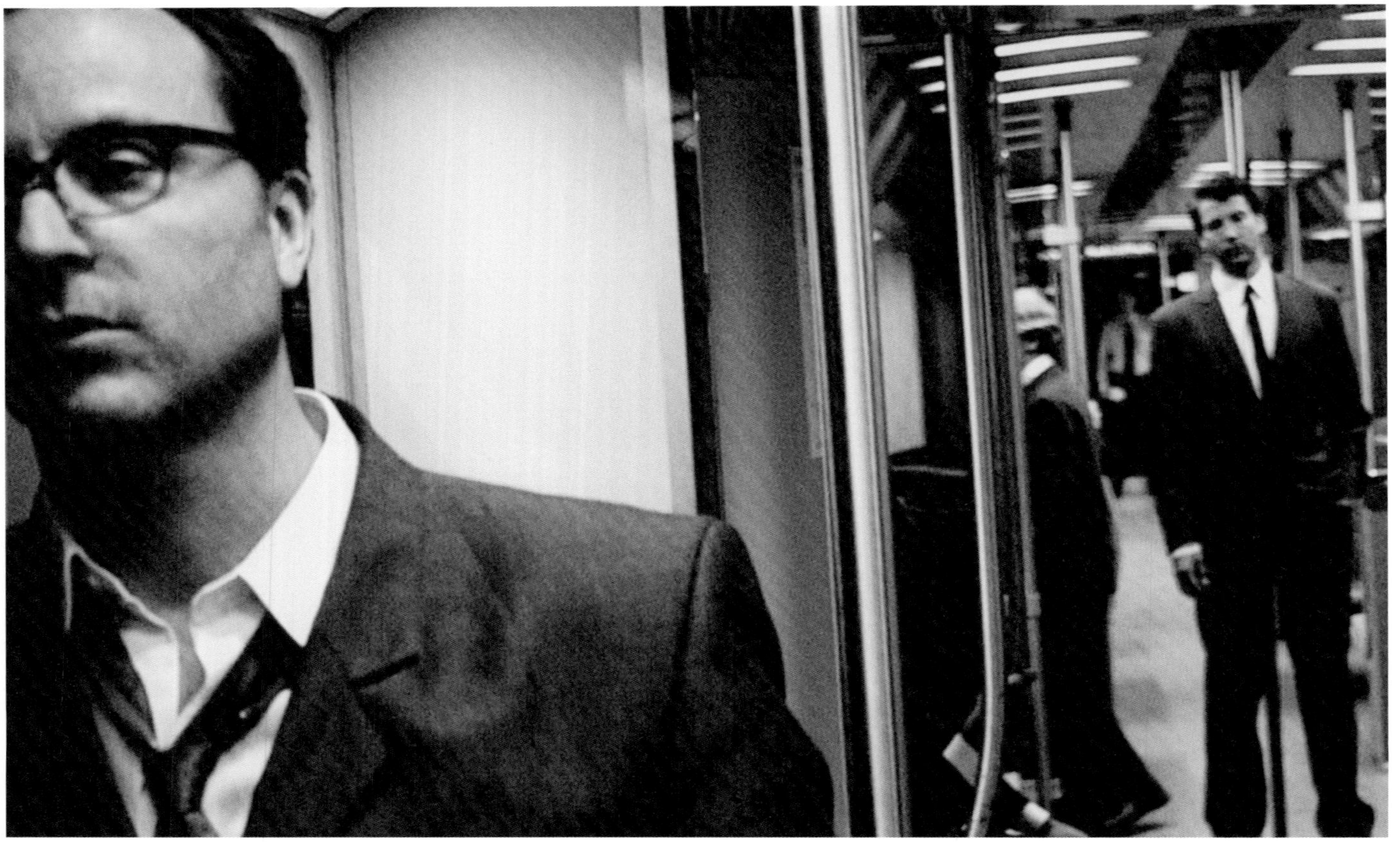

Meanwhile Rome was growing. More and more ground was coming within the circuit of its walls. They built their defenses with an eye rather to the future population than to any present overcrowding. Romulus resorted to a plan for increasing the inhabitants which had long been employed as ancient policy for founders of new cities, gather about an obscure and lowly multitude of people and then to spread the fiction that they were the children of the soil, 'born of earth' to be his progeny. In accordance with this policy, Romulus opened a place of refuge... A promiscuous crowd of freemen and slaves, eager for change, fled thither . . .

The Early History of Rome, 1.8, Livy

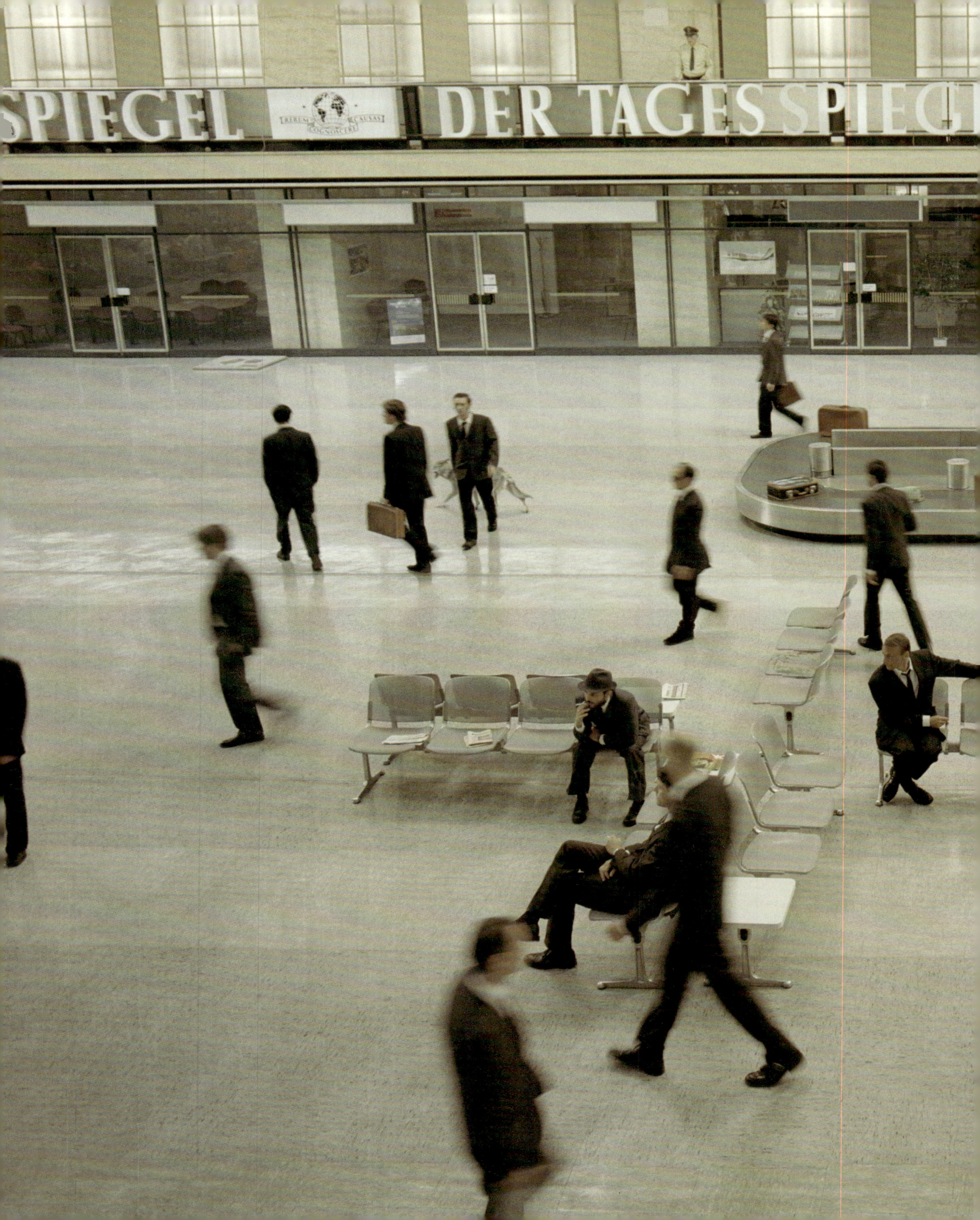
SPIEGEL
RERUM COGNOSCERE CAUSAS
DER TAGESSPIEGEL

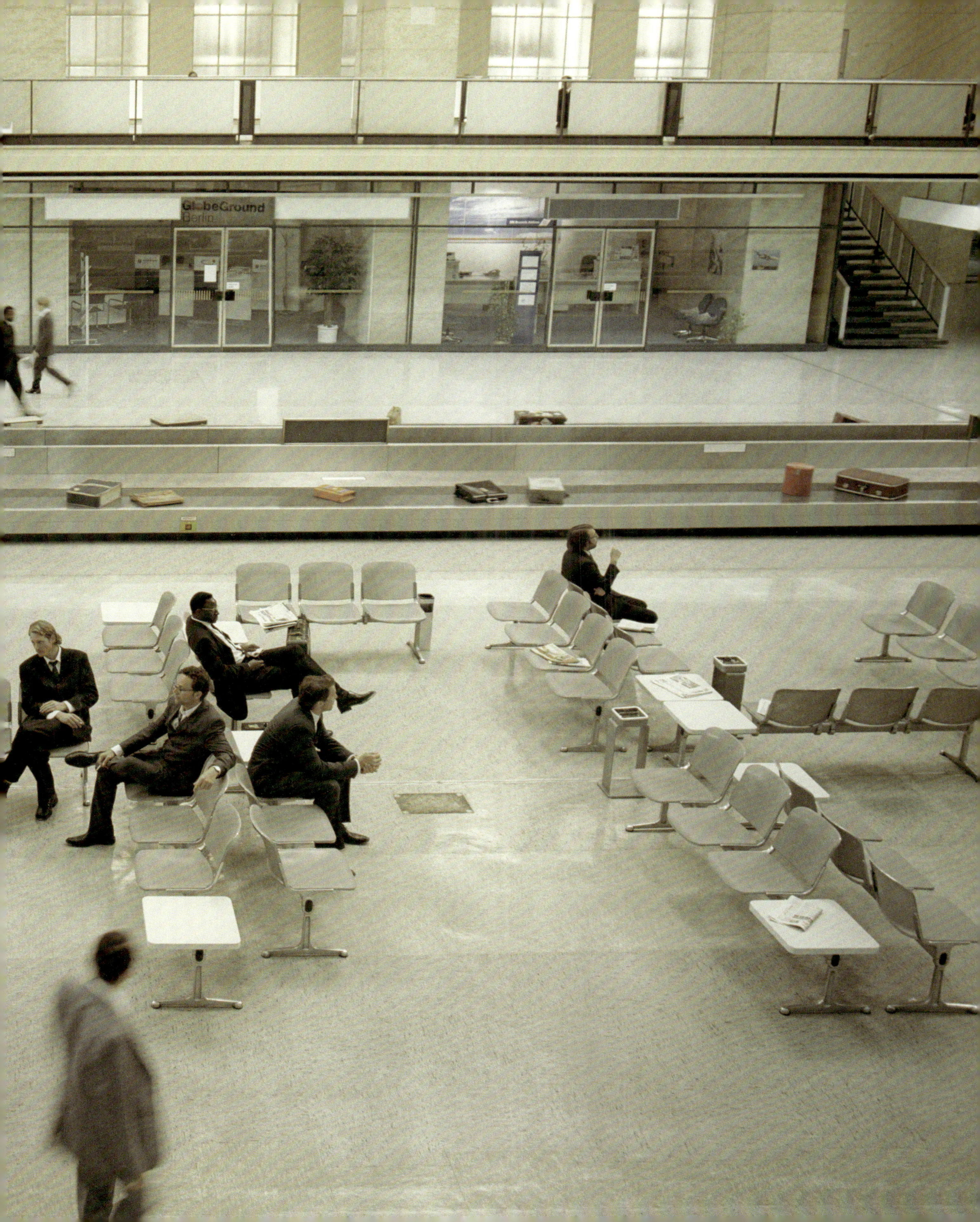
GlobeGround
Berlin

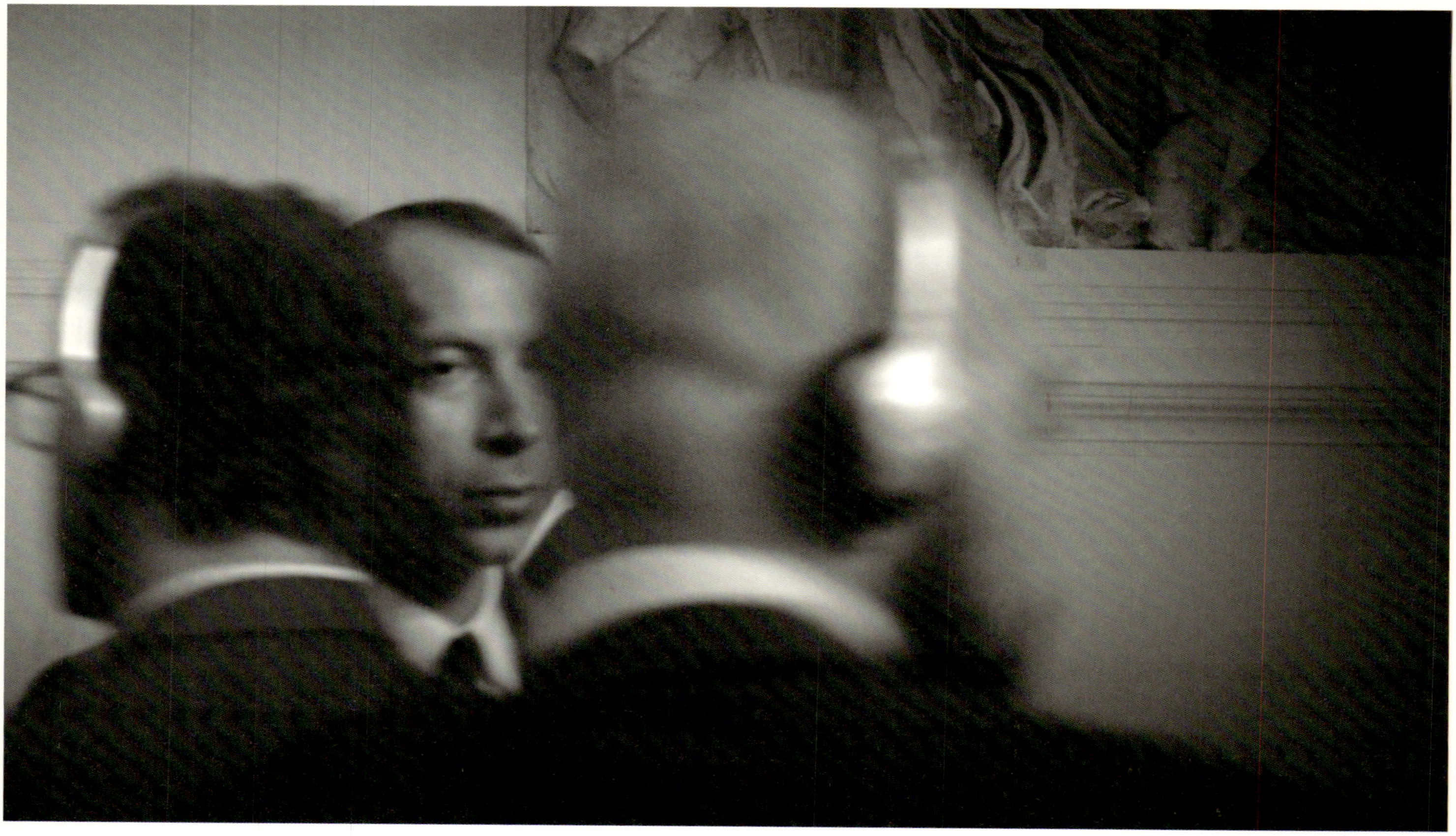

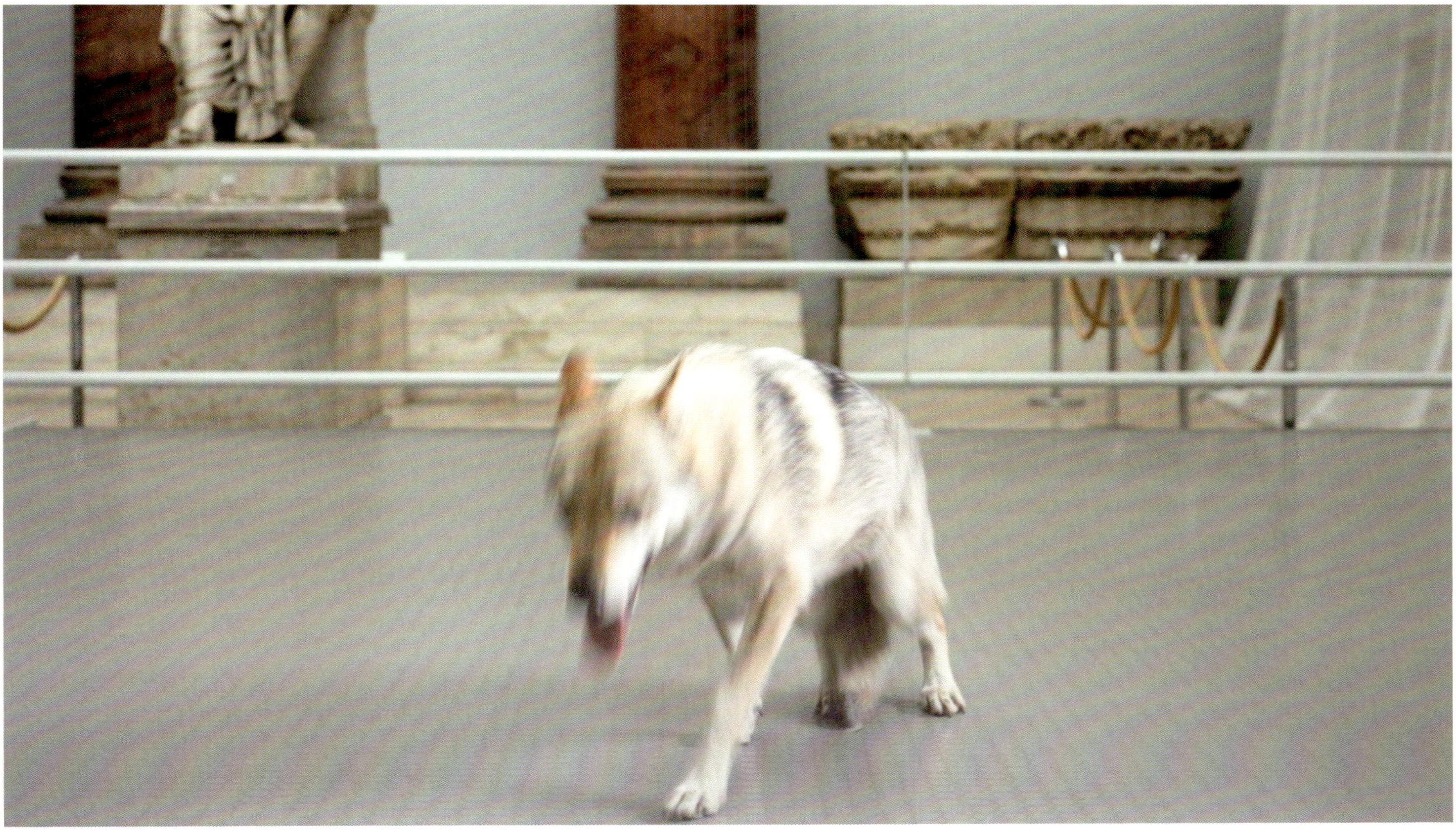

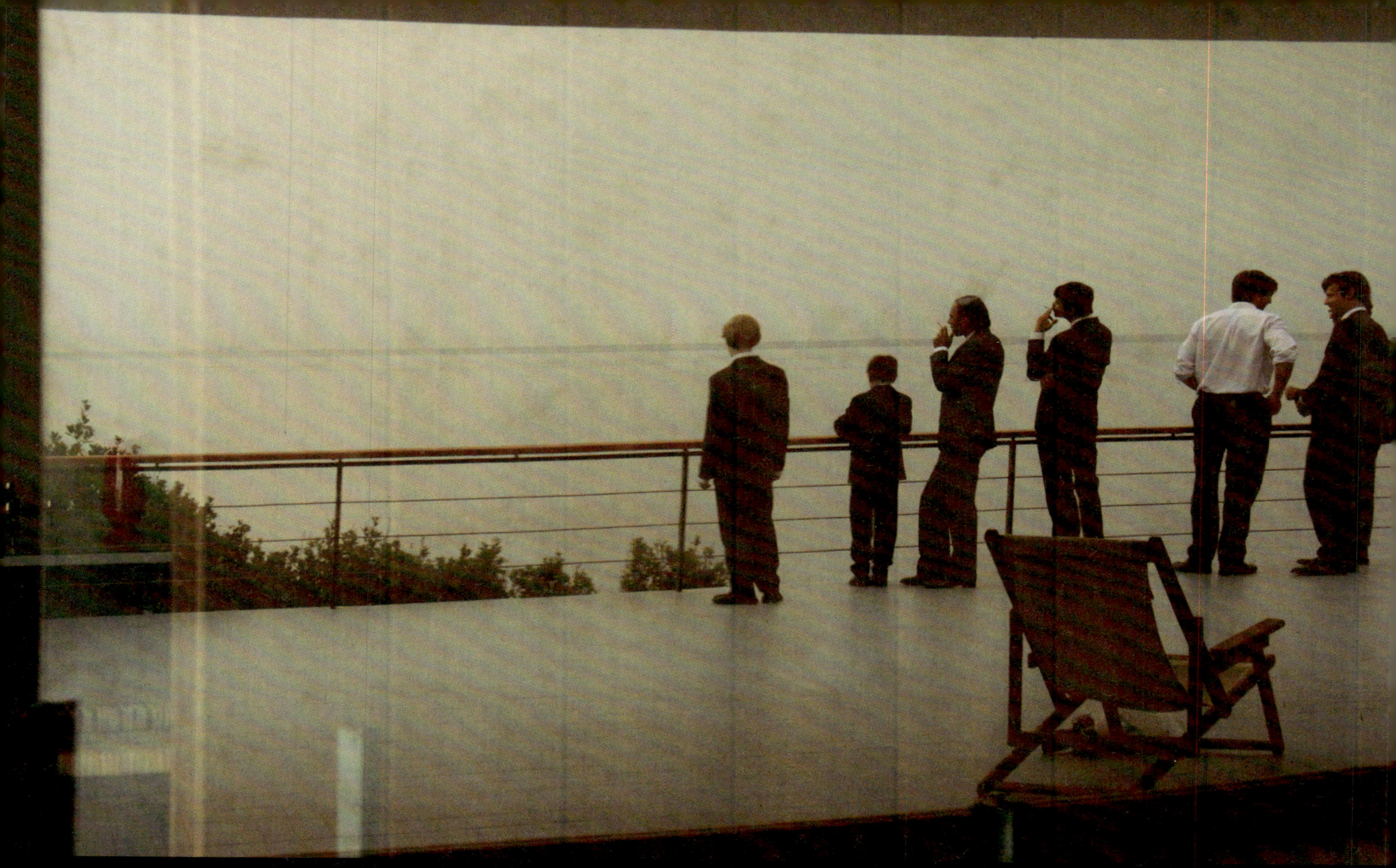

I am aware, too, that most readers will take little pleasure in my account of how Rome began and in her early history; they will wish to hurry on to more modern times and to read of the period, already a long one, in which the might of an imperial people is beginning to work its own ruin.

The Early History of Rome, 1.1, Livy

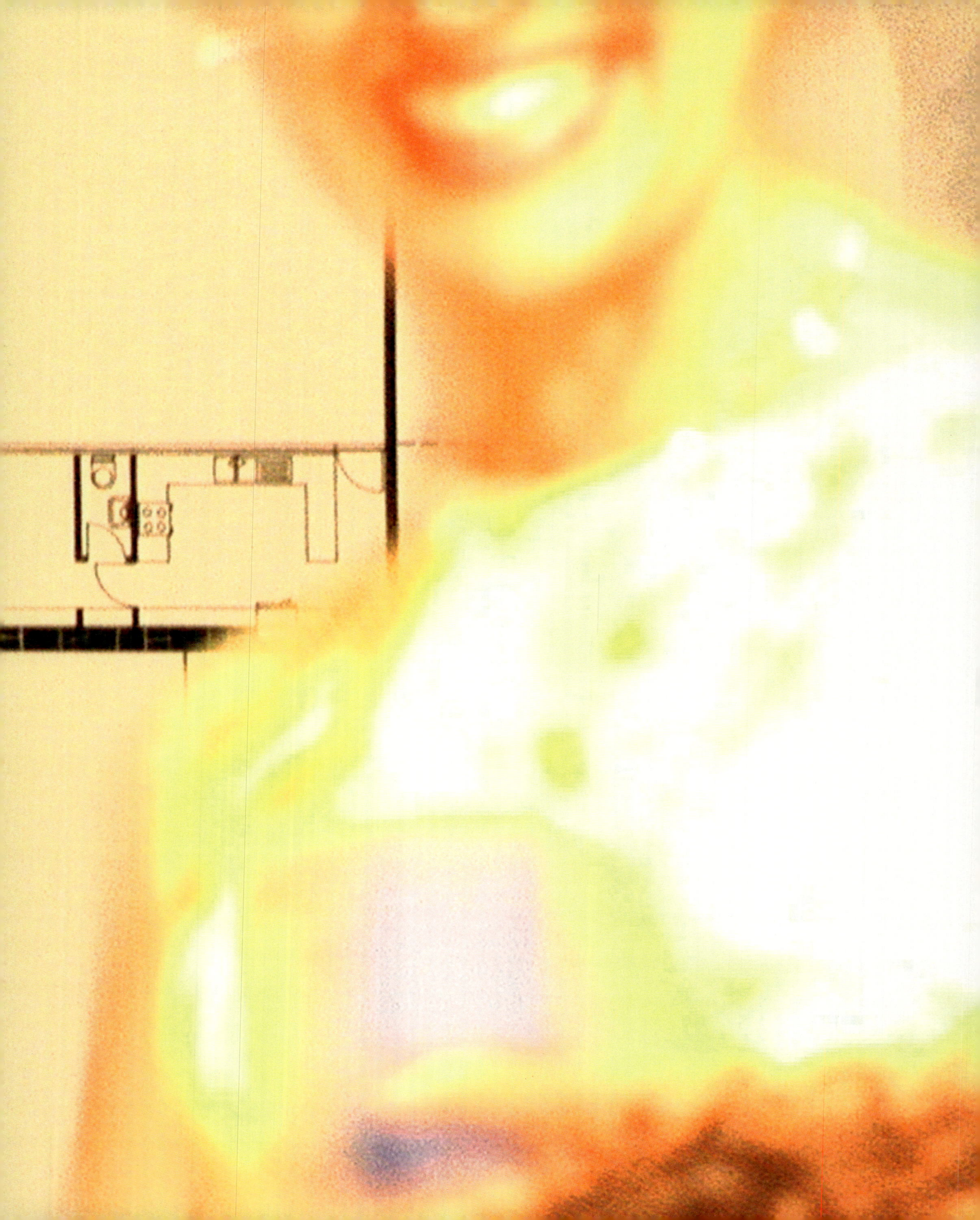

The Roman State had now become so strong that it was a match for any of its neighbours, but her greatness threatened to last for only a single generation. For want of women there was no hope of offspring, since she had neither prospect of posterity at home nor the right of intermarriage with her neighbours. Acting on the advice of the senate, Romulus accordingly sent envoys amongst the surrounding peoples to solicit for the men an alliance and the privilege of intermarriage for his newly founded state. The envoys were instructed to point out that "cities, like everything else, sprung from the lowliest beginnings, and those who were helped on by their own courage and the favour of heaven, some at least, will win for themselves great power and great renown, and of these Rome will assuredly be one." As to the origin of Rome, it was well known that whilst it had received divine assistance, courage and self-reliance were not wanting.

The Early History of Rome, 1.9, Livy

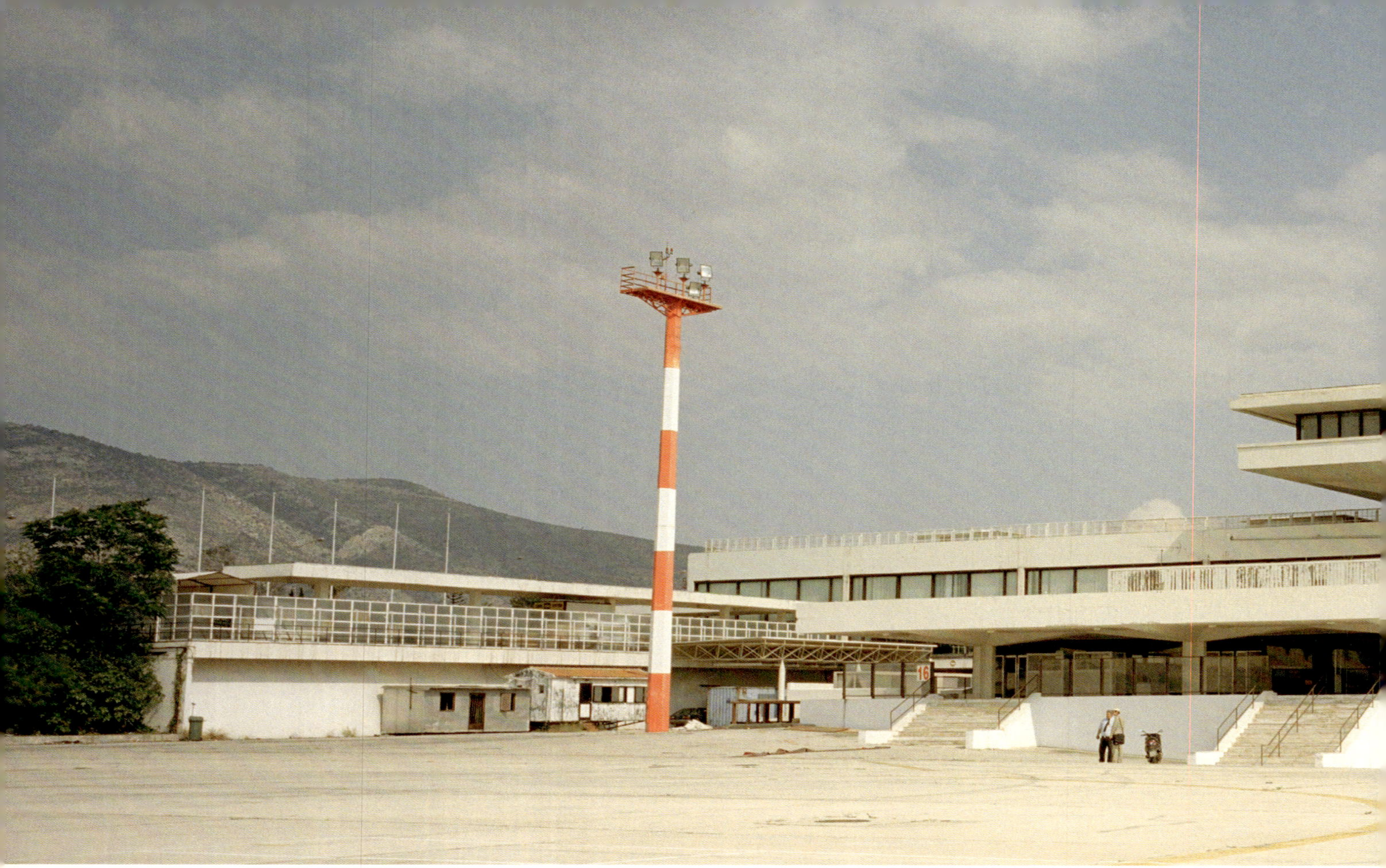

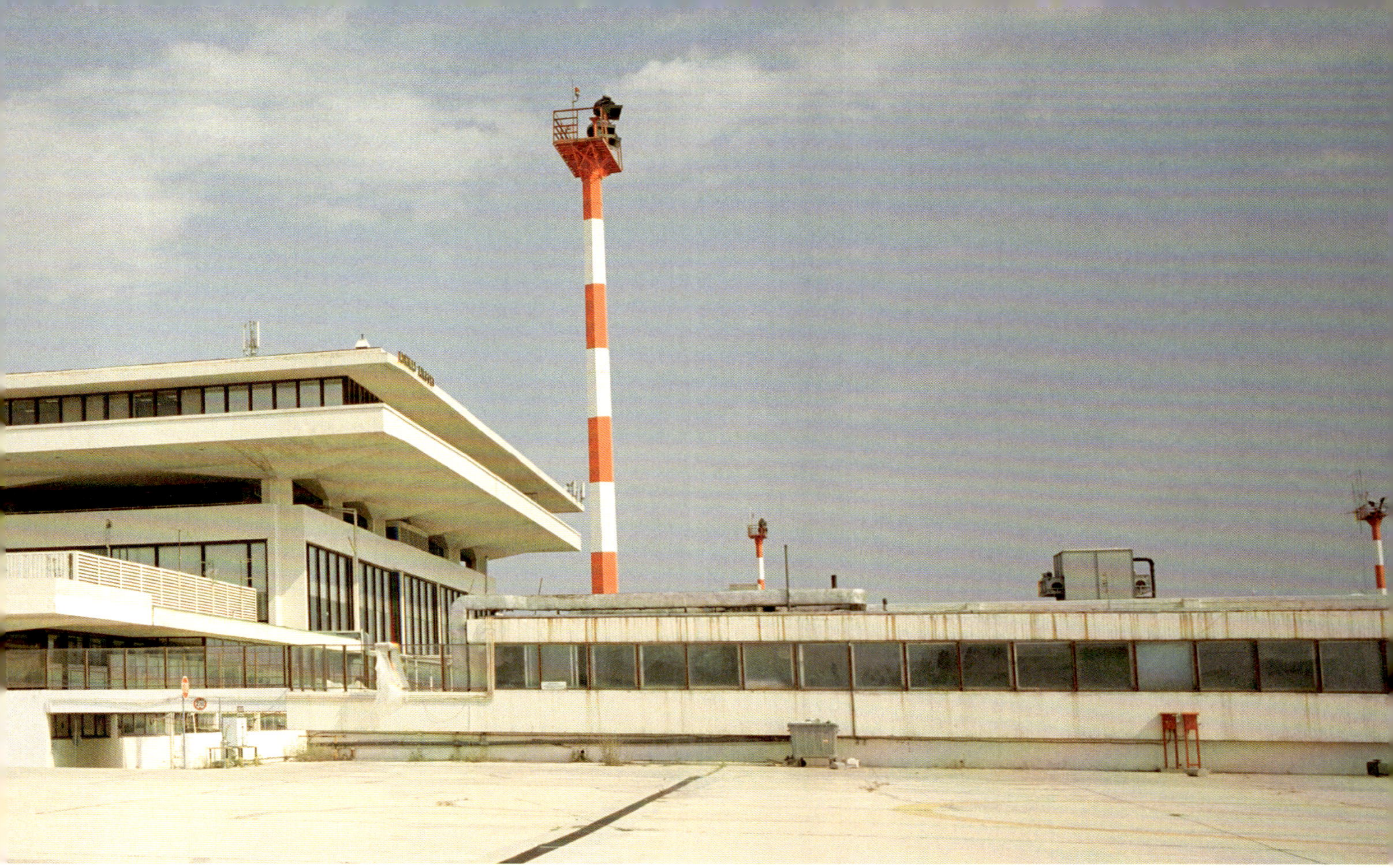

The Romans were men as they were; why then be reluctant? There should, therefore, be no hesitation for these Sabines to mingle their blood with their fellow-men. Nowhere did the embassy obtain a friendly hearing. It was clear that everyone despised the new community. Whilst their proposals were treated with contumely, there was at the same time a general feeling of alarm at the power so rapidly growing in their midst. More often than not his envoys were dismissed with the question, "whether Rome had thrown open her doors to female as well as male runaways and vagabonds, as that would have been the most suitable way for Romans to get wives." The Roman youth could ill brook such insults, and matters began to look like an appeal to force. Expressly to afford a fitting time and place for this, Romulus concealed his resentment...

The Early History of Rome, 1.9, Livy

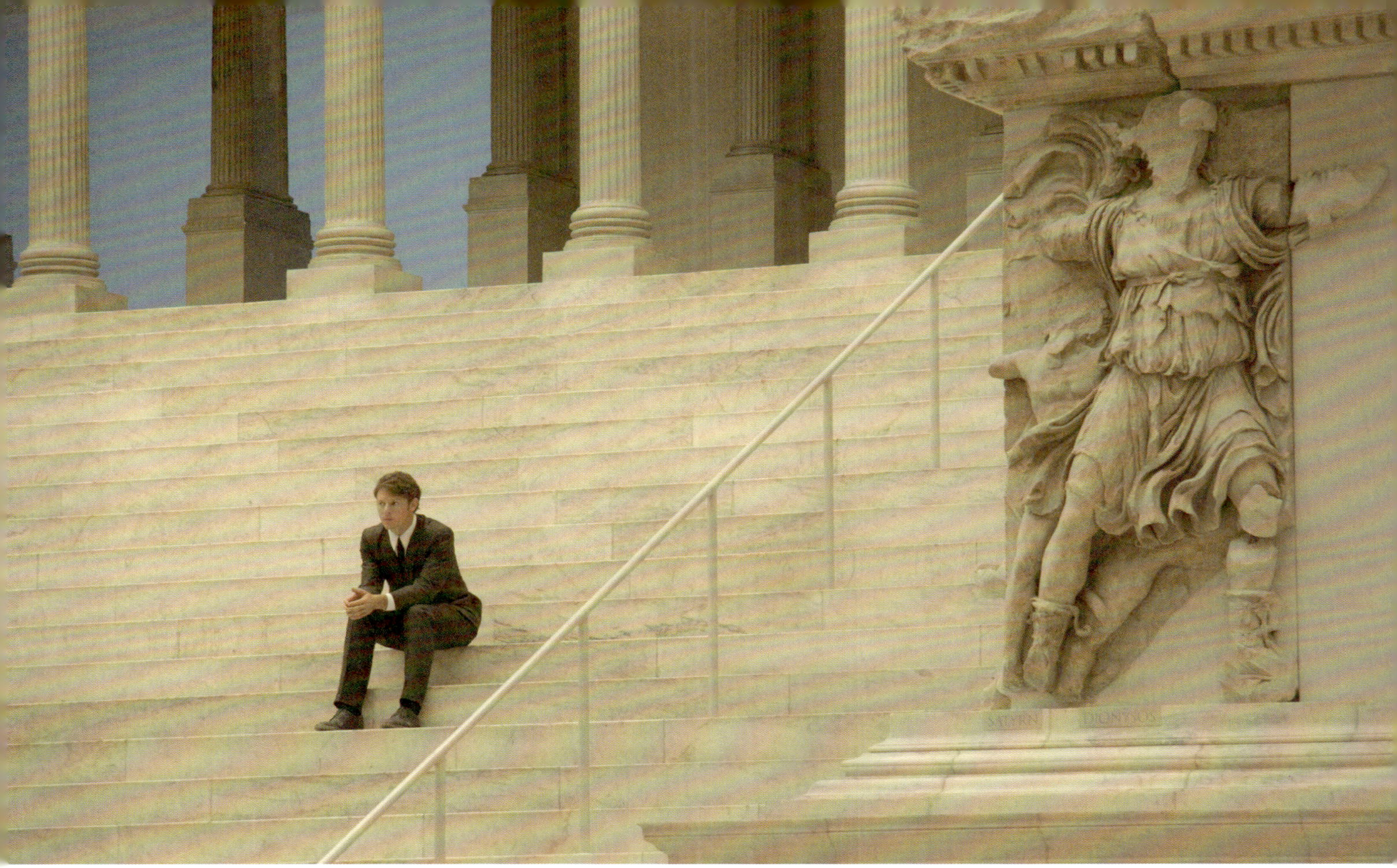

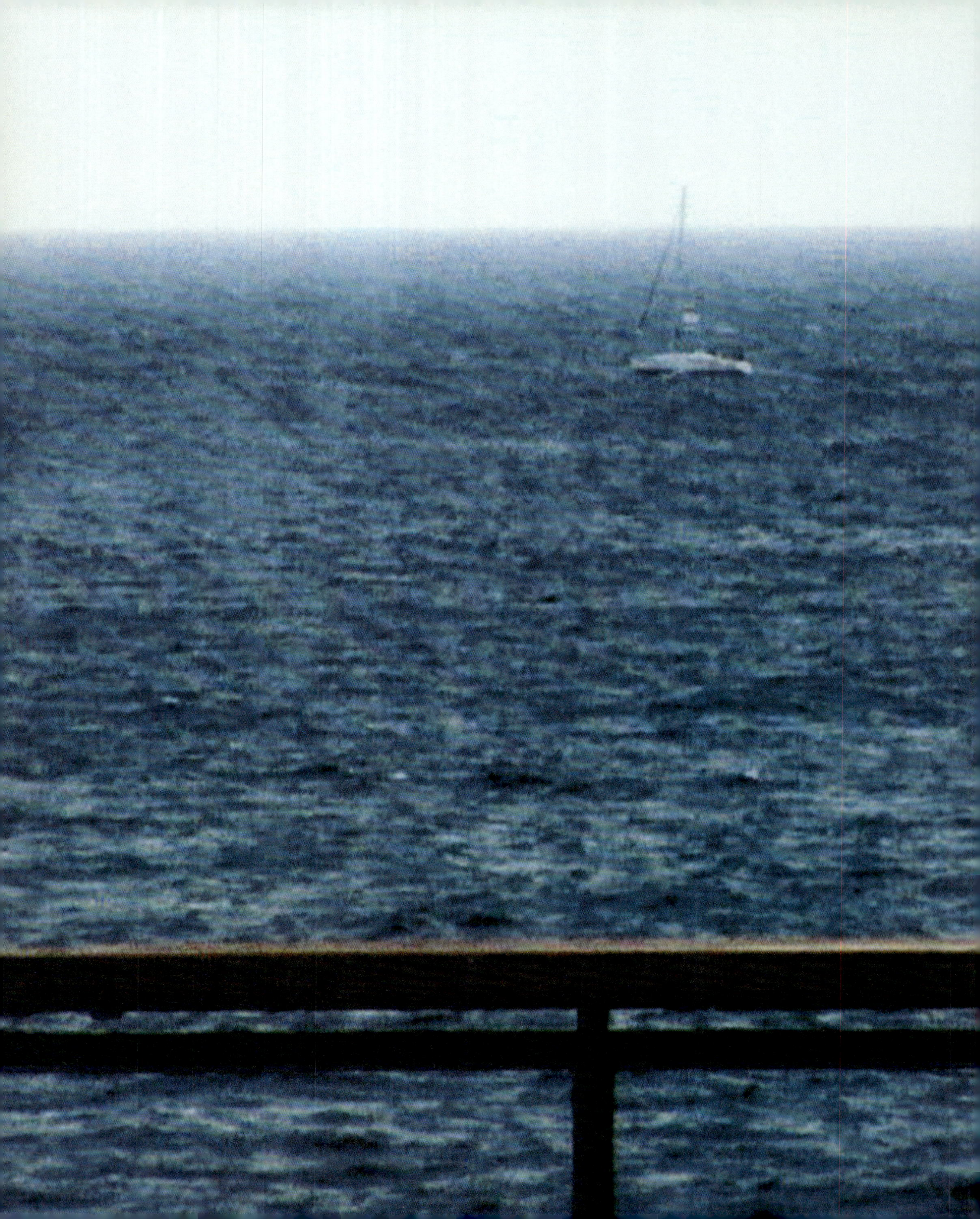

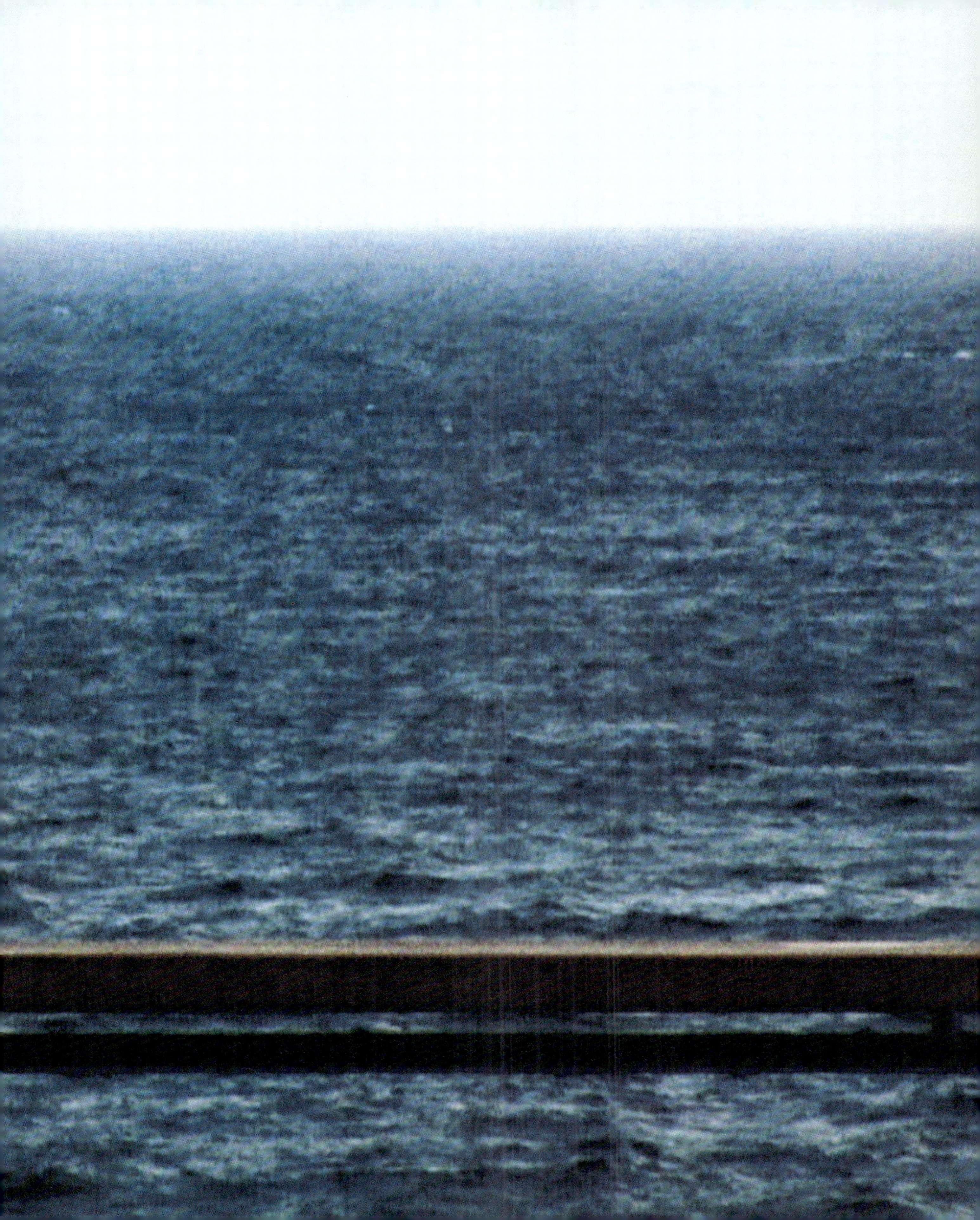

This was the first accession of strength to the nascent greatness of the city. When he was satisfied as to its strength, his next step was to provide for that strength being wisely directed. He created a hundred senators; either because that number was adequate, or because

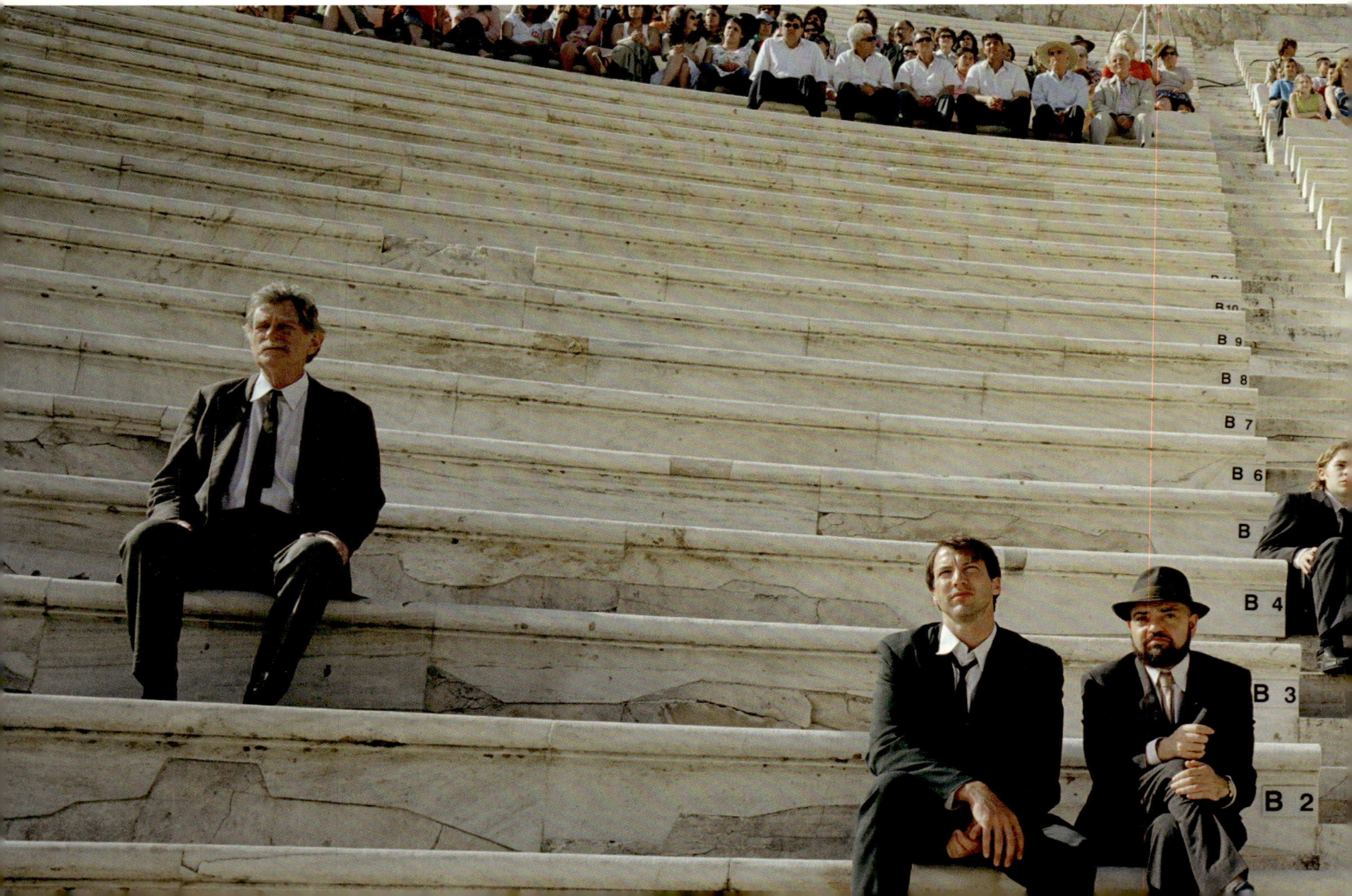

there were only a hundred heads of houses who could be created. In any case, they were called the "Patres" in virtue of their rank, and their descendants were called "Patricians."

The Early History of Rome, 1.8, Livy

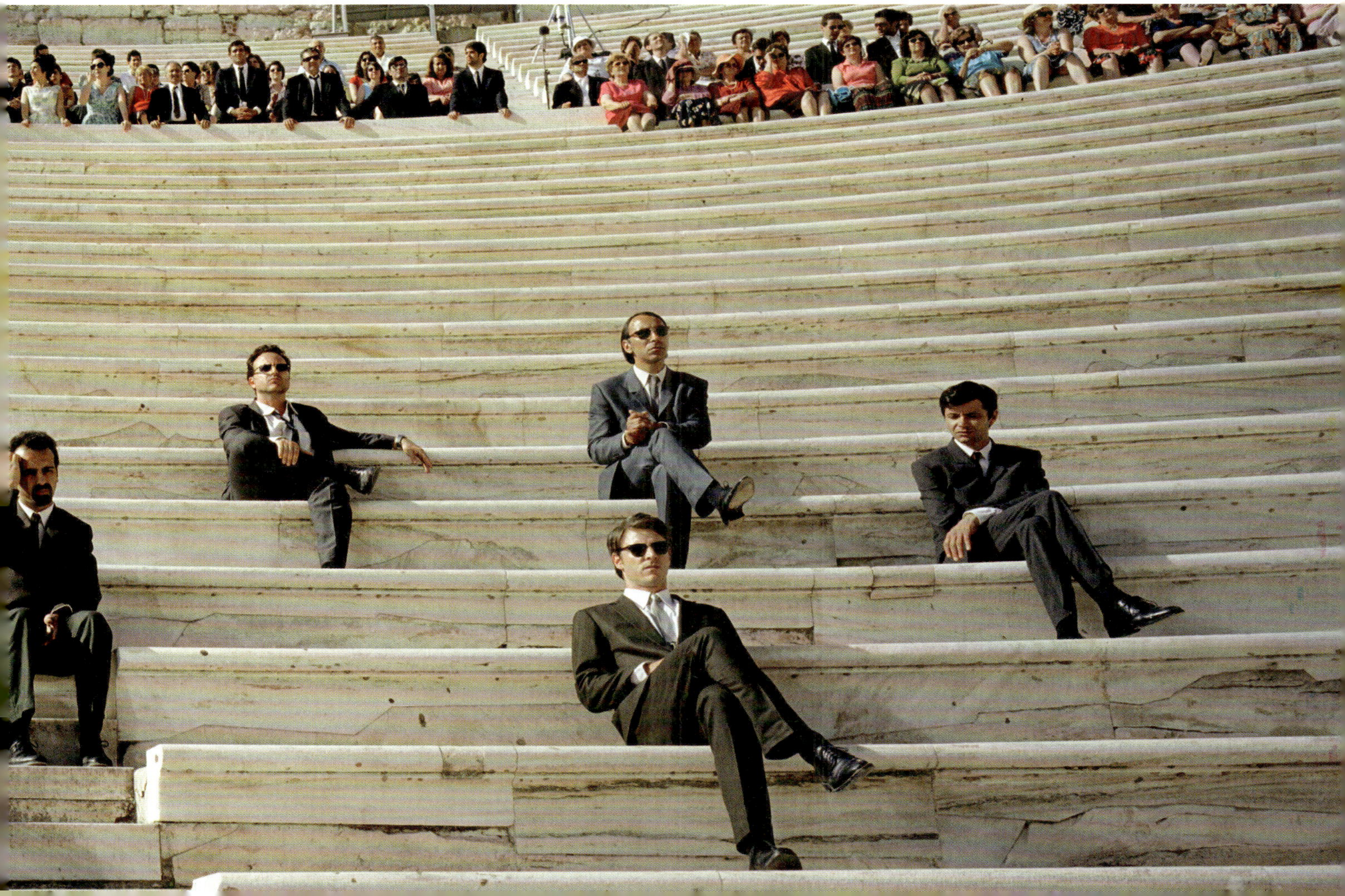

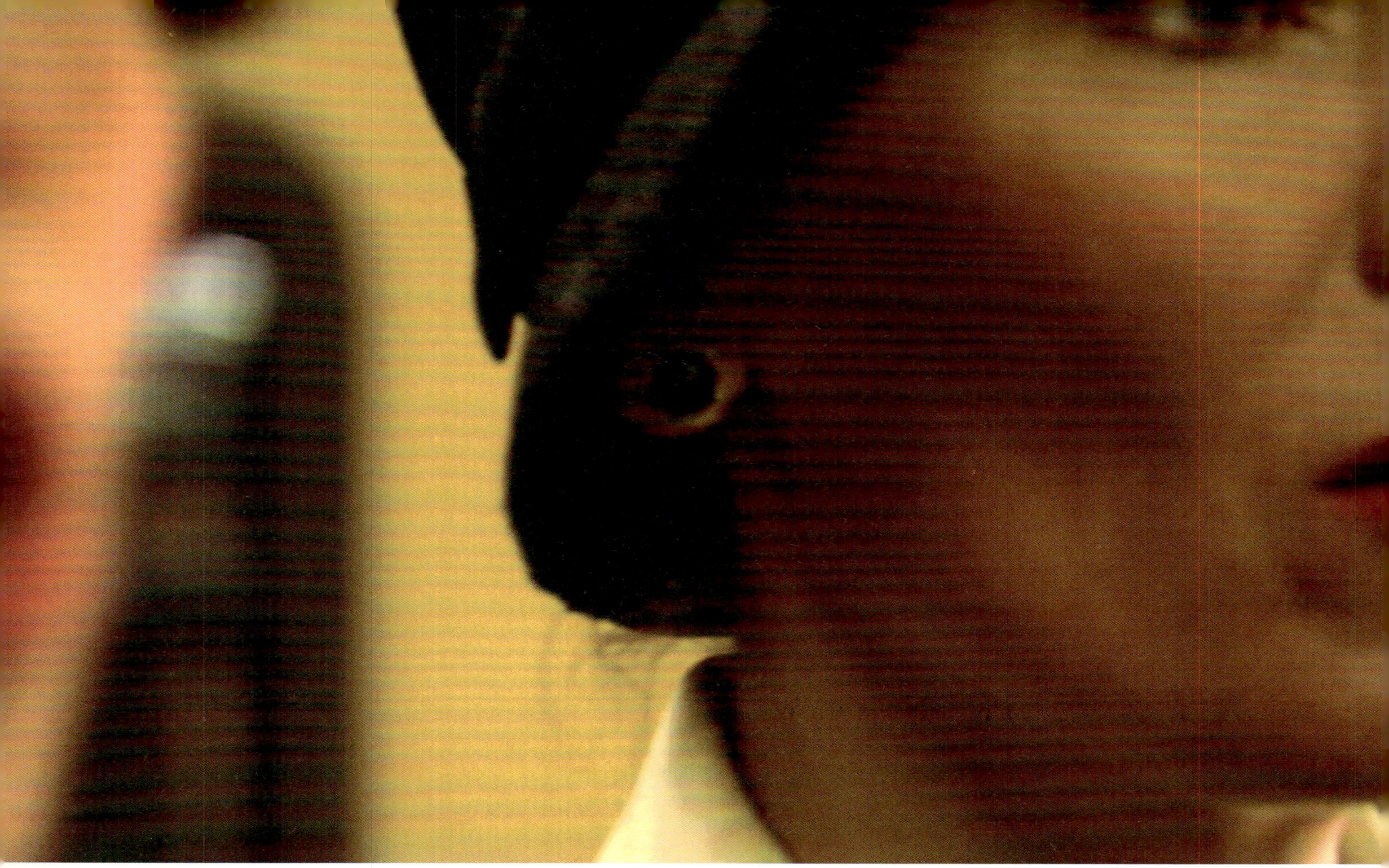

Therefore pass these Sirens by, and stop your men's ears with wax that none of them may hear; but if you like you can listen yourself, for you may get the men to bind you as you stand upright on a cross-piece half way up the mast, and they must lash the rope's ends to the mast itself, that you may have the pleasure of listening. If you beg and pray the men to unloose you, then they must bind you faster.

The Odyssey, Homer

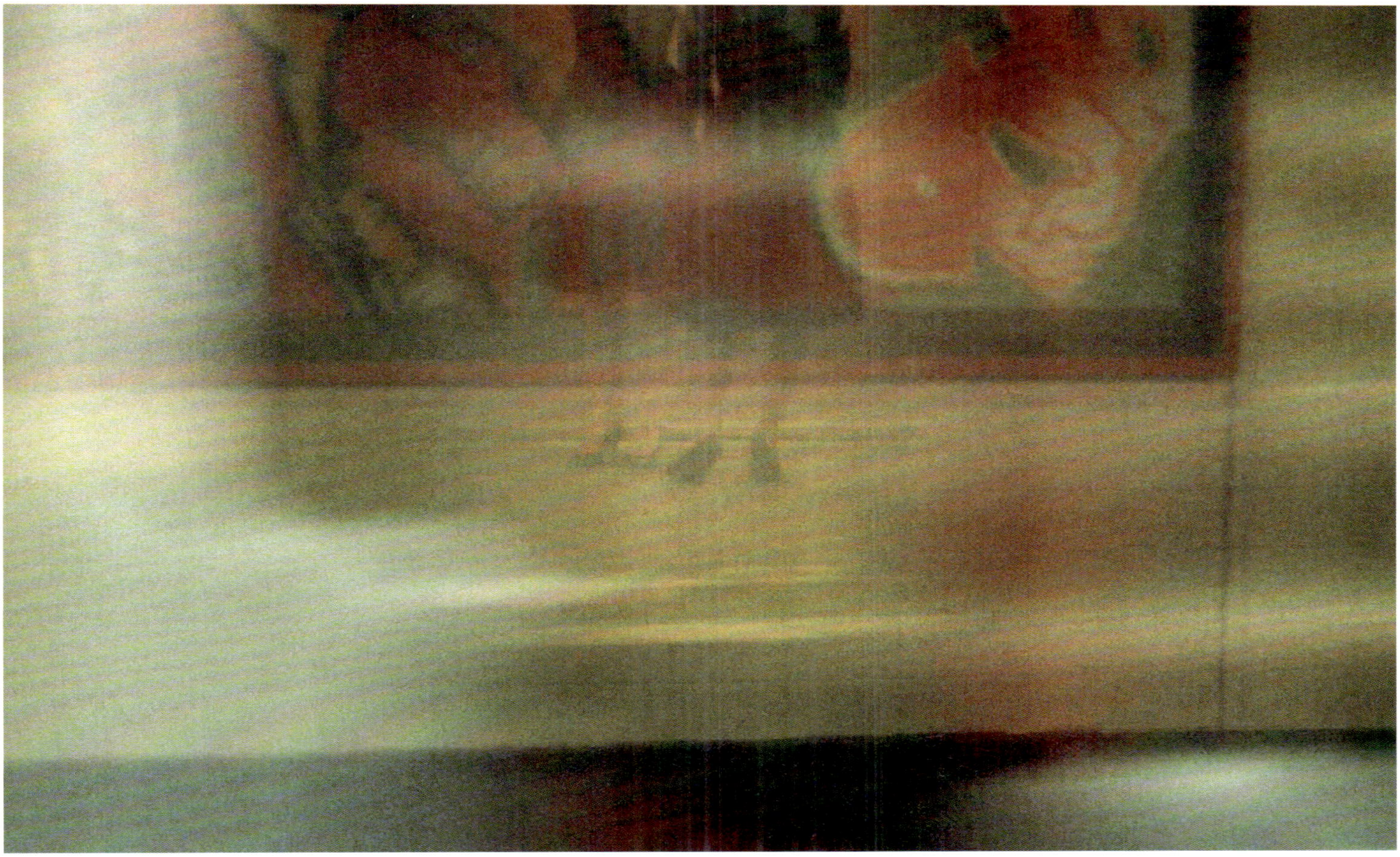

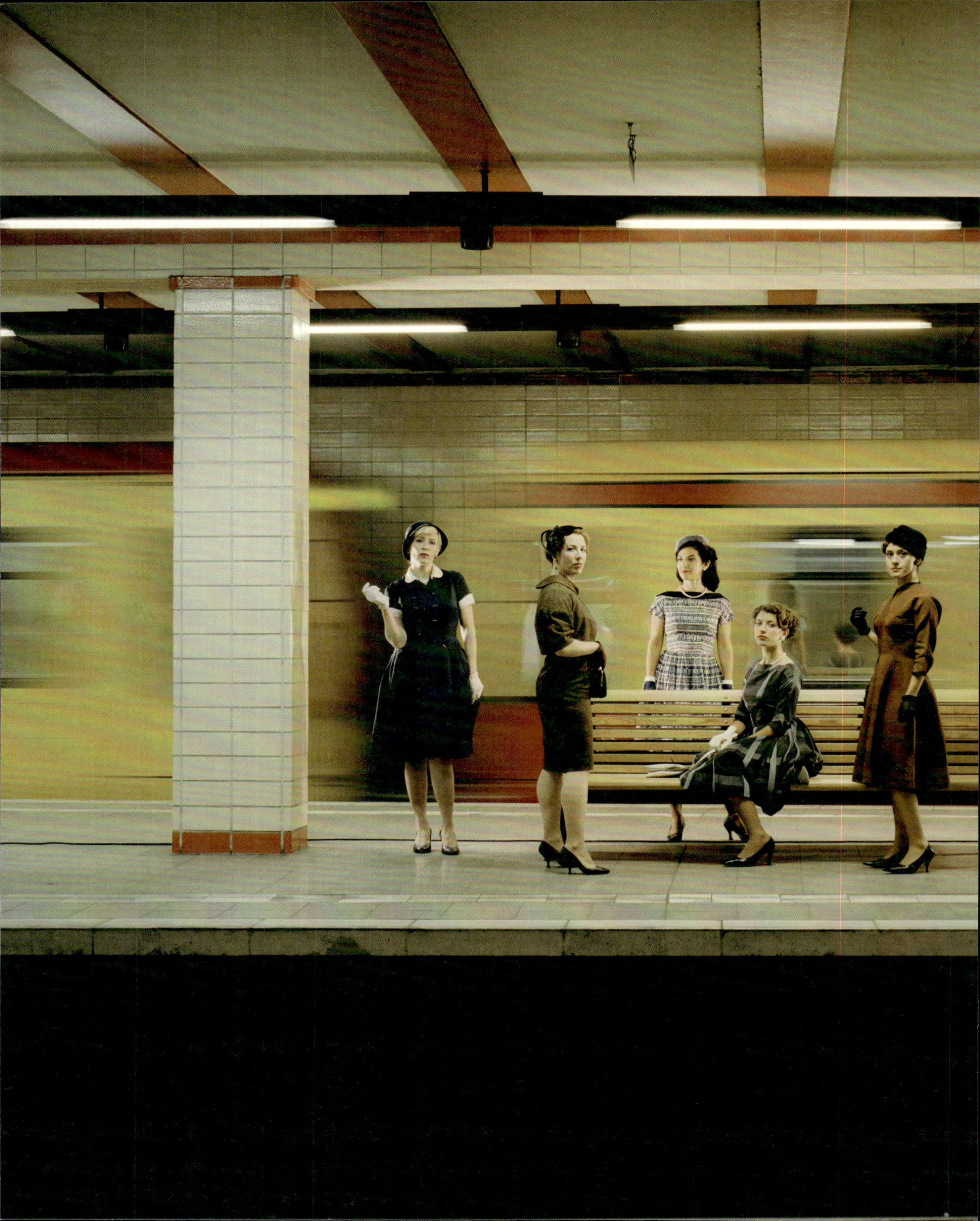

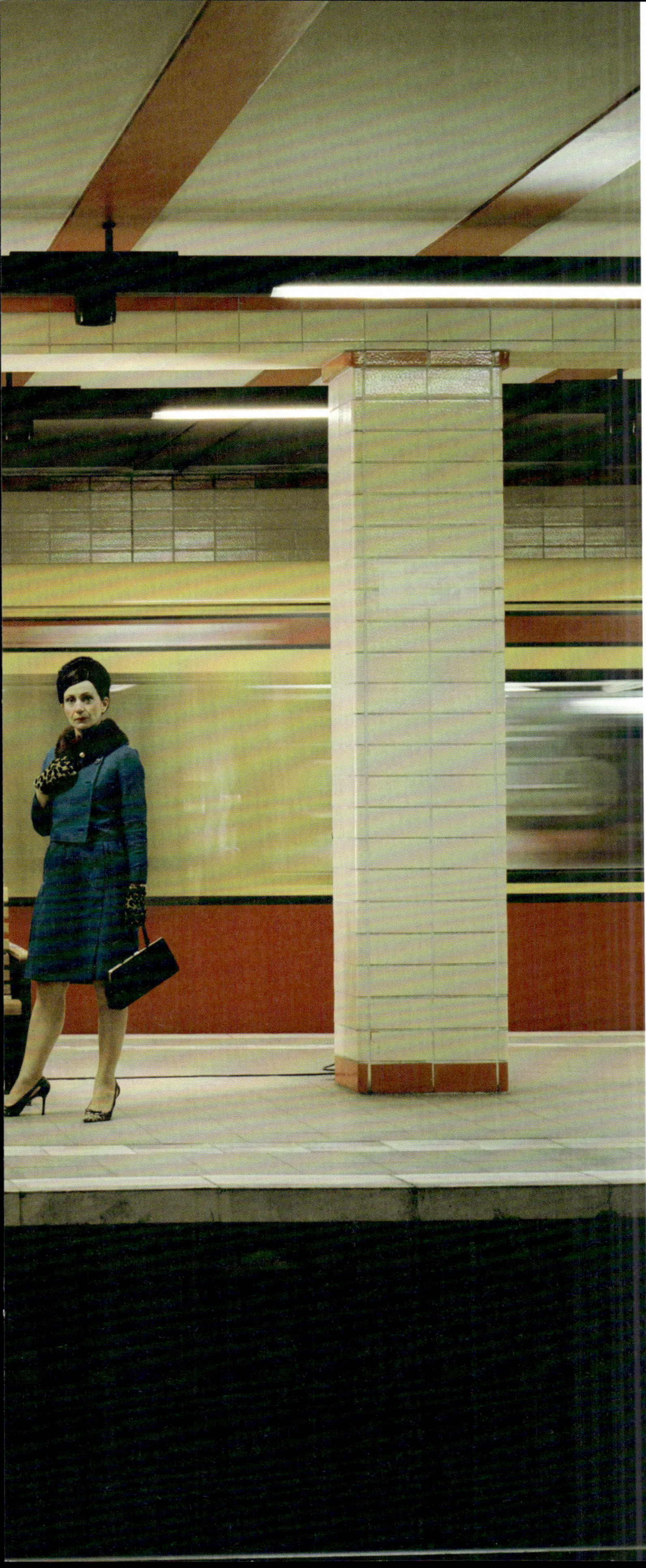

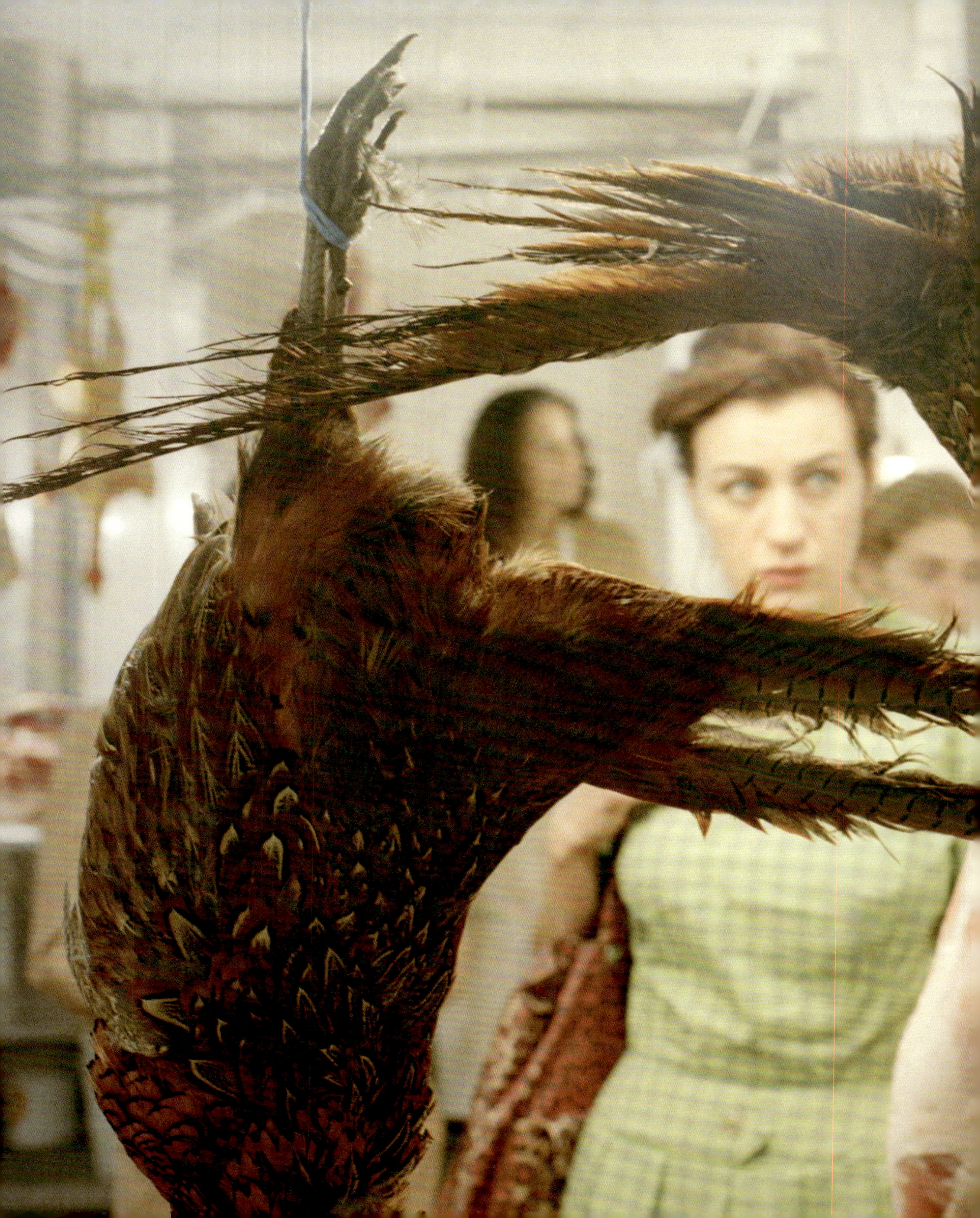

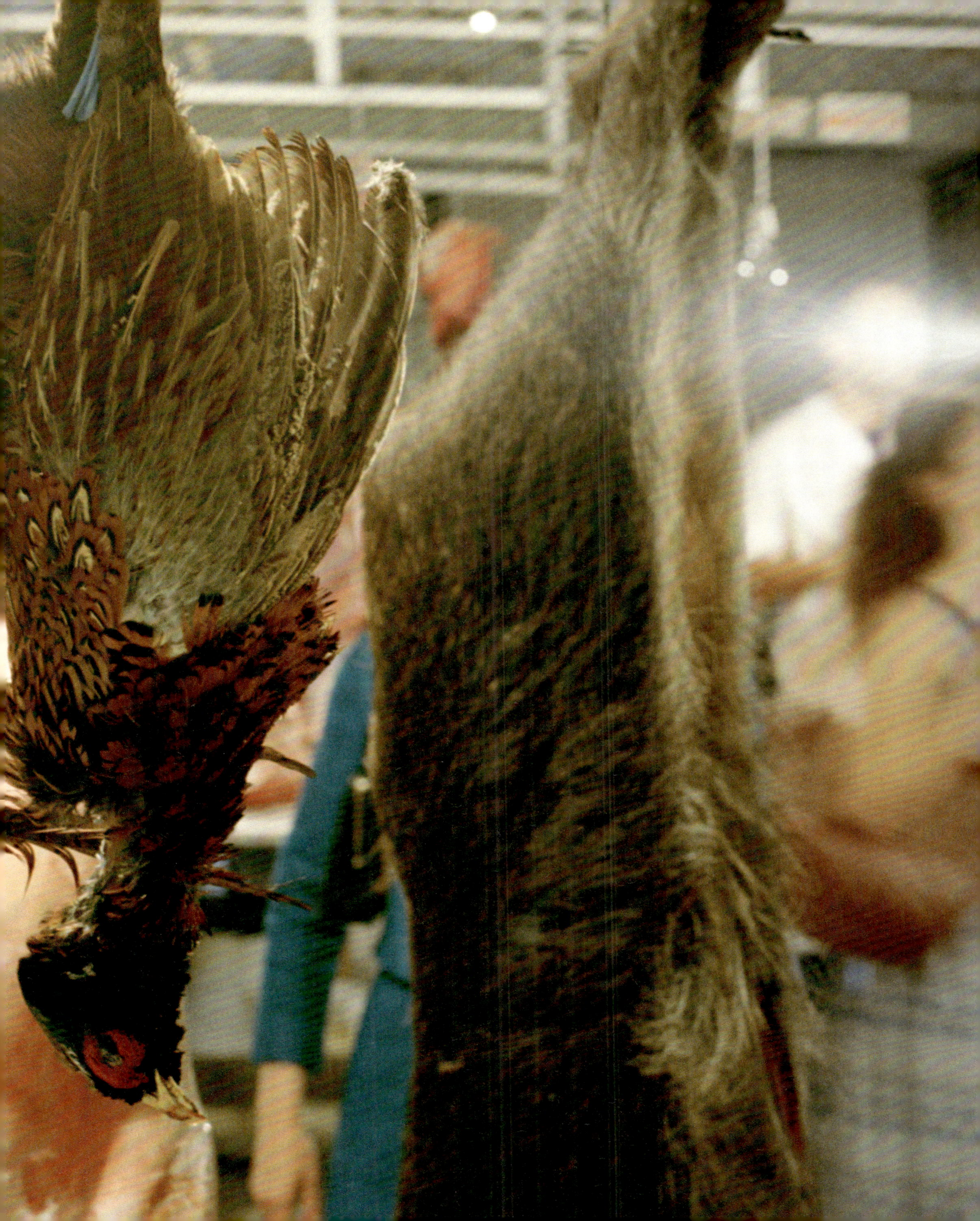

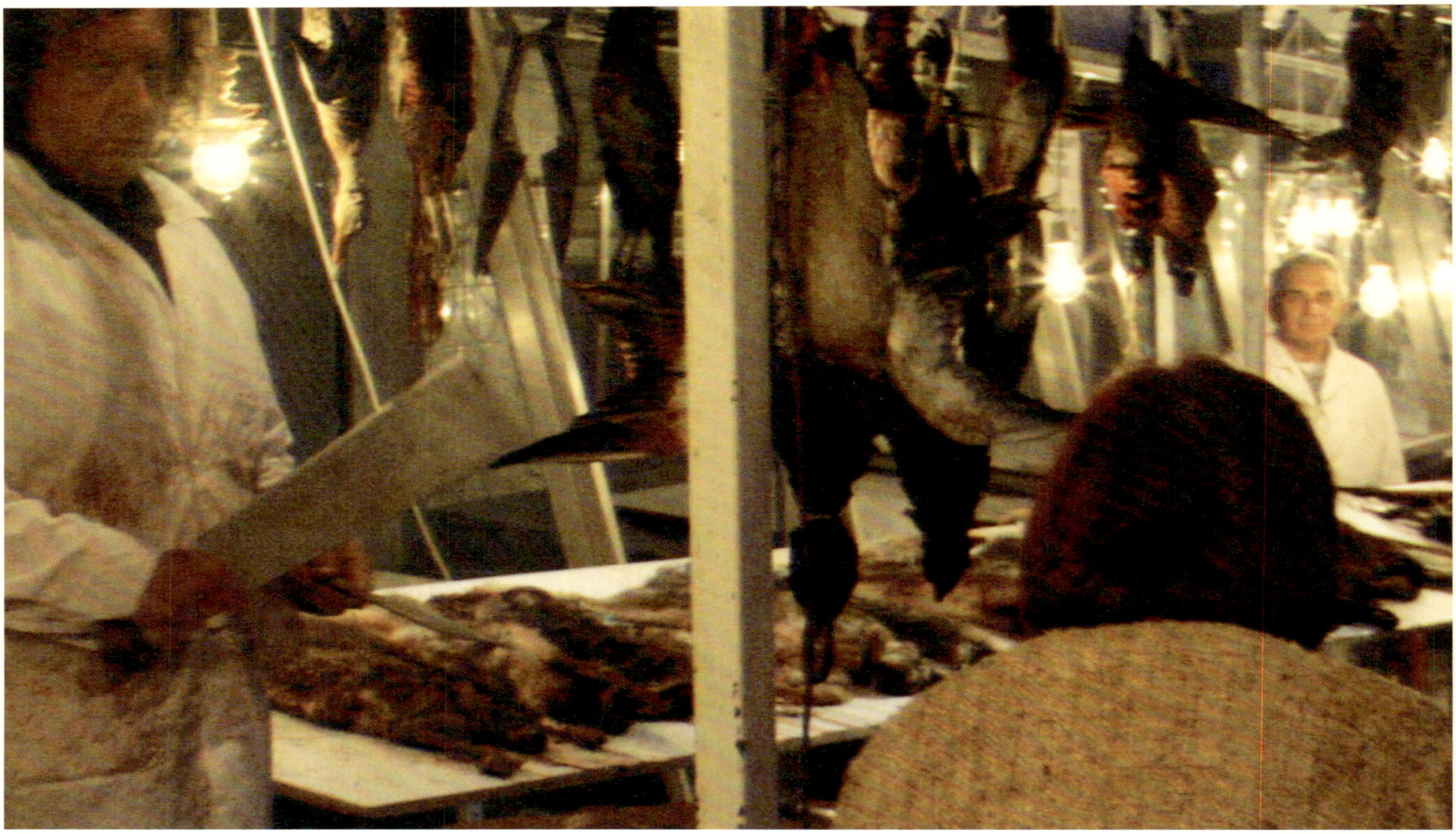

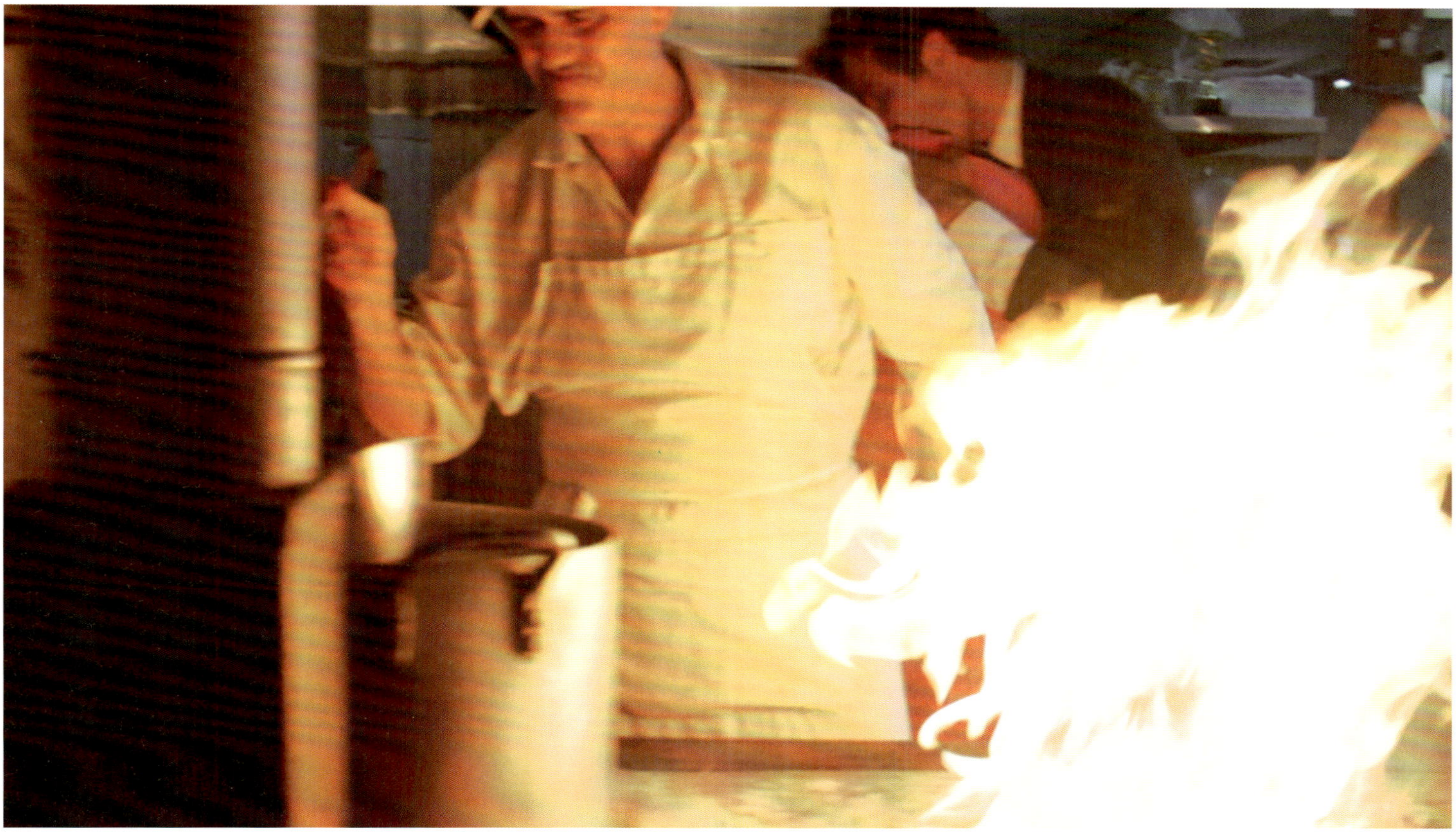

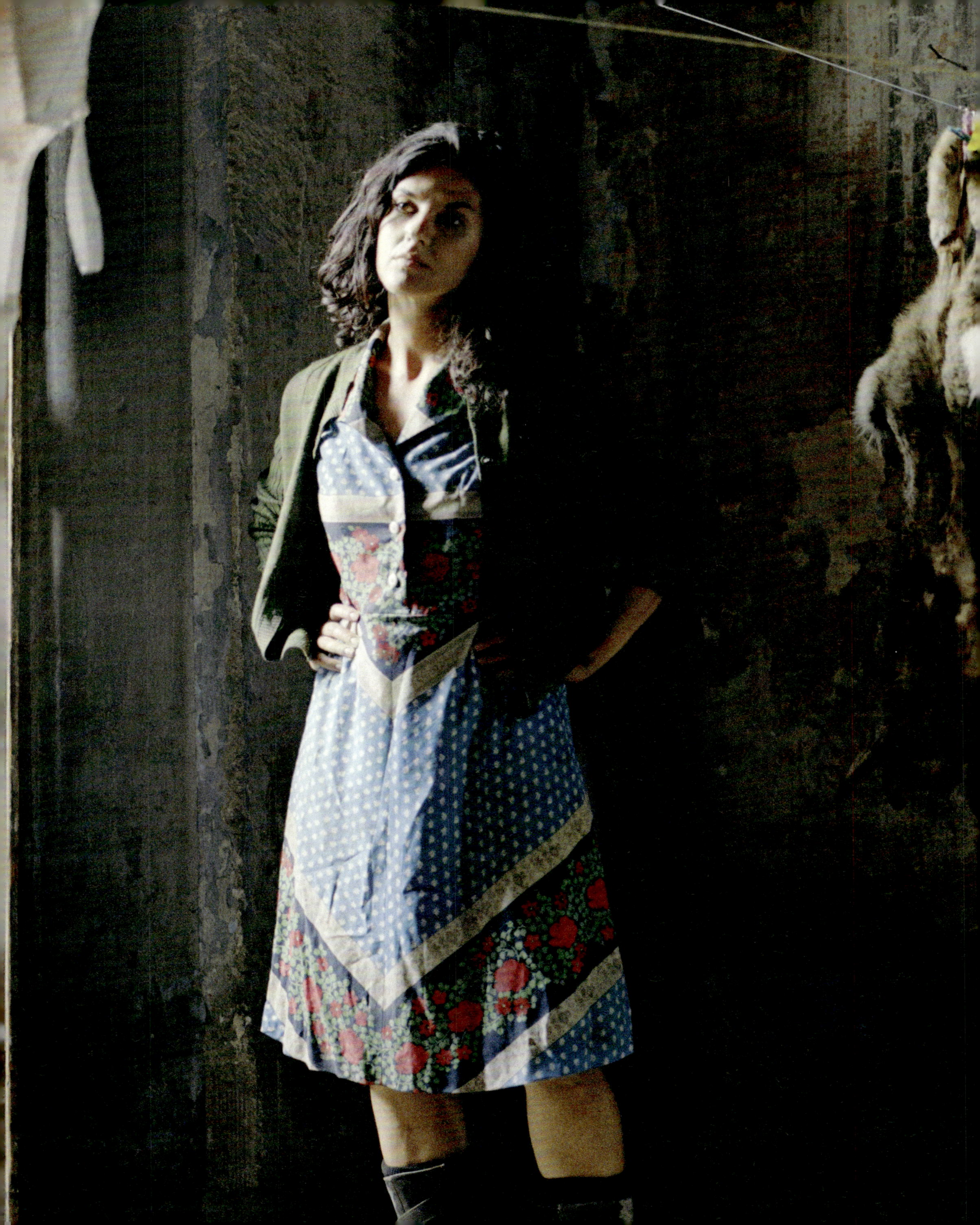

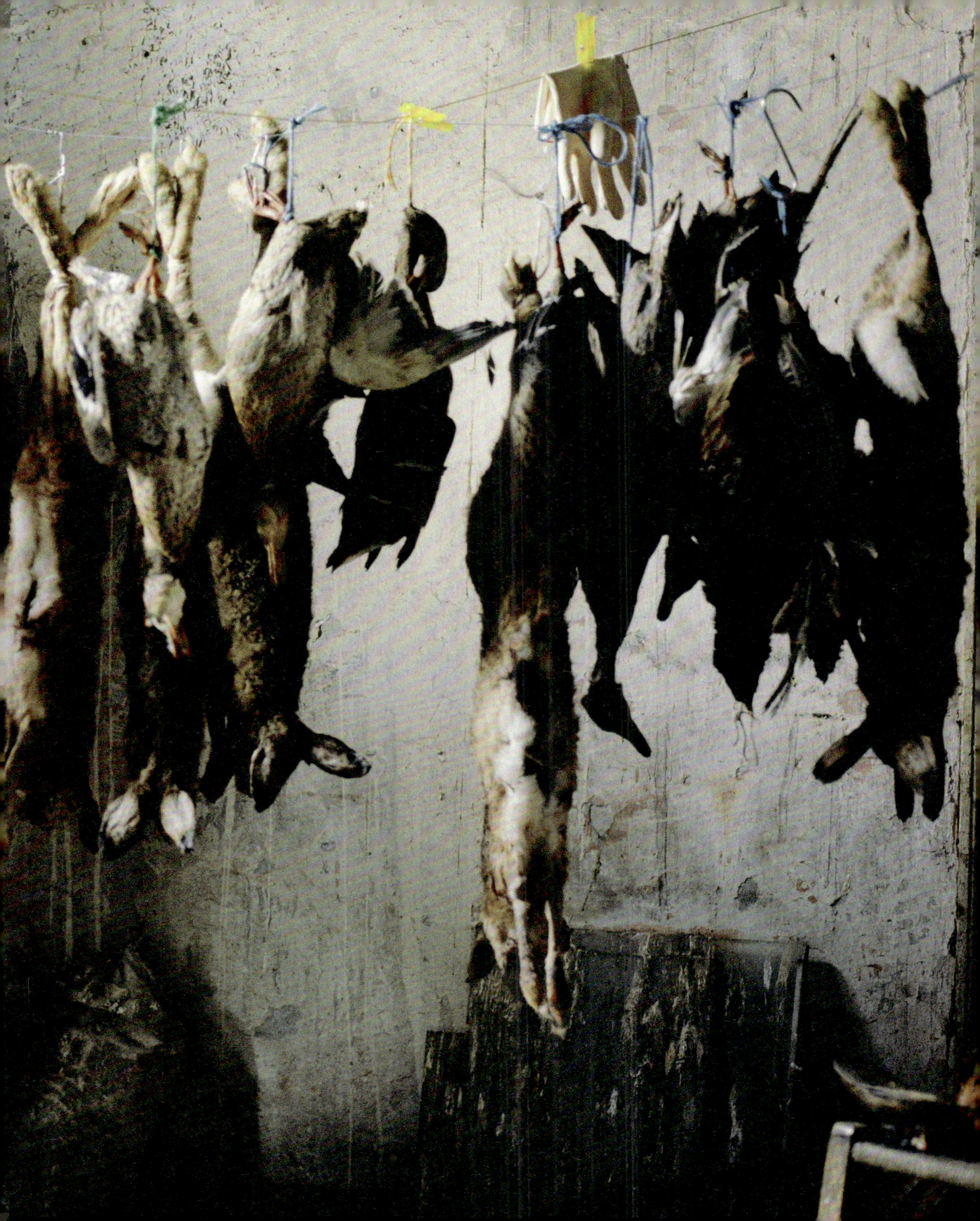

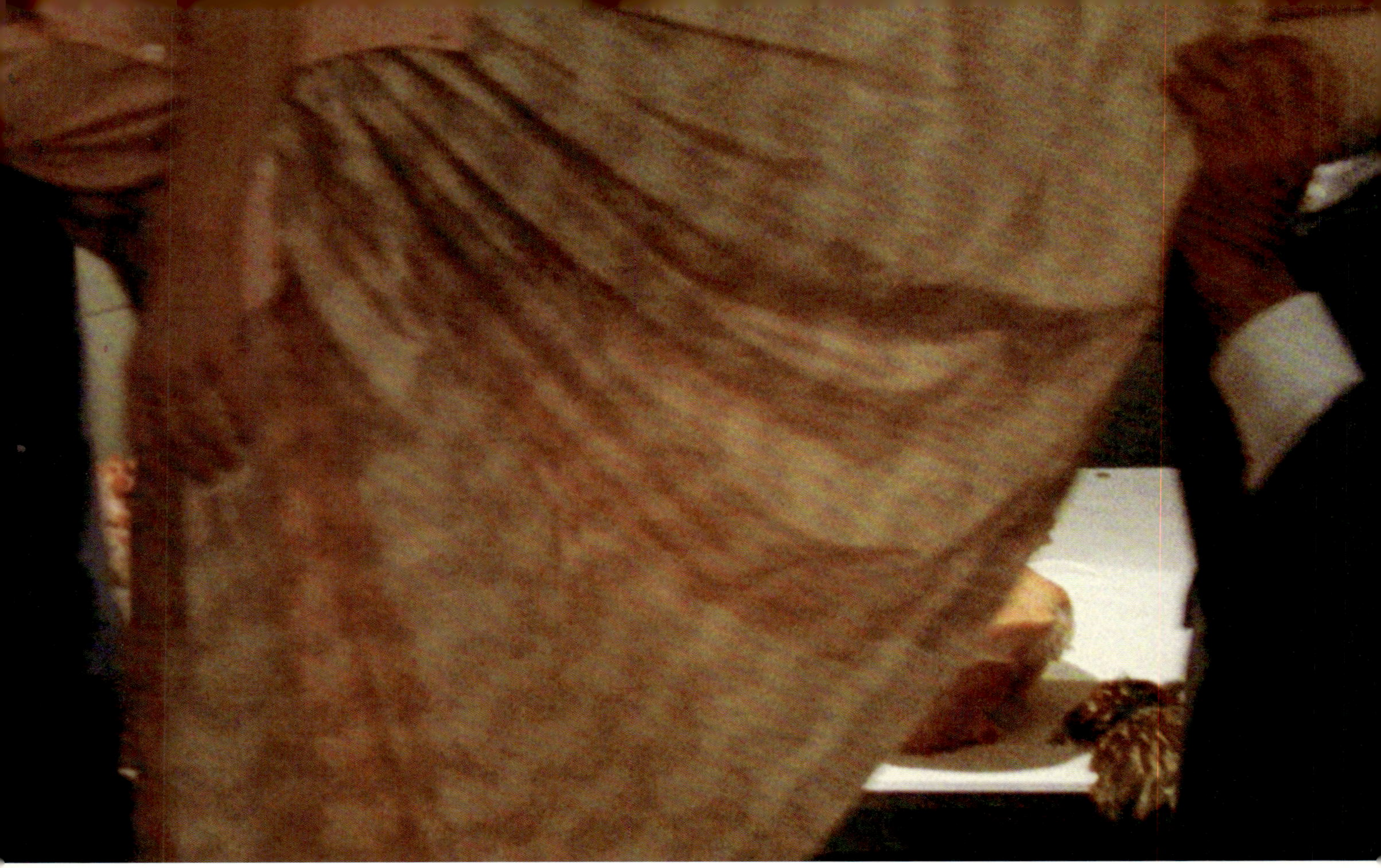

Then the great moment came; the show began. Nobody had eyes or minds for anything else. This was the Romans' opportunity: at a given signal all the Roman men burst through the crowd and seized the young women. Most of the girls were the prize of whoever got

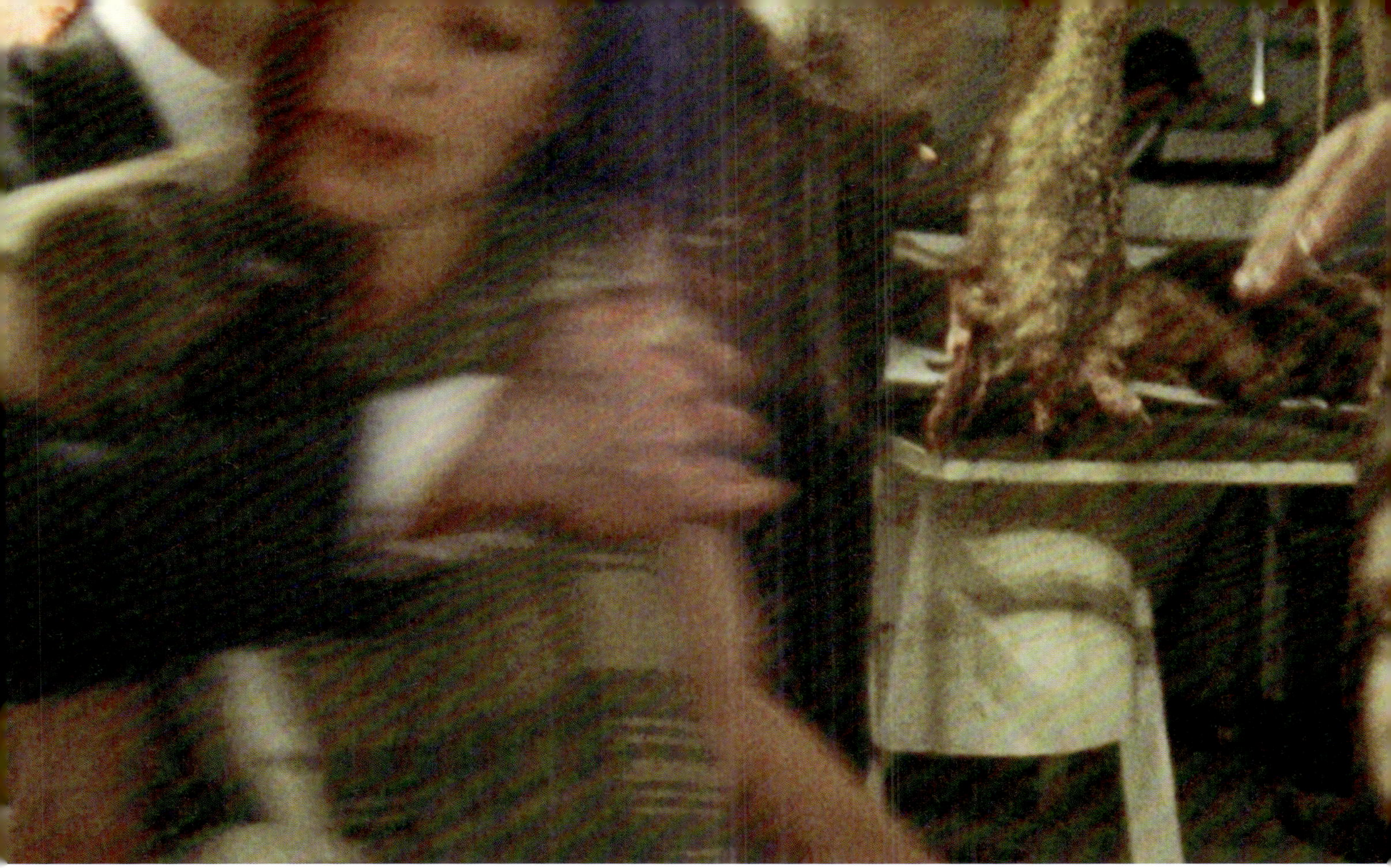

hold of them first, but a few conspicuously handsome ones had previously been marked down for leading patricians and these were carried to their houses by plebeians, special gangs told off for the task.

The Early History of Rome, 1.9, Livy

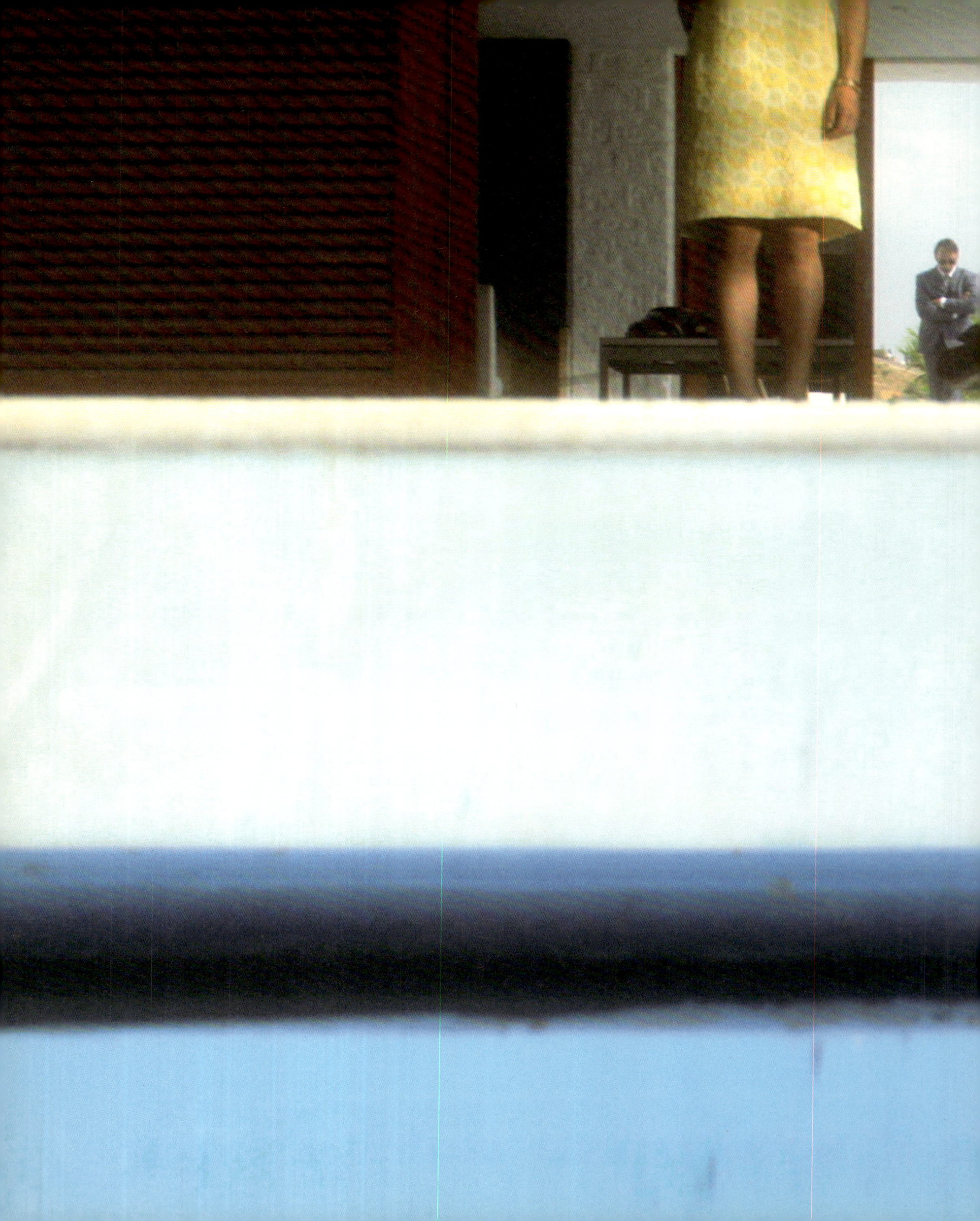

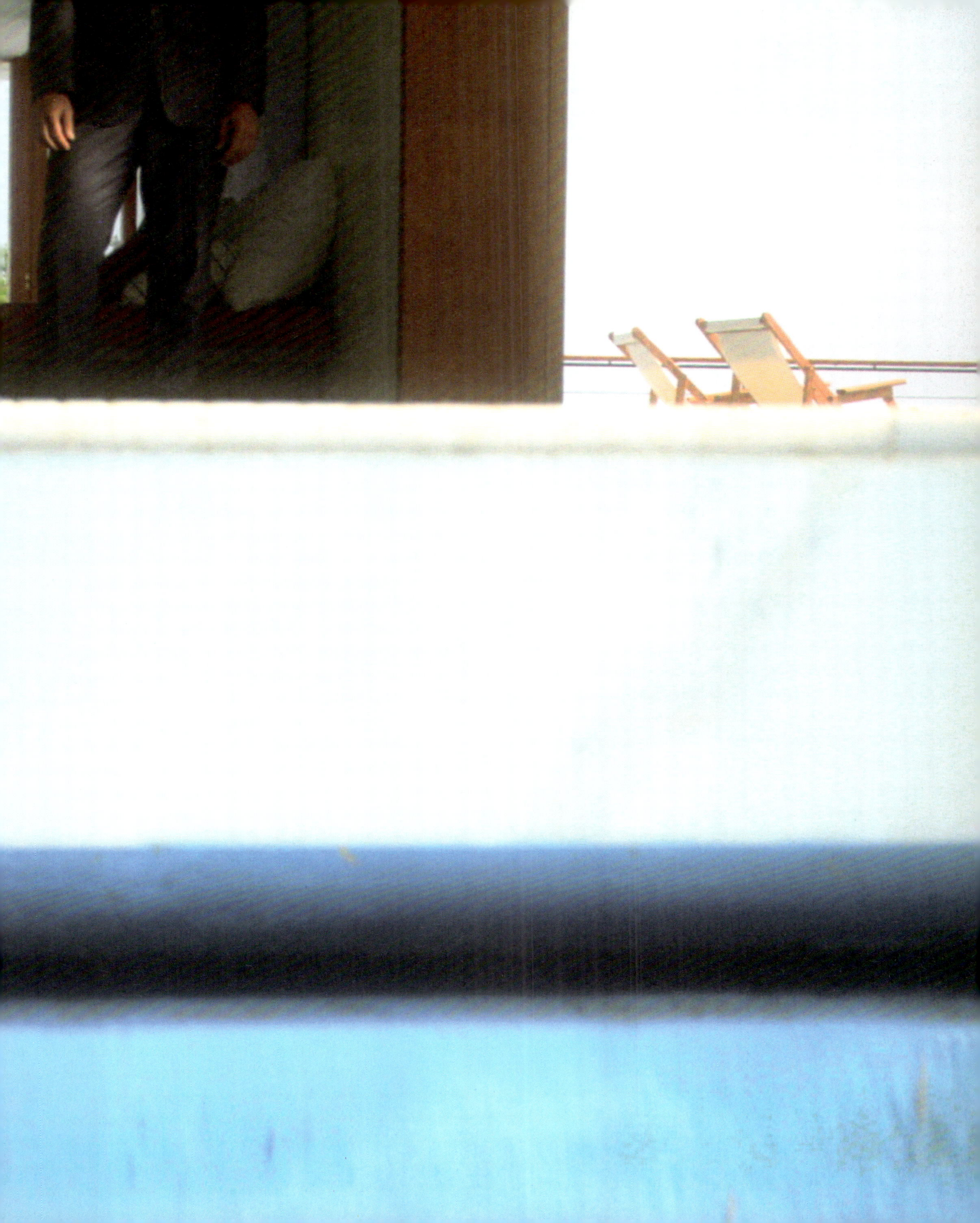

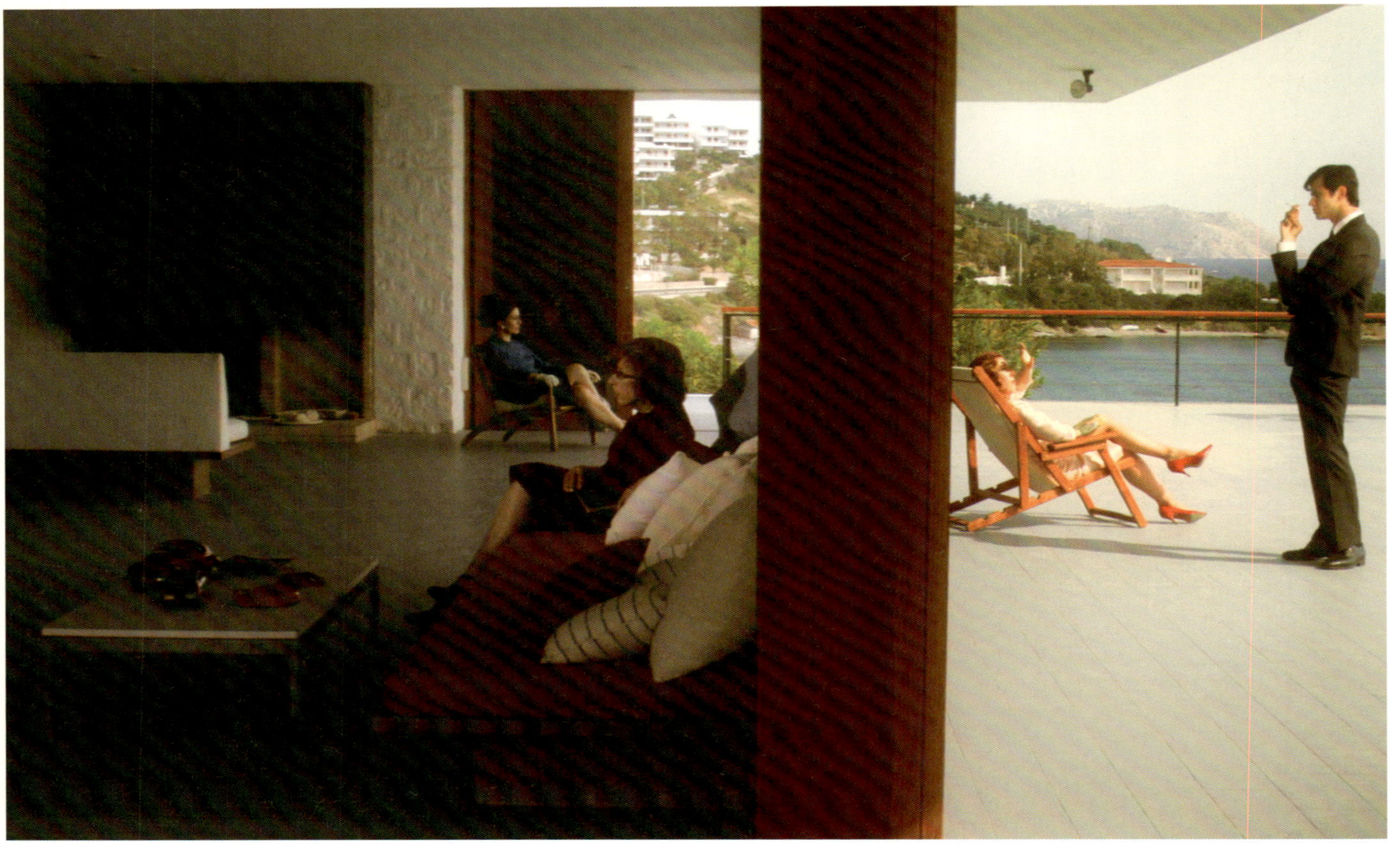

The abducted maidens were quite as despondent and indignant. Romulus, himself went amongst them, and pointed out to them that it was the pride of their parents that had caused this deed by denying right of intermarriage to their neighbours. They need not fear; they would live in honourable wedlock, and share

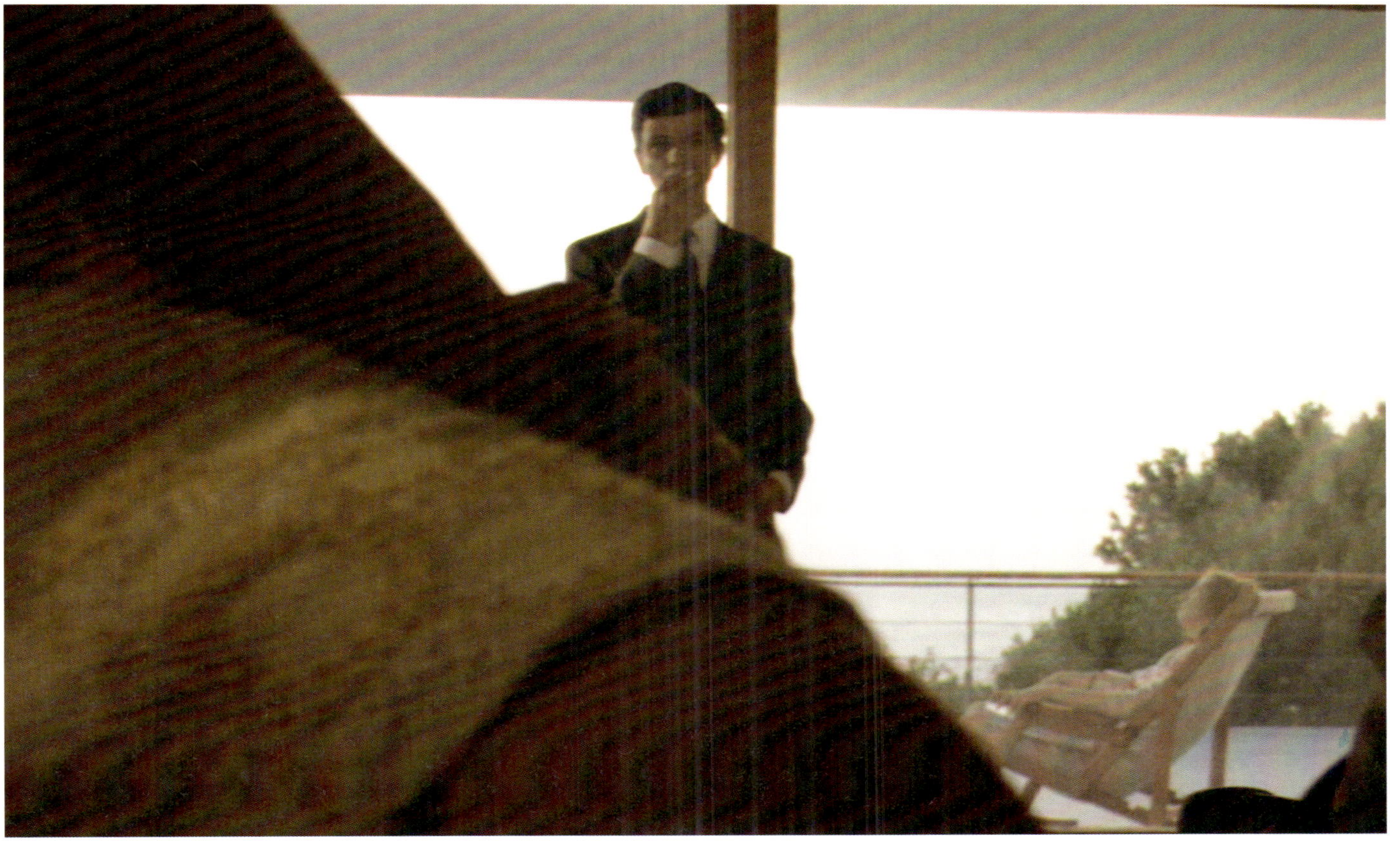

all the fortunes of Rome, all property and civil rights and – dearest of all to human nature – would be the mothers of freemen. He urged them to forget their wrath and give their hearts to those to whom chance had given their bodies.

The Early History of Rome, 1.9, Livy

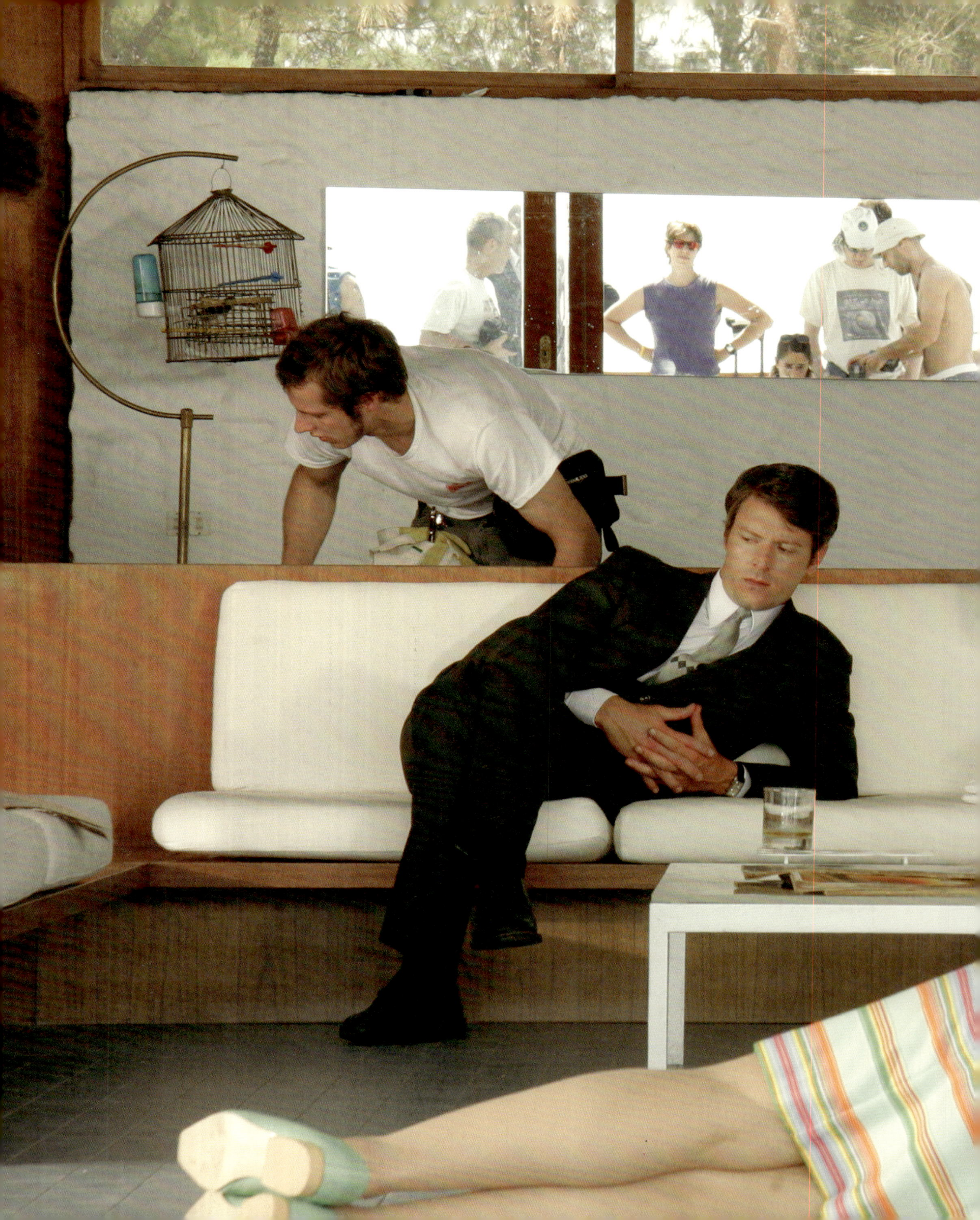

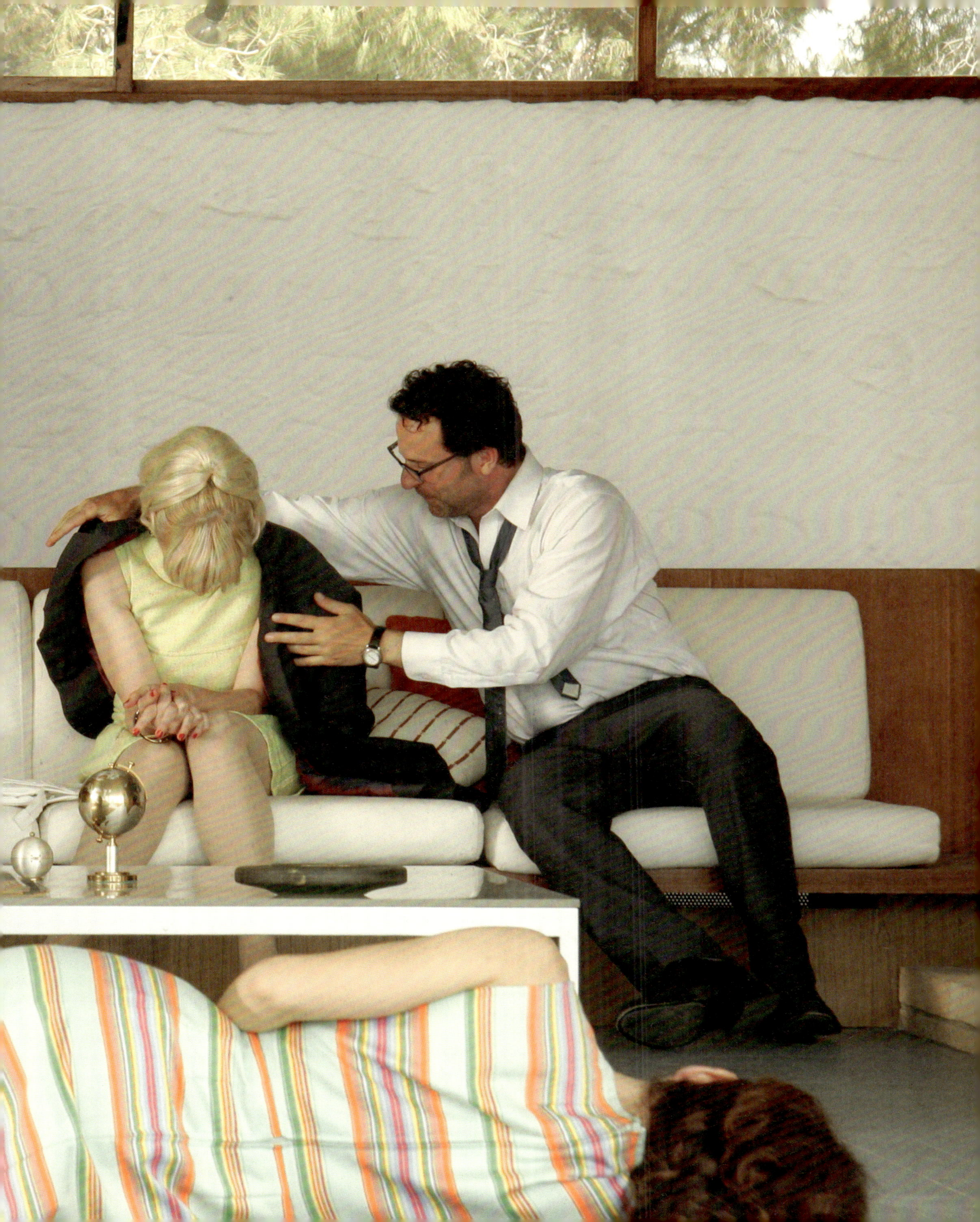

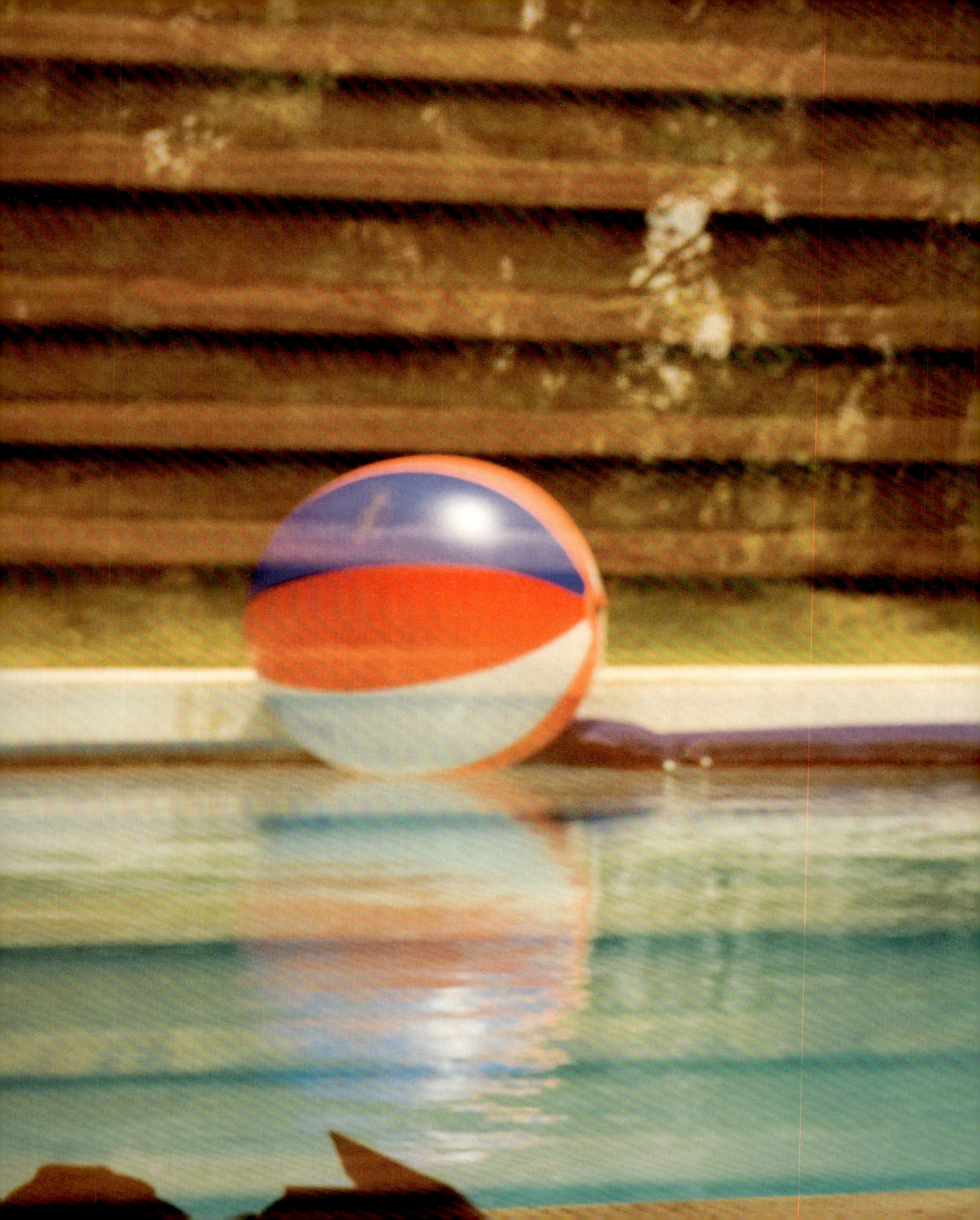

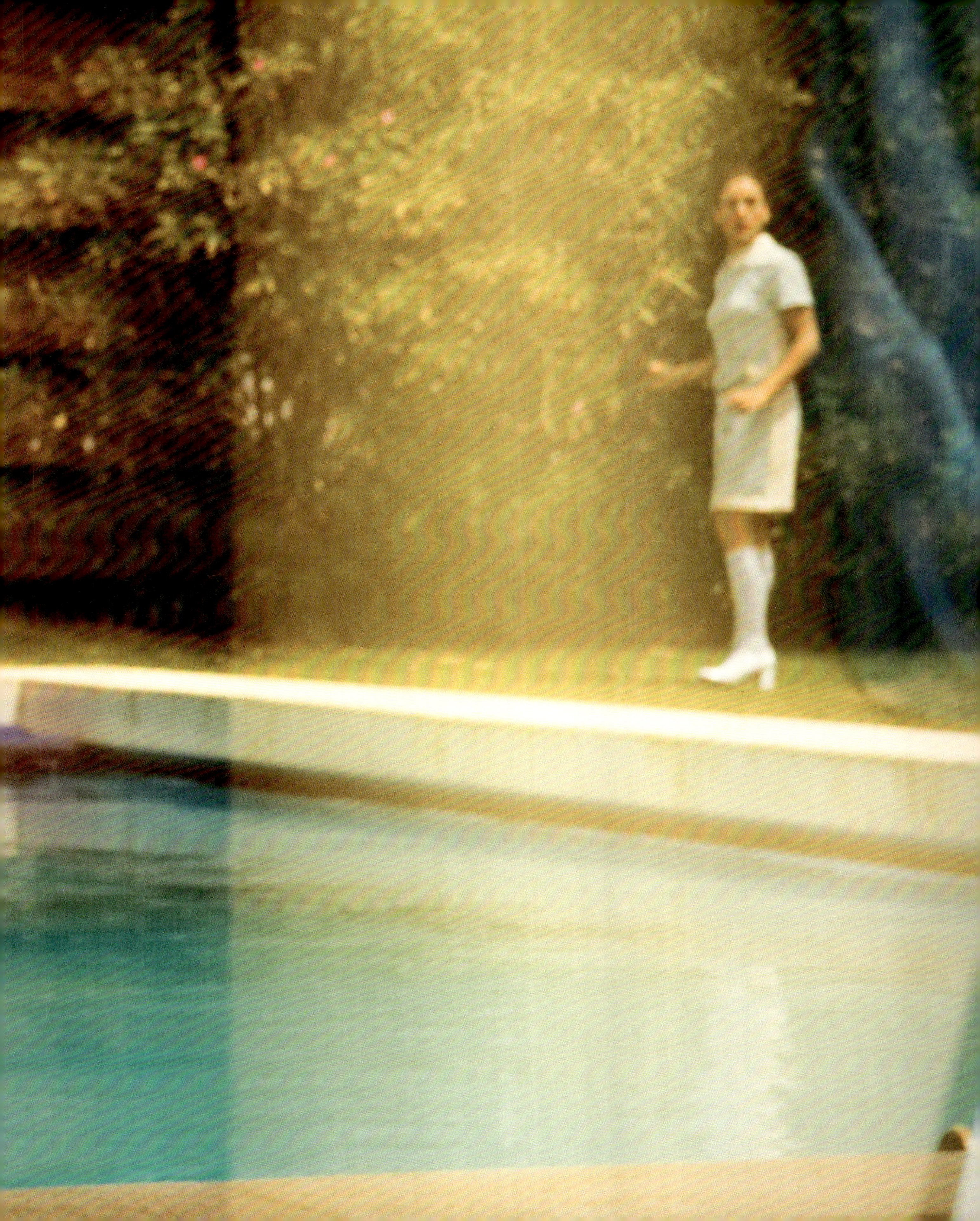

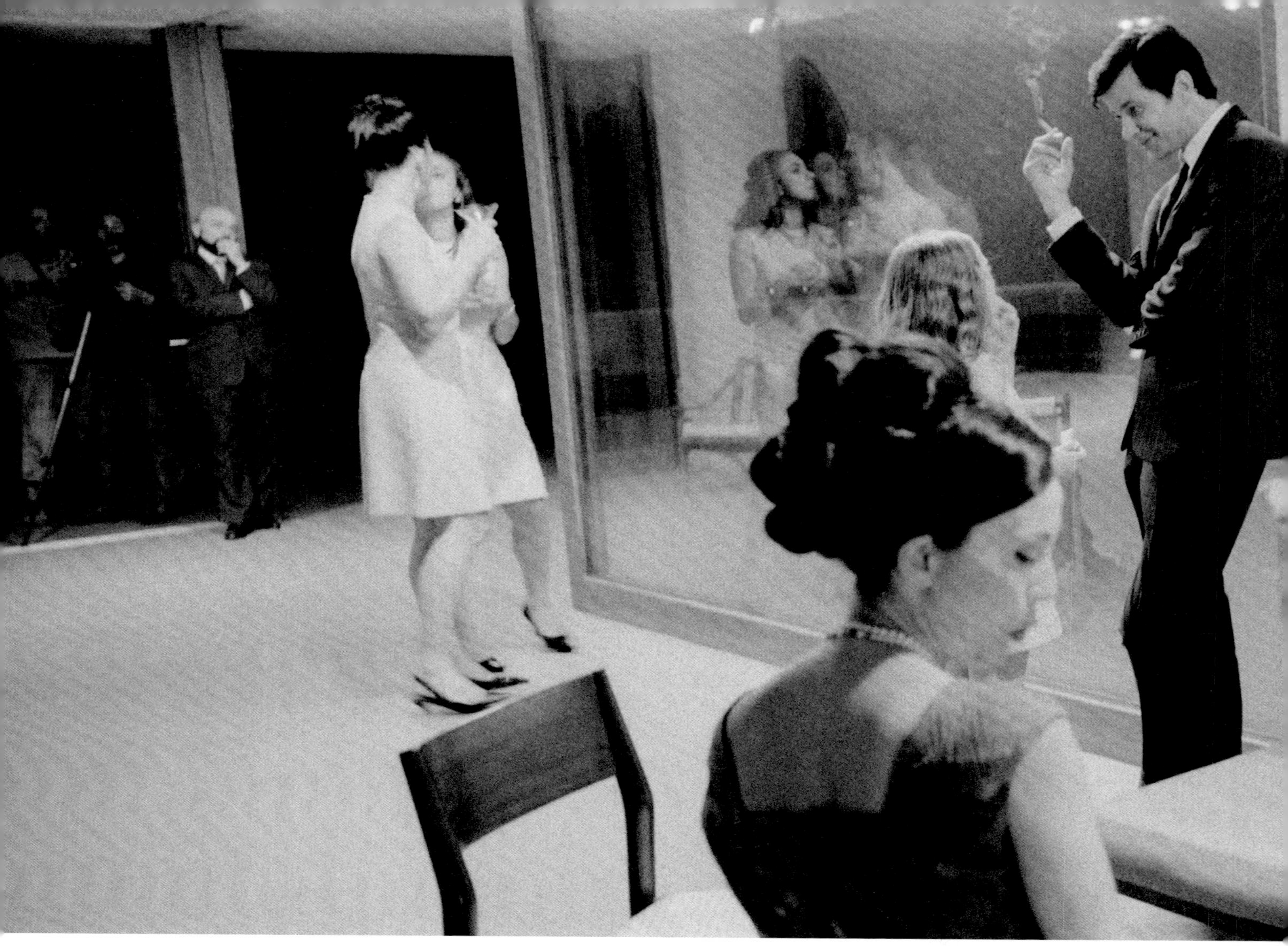

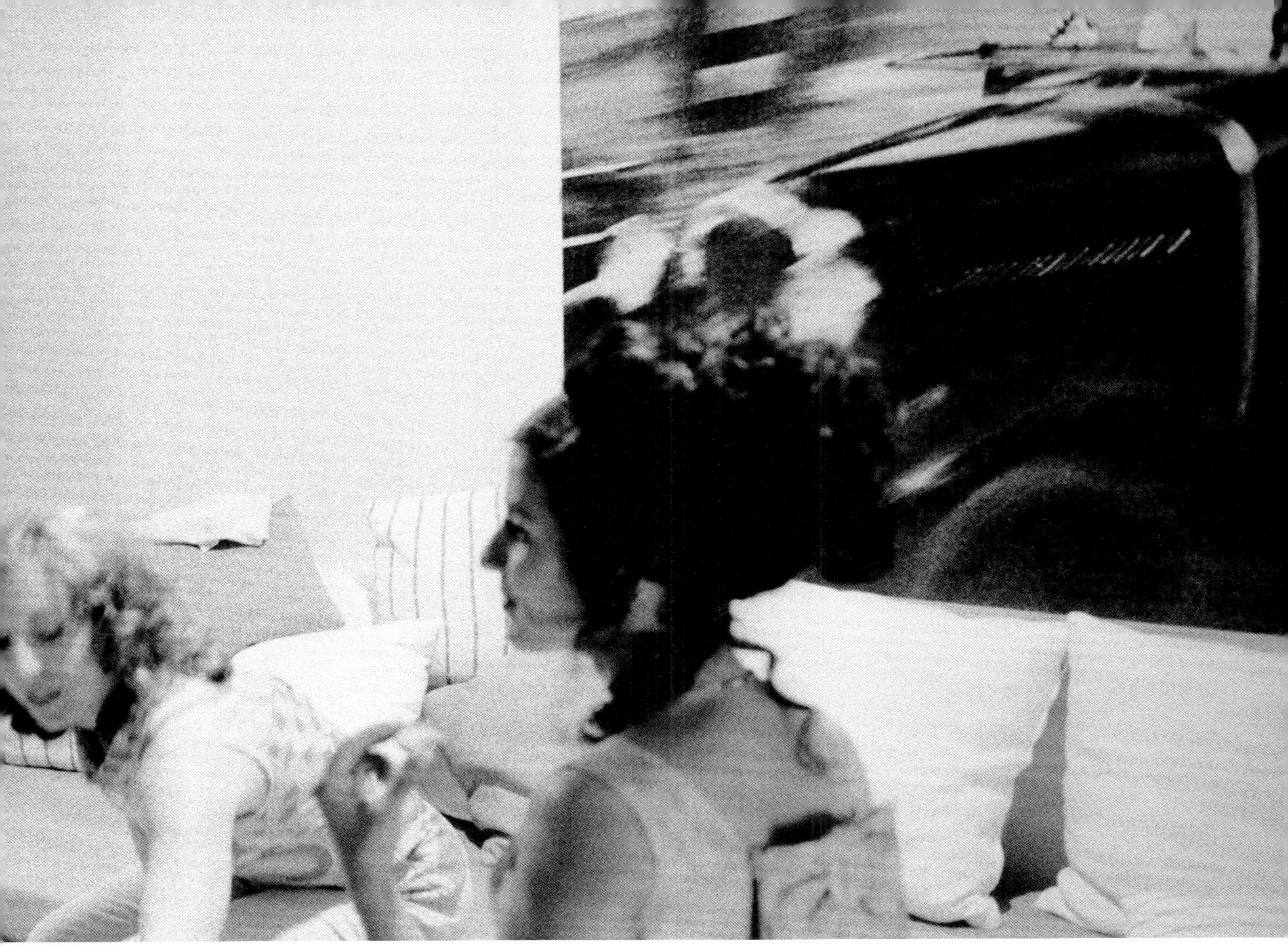

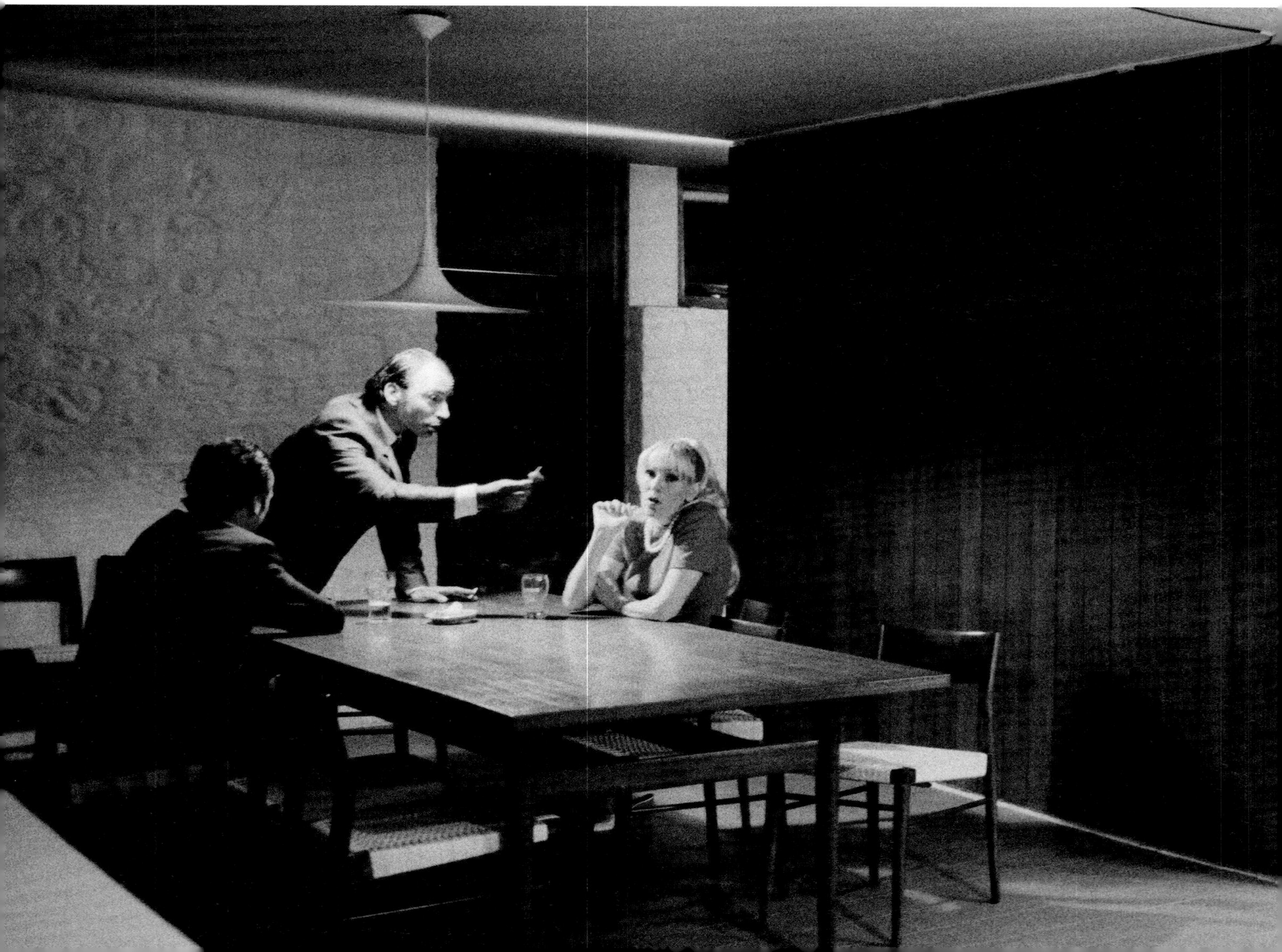

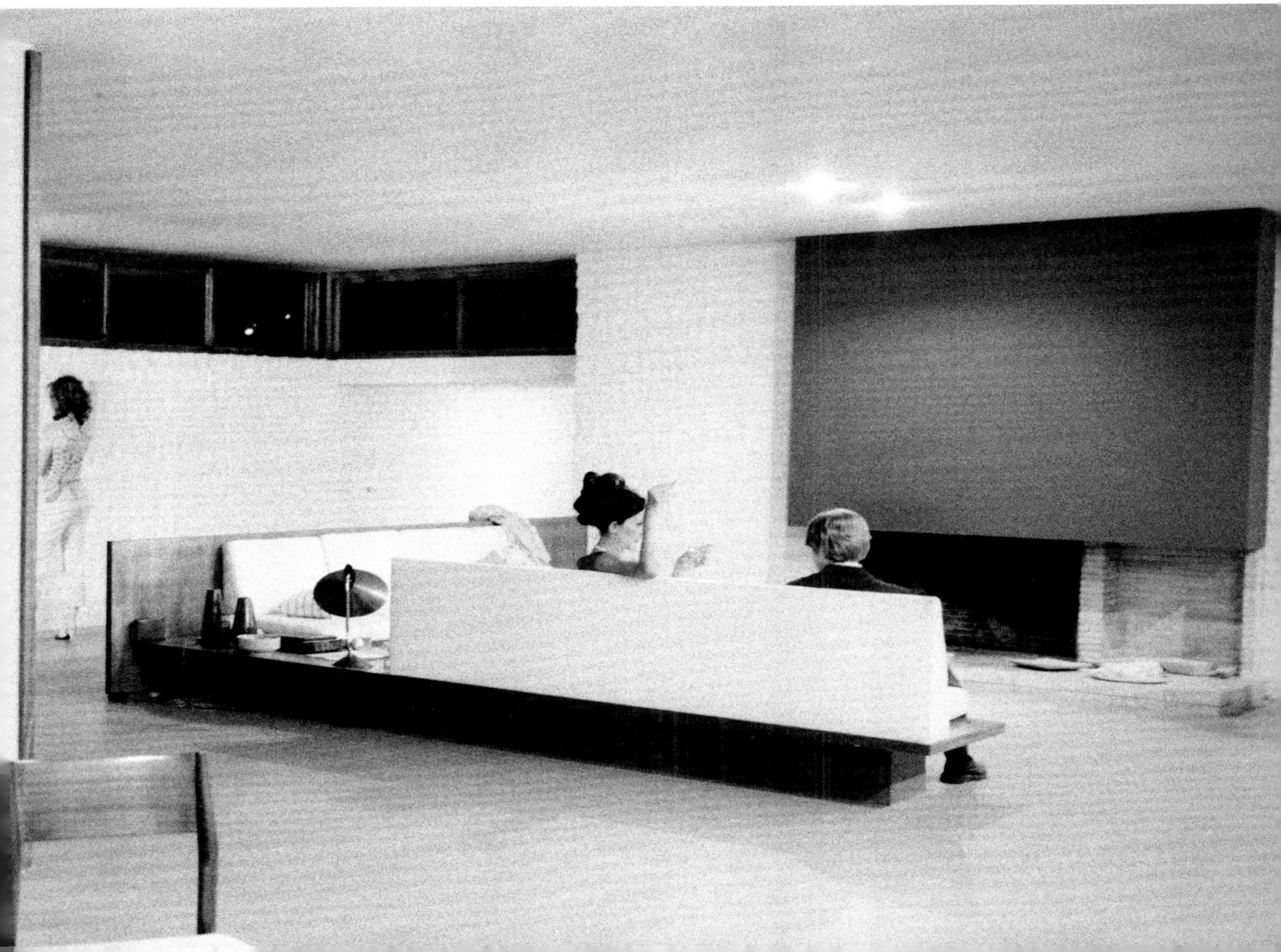

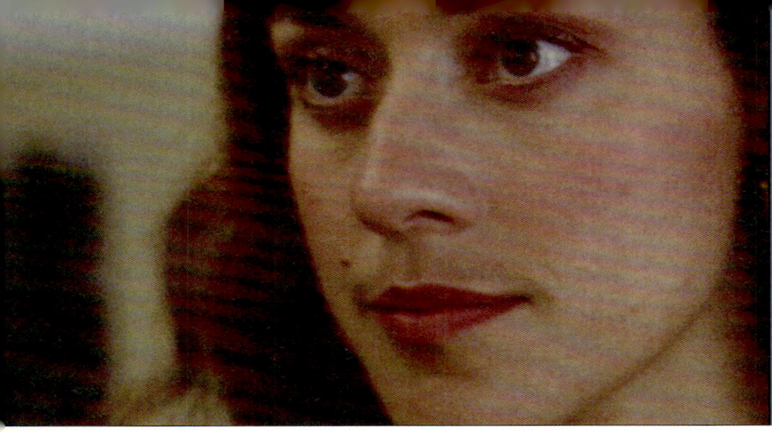
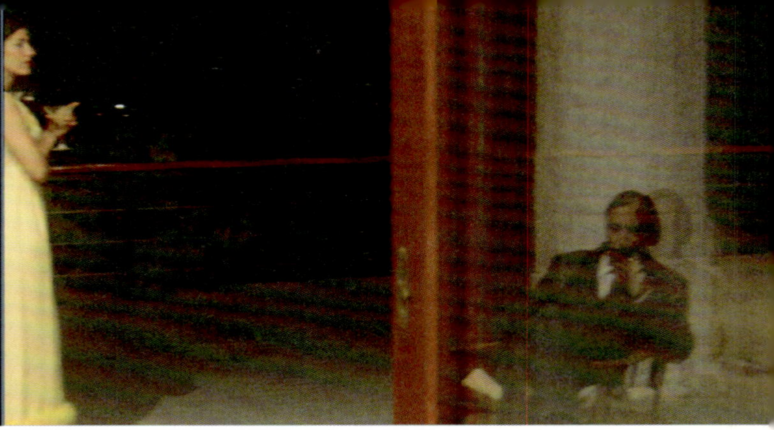
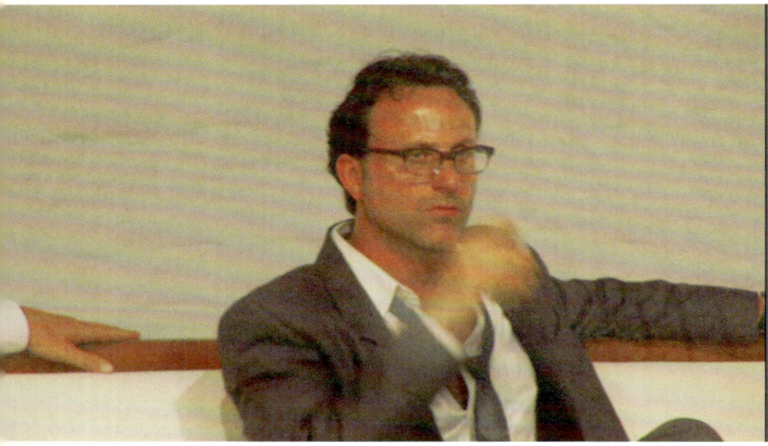
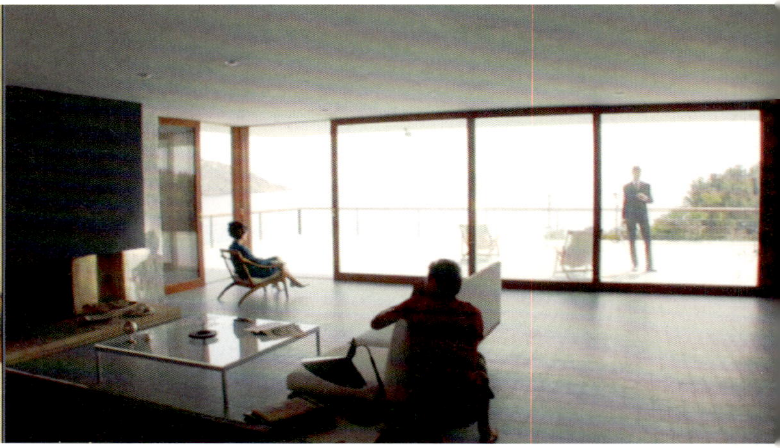
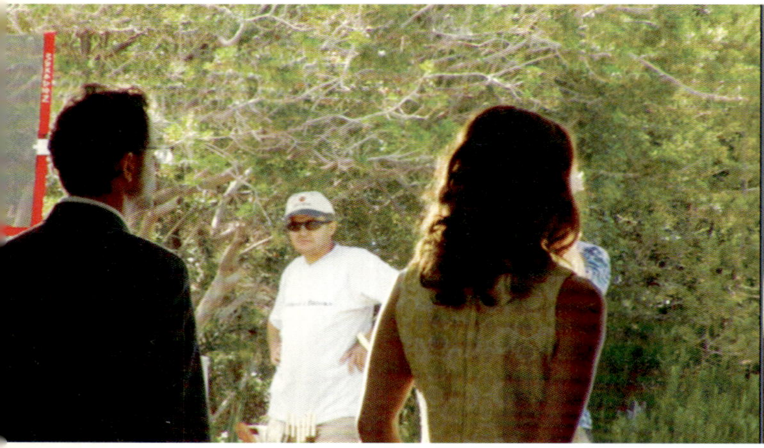
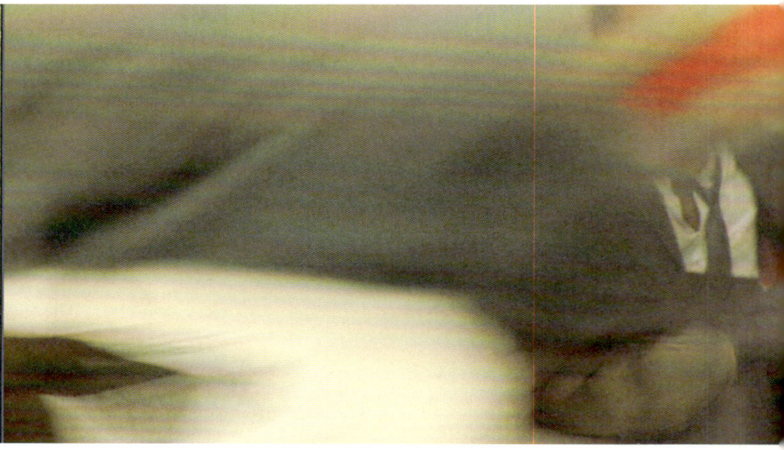
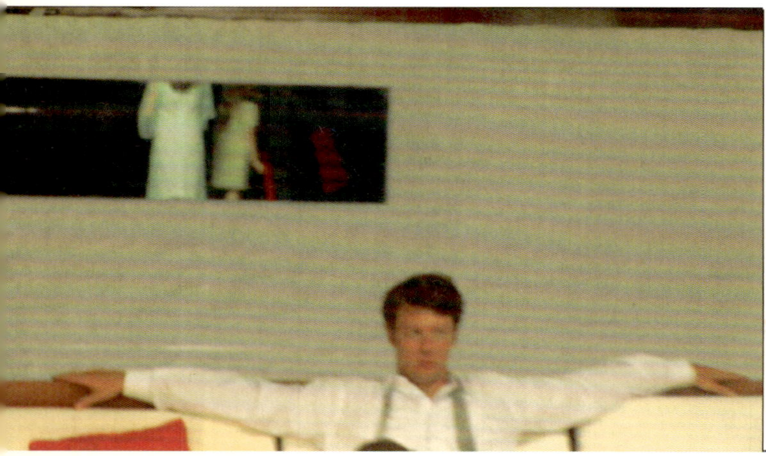
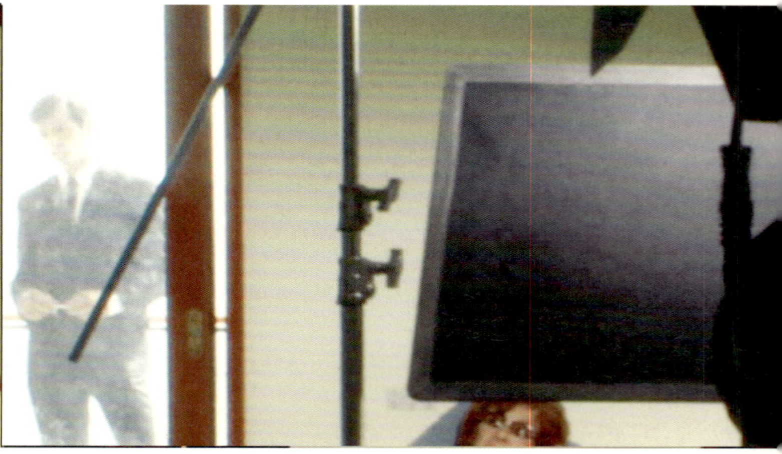

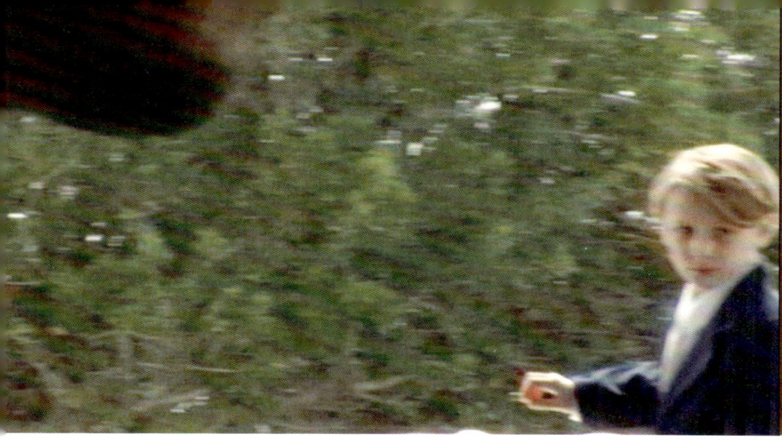
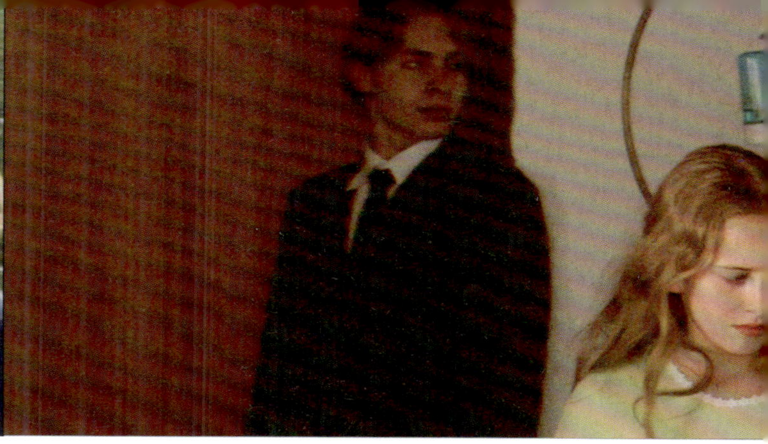
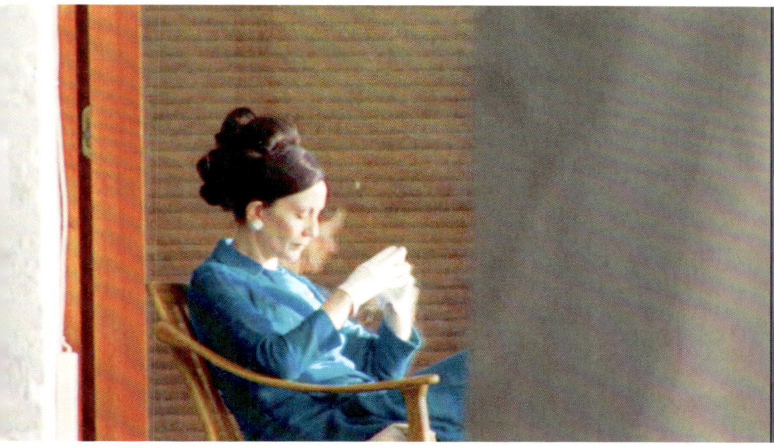
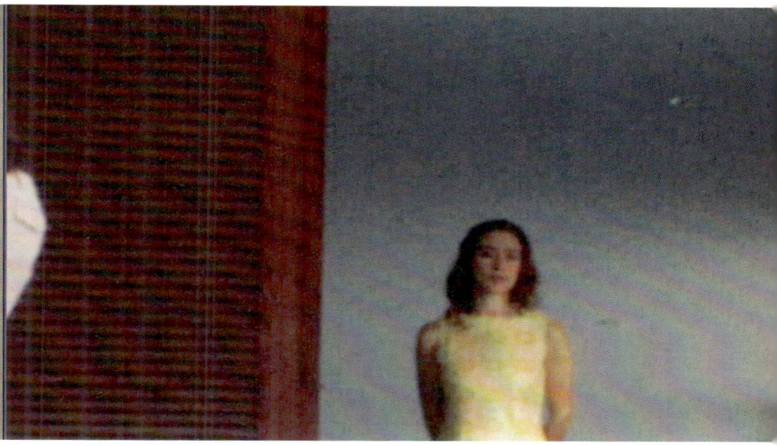
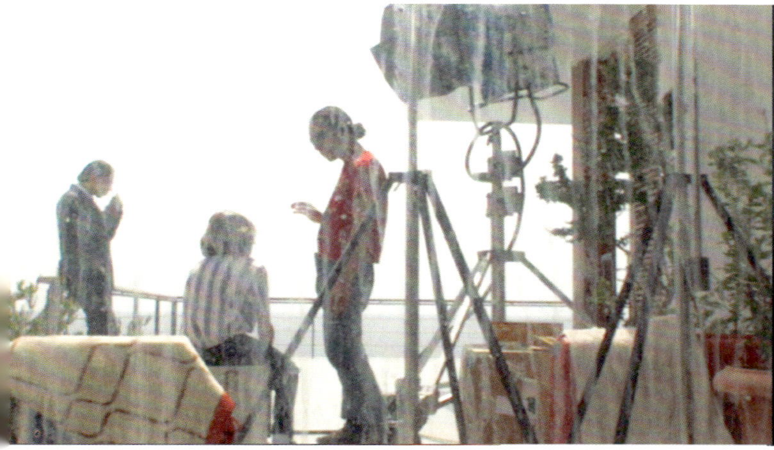
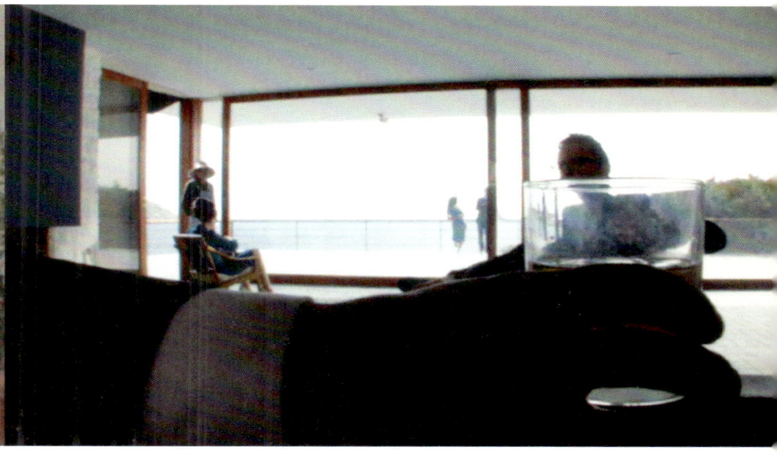
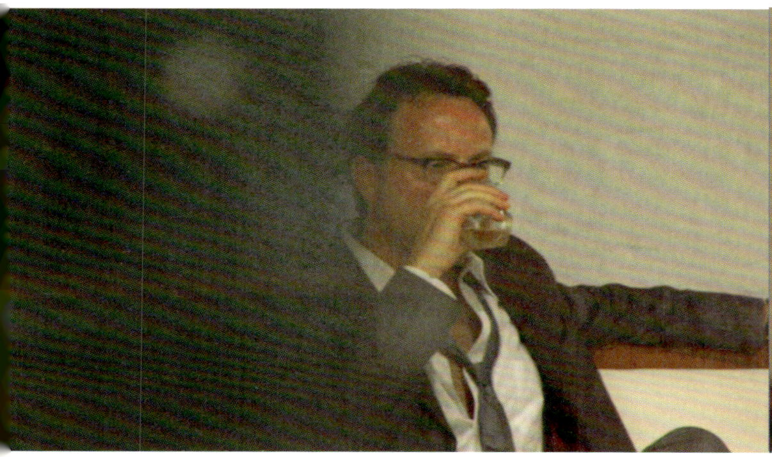
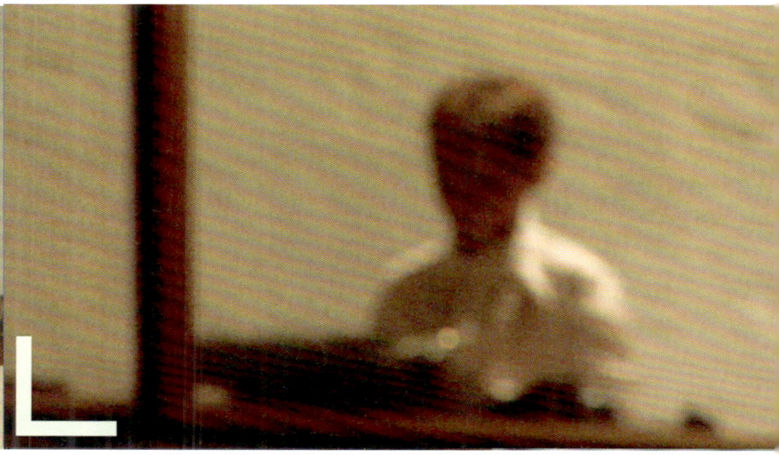

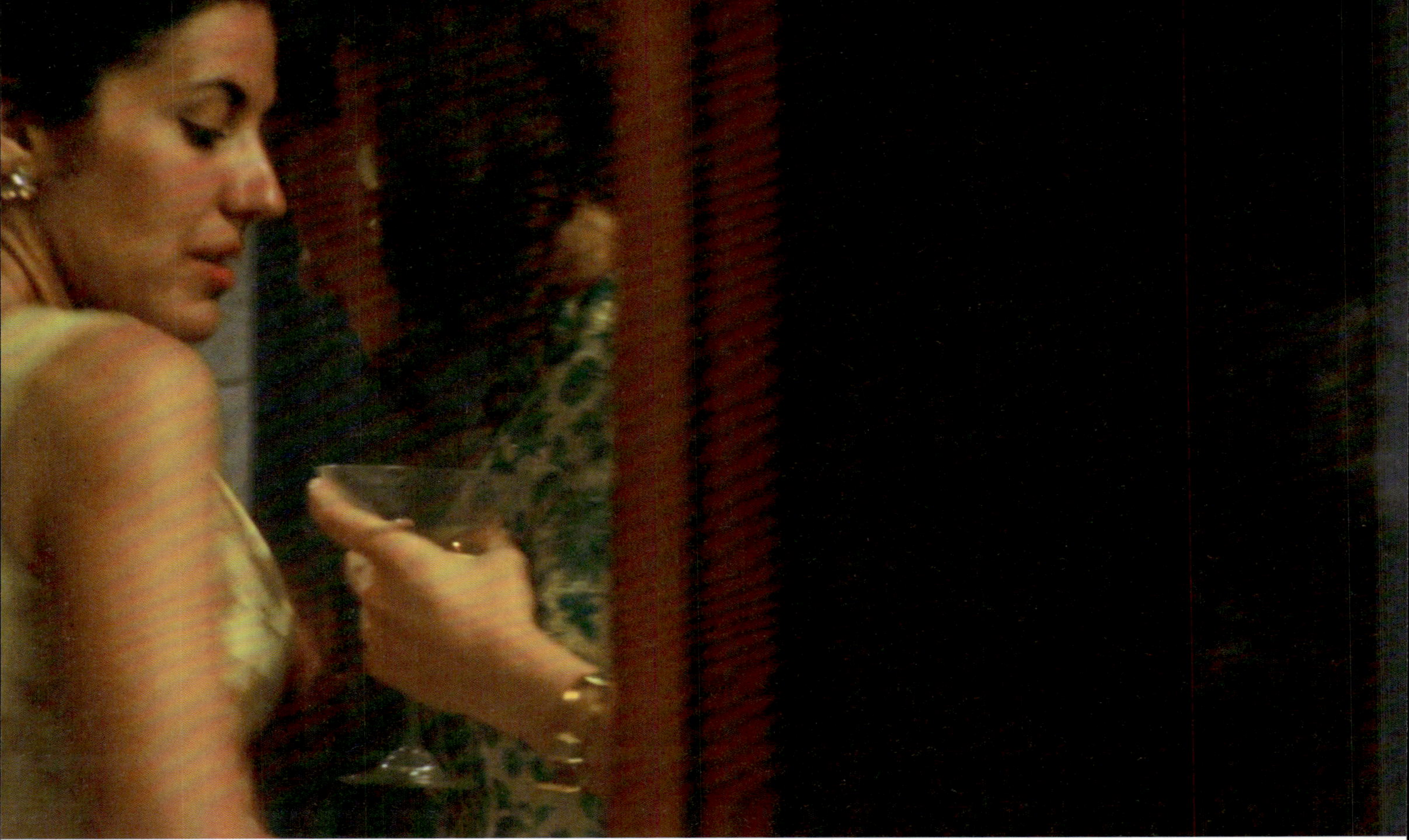

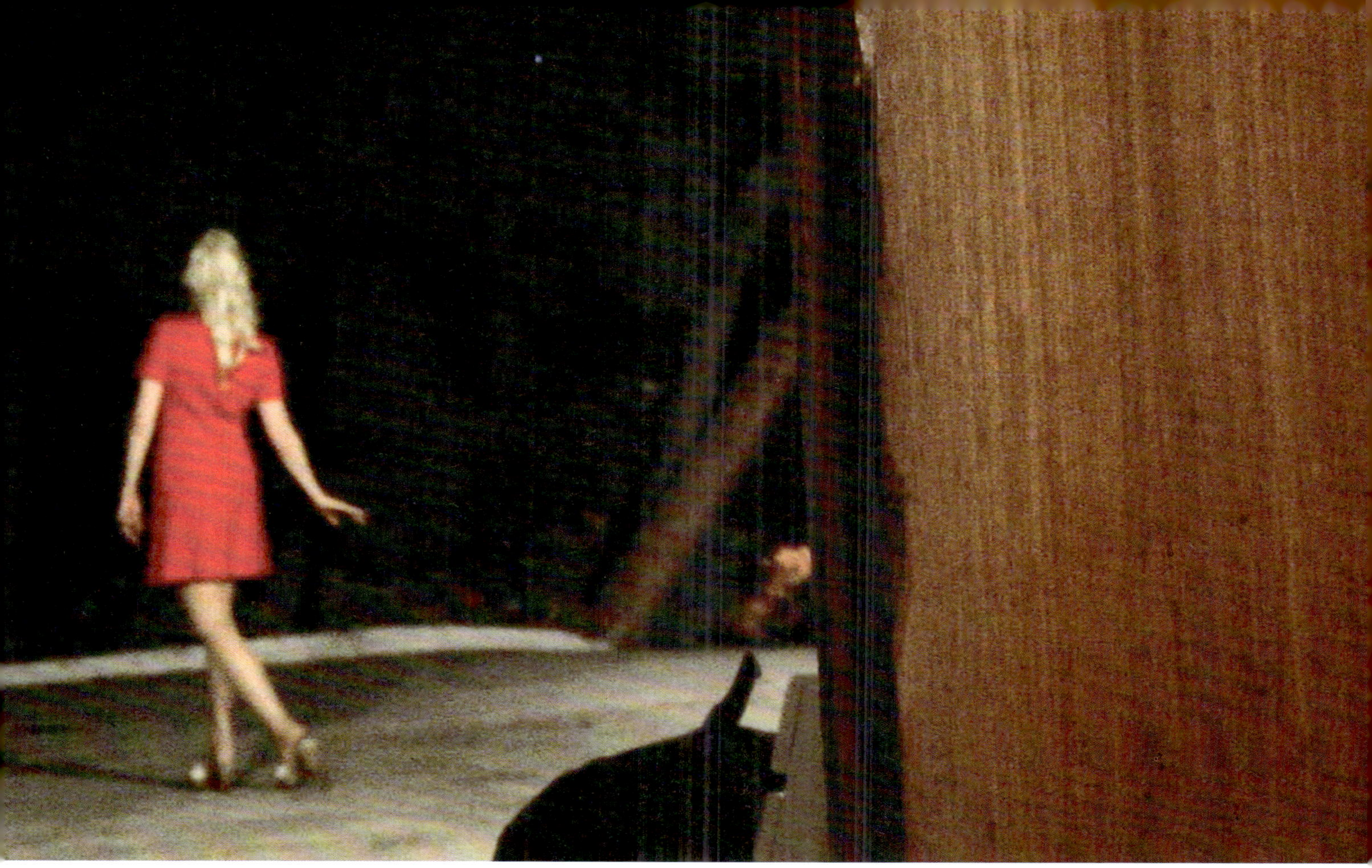

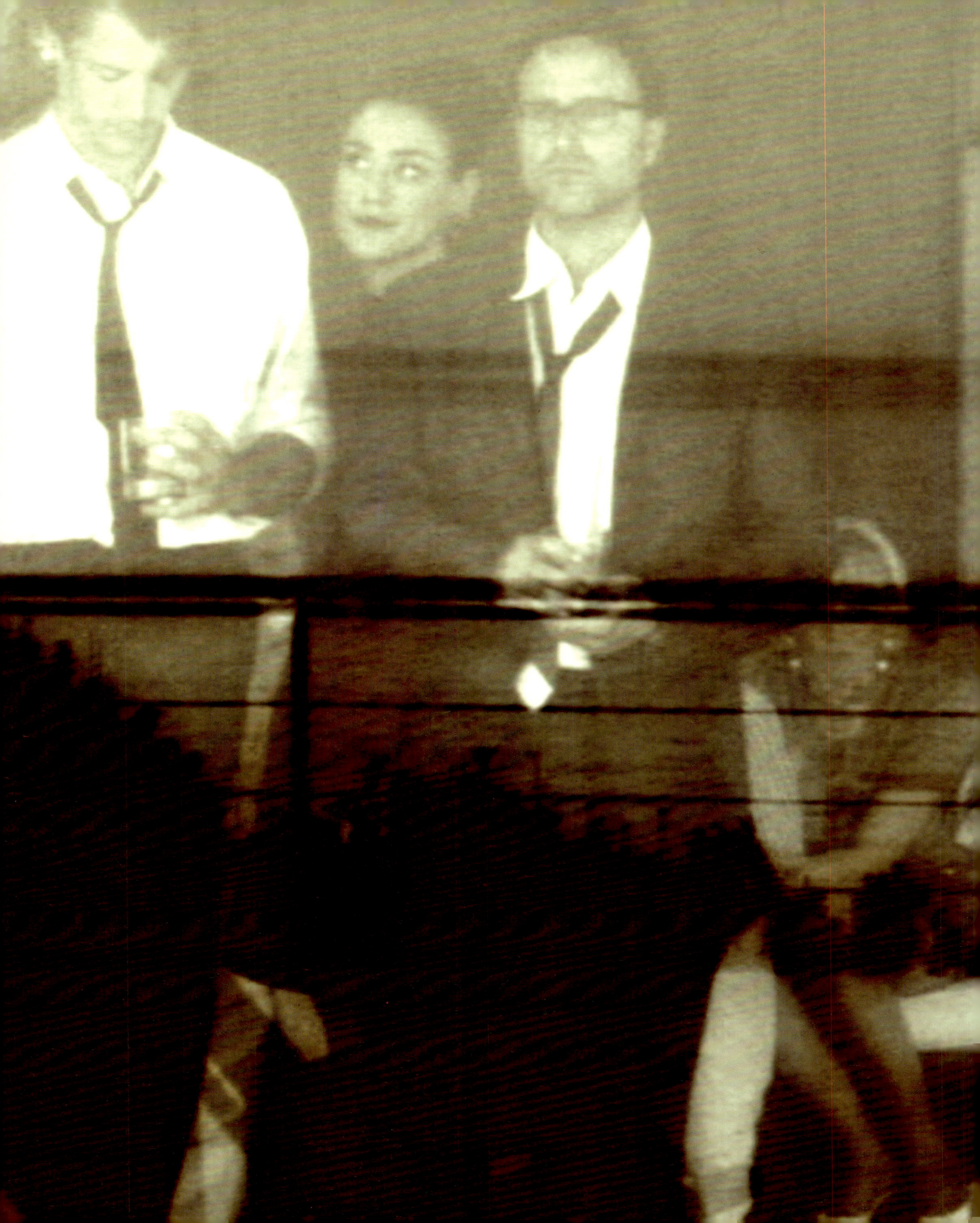

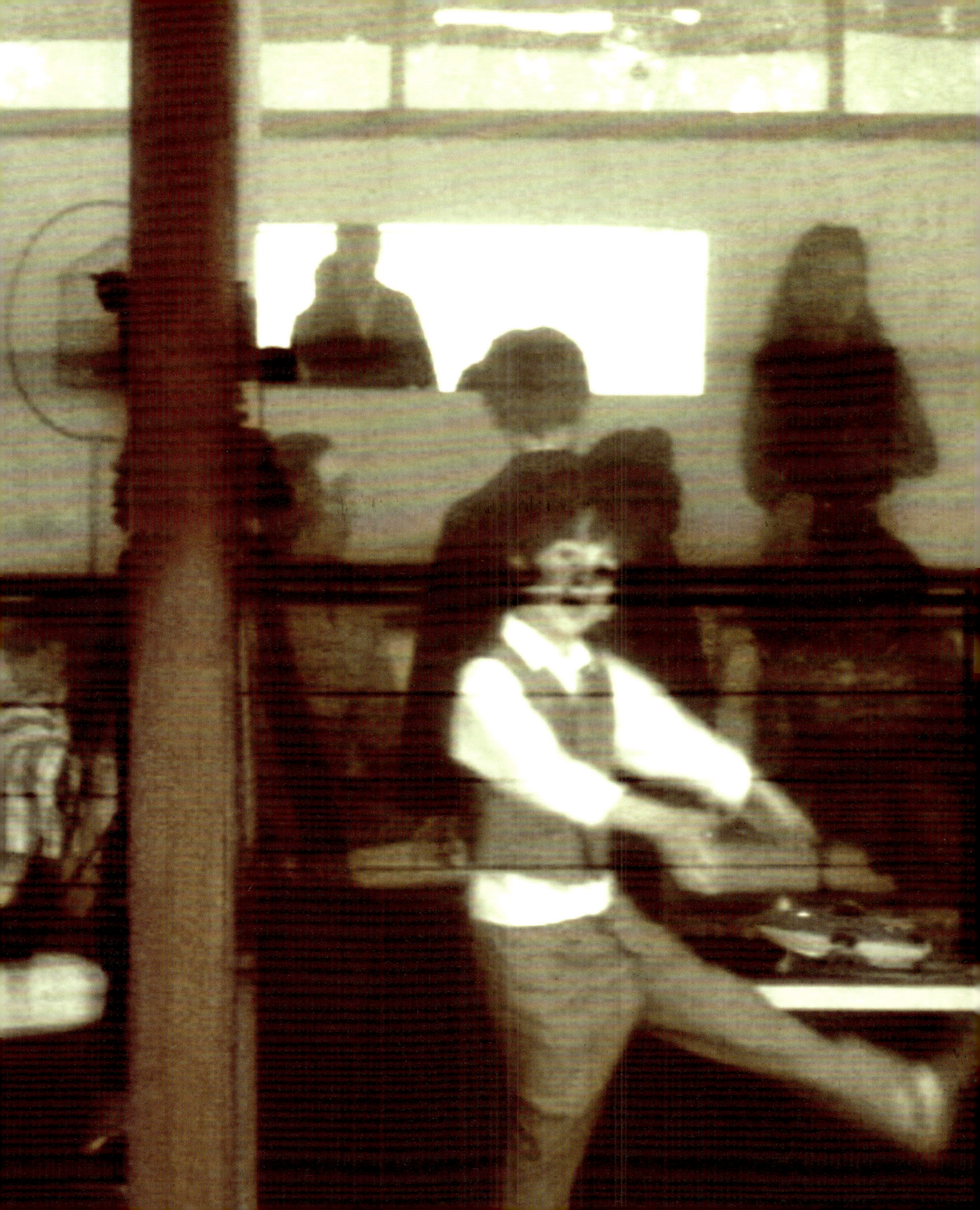

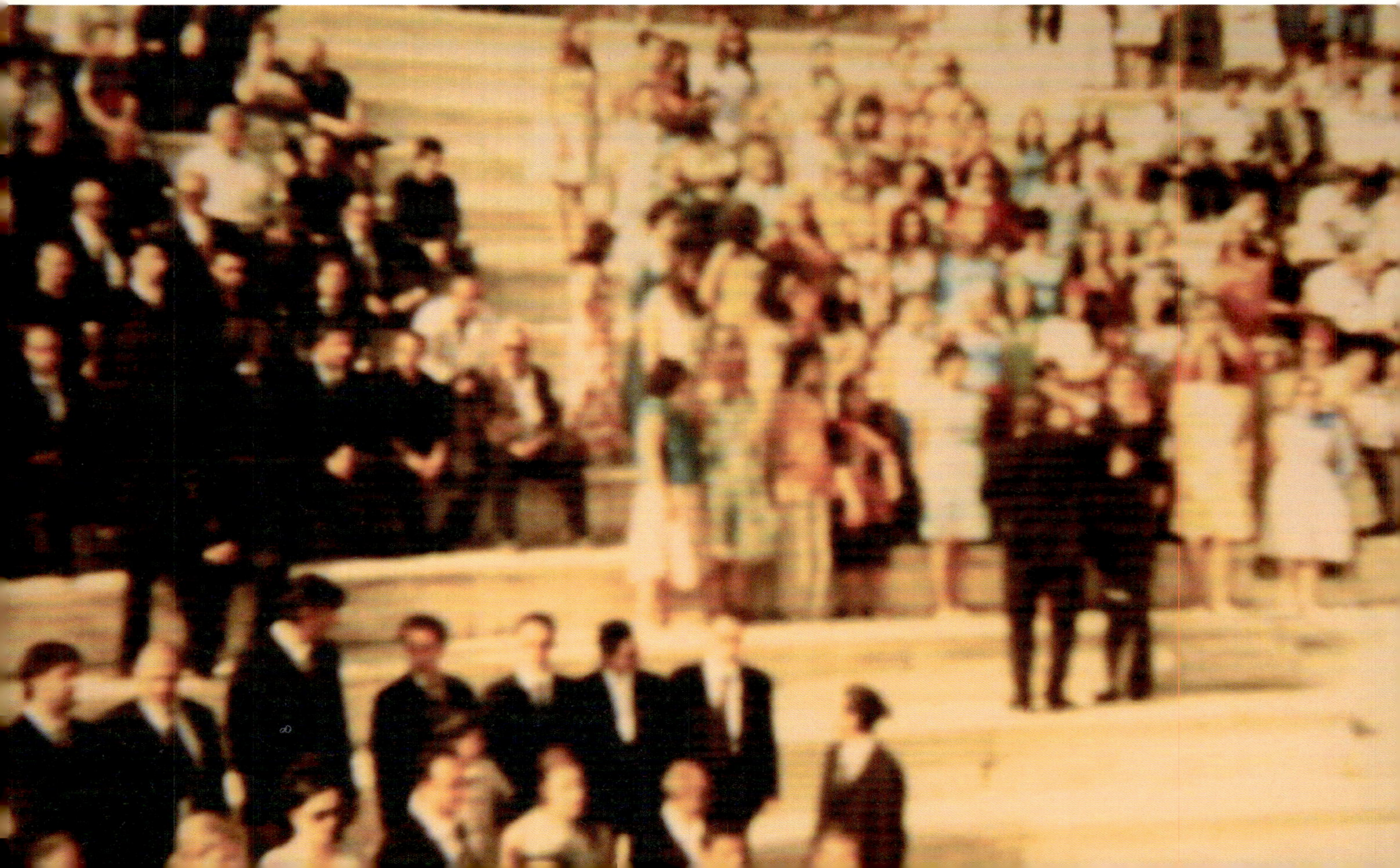

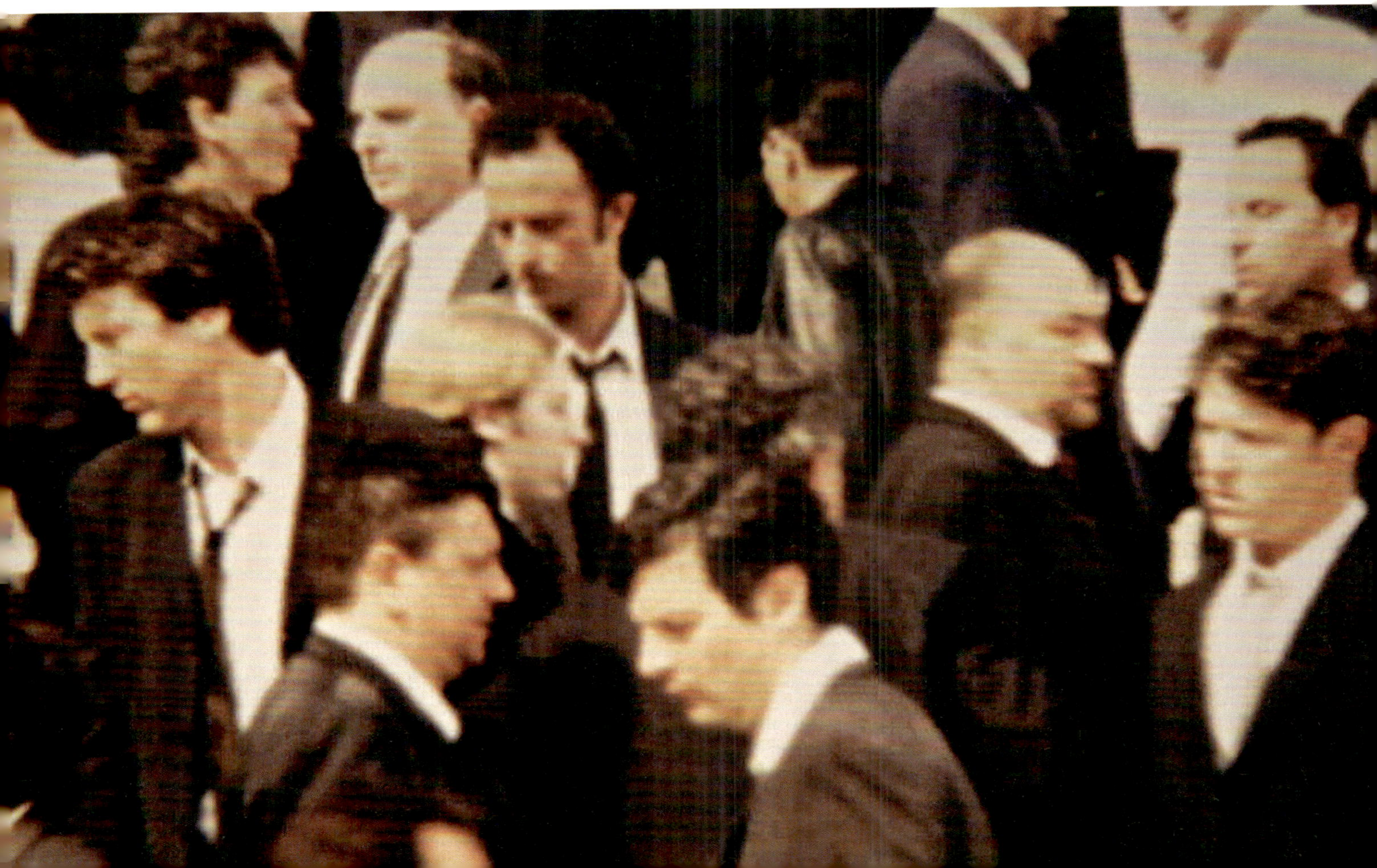

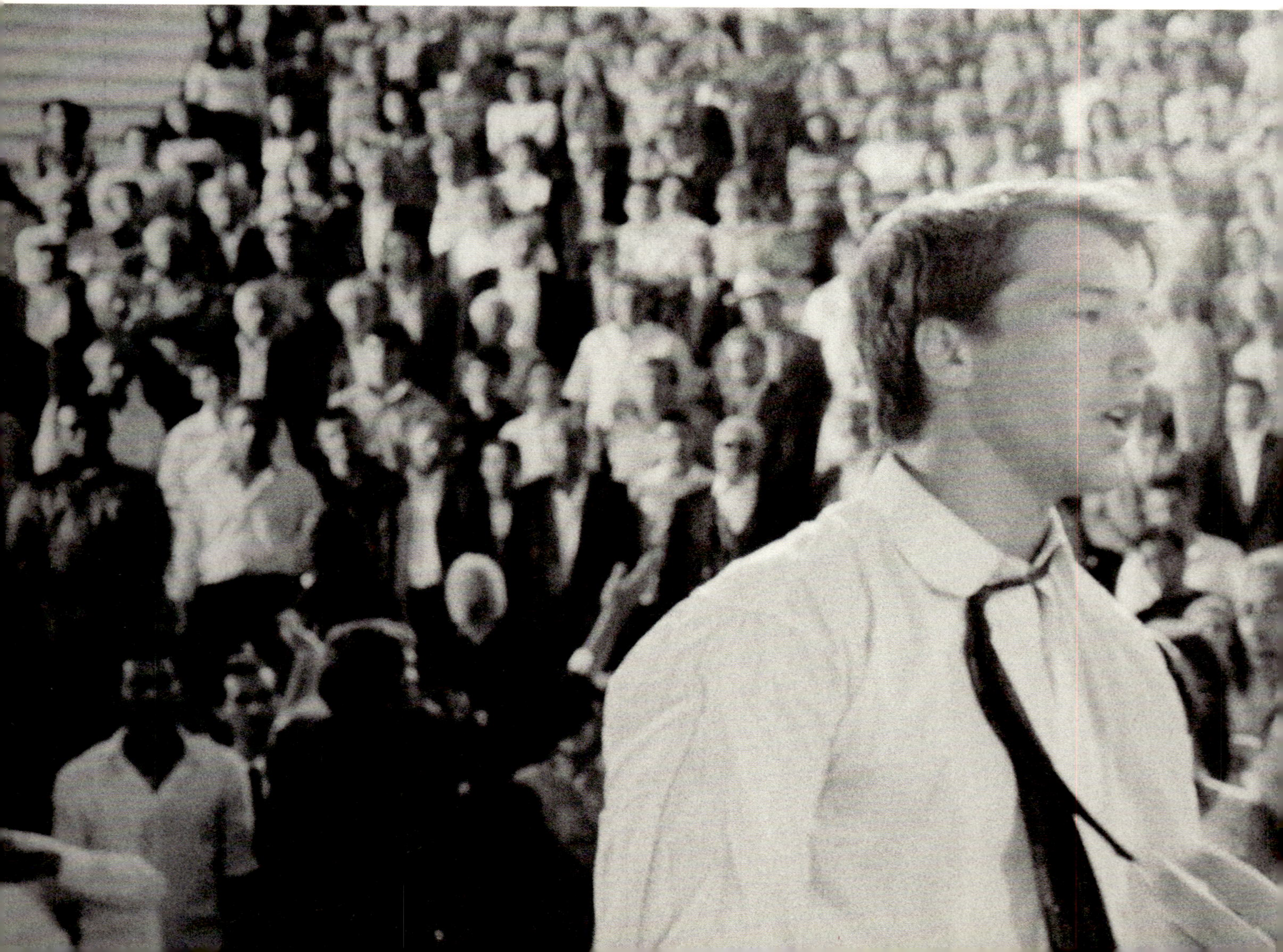

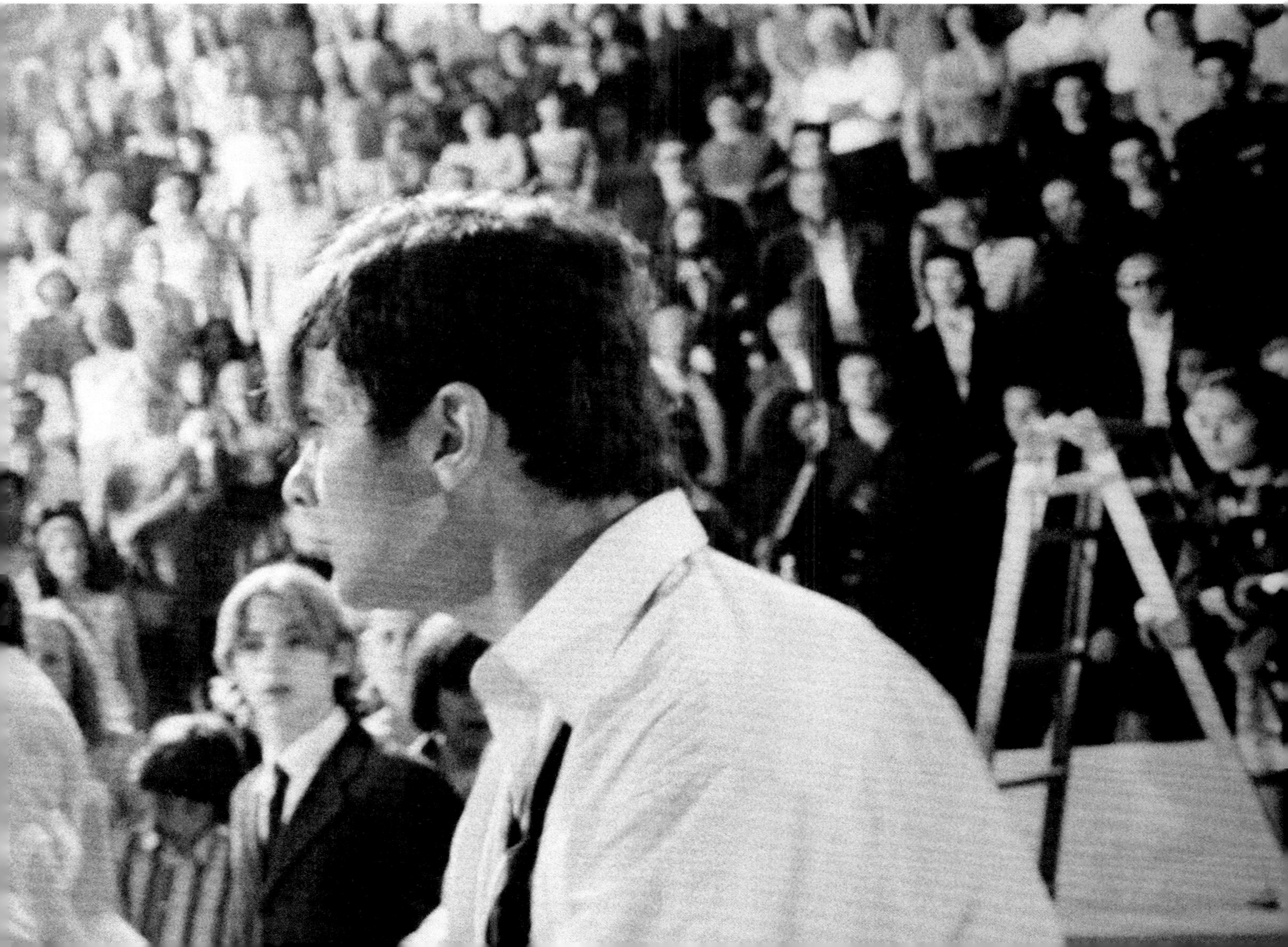

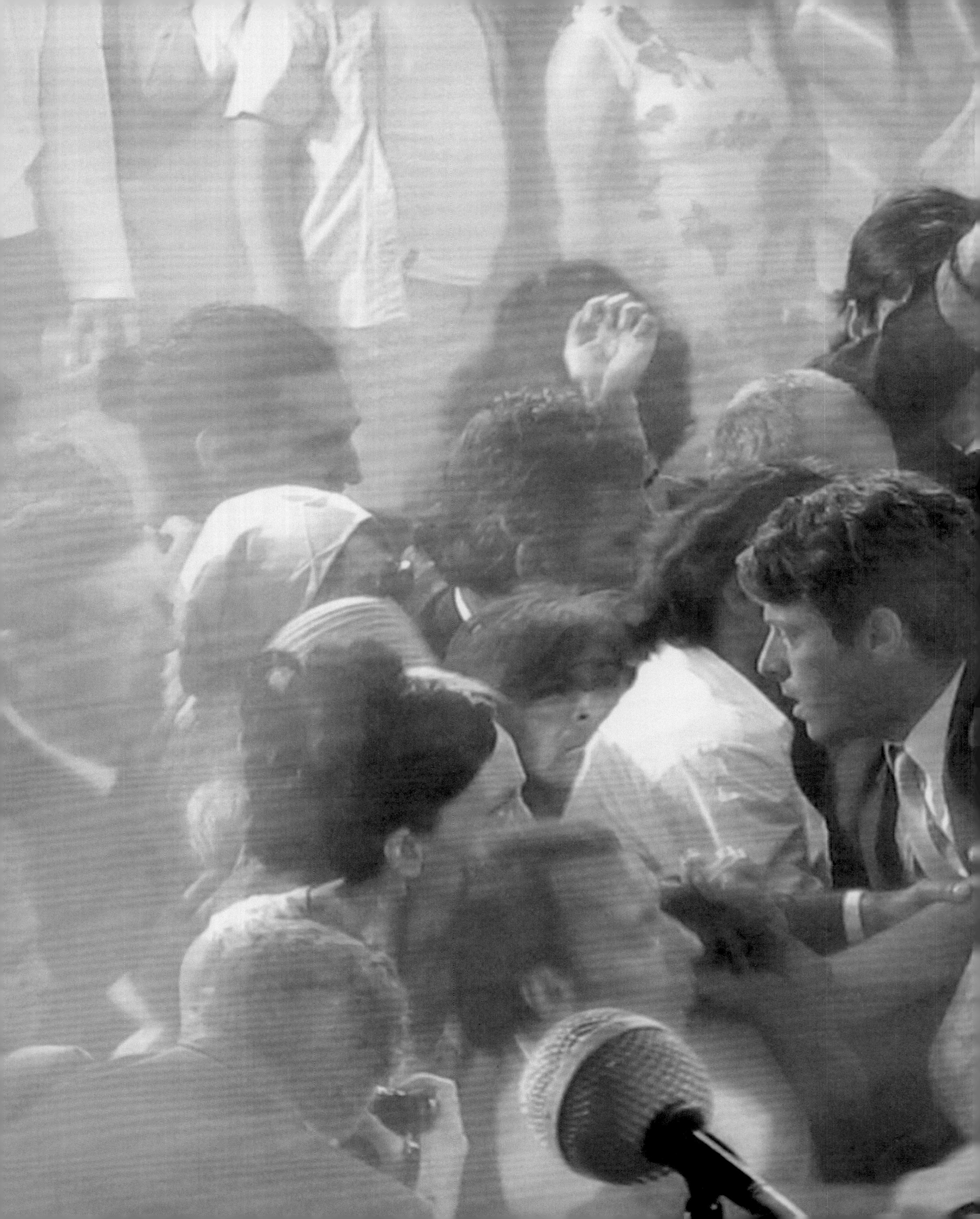

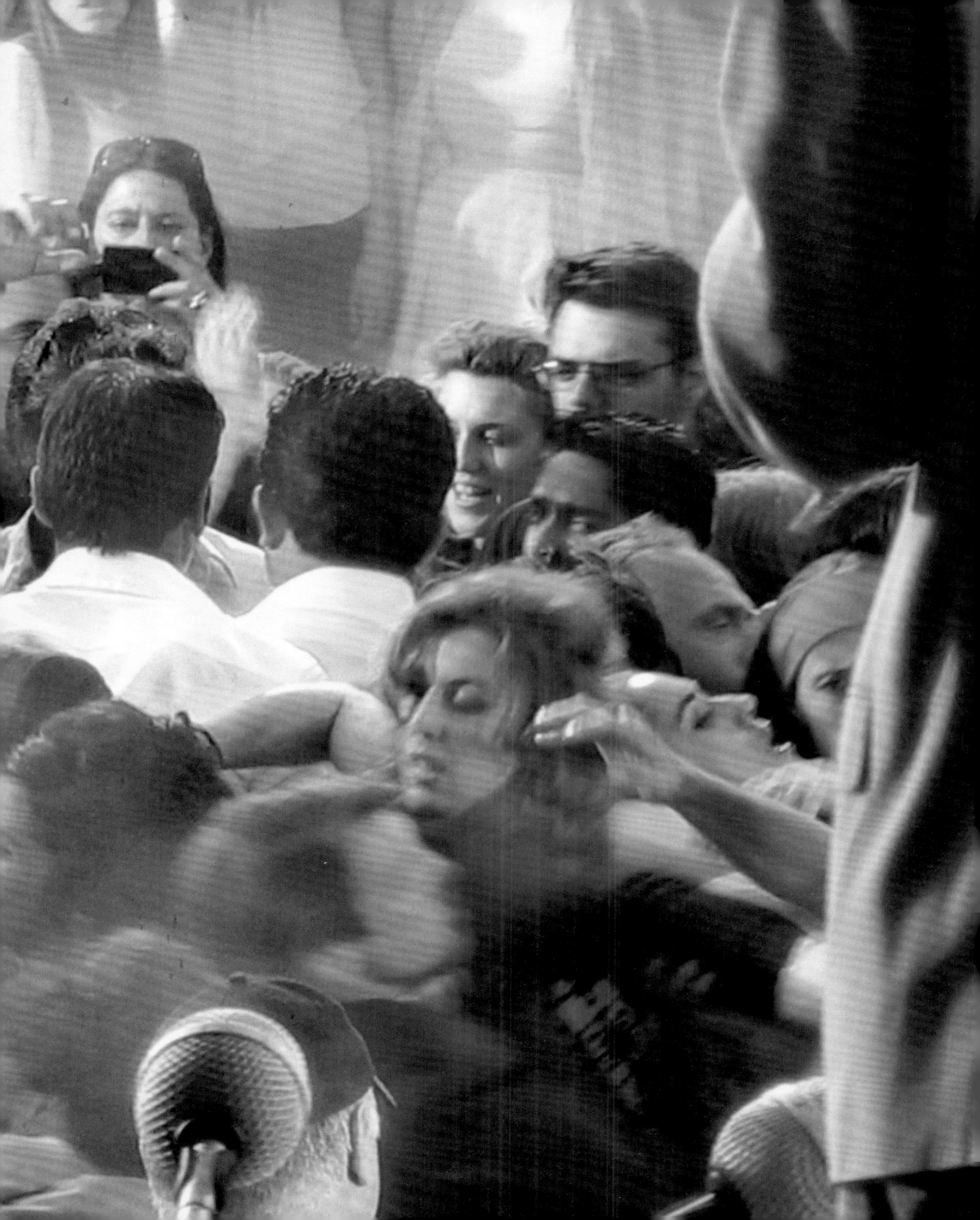

Then it was that the Sabine women, whose wrongs had given rise to war, throwing off all womanish fears in their distress, went boldly into the midst of the flying missiles with dishevelled hair and rent garments. Running across the space between the two they tried to stop any further fighting and calm the excited passions by appeals...

The Early History of Rome, 1.13, Livy

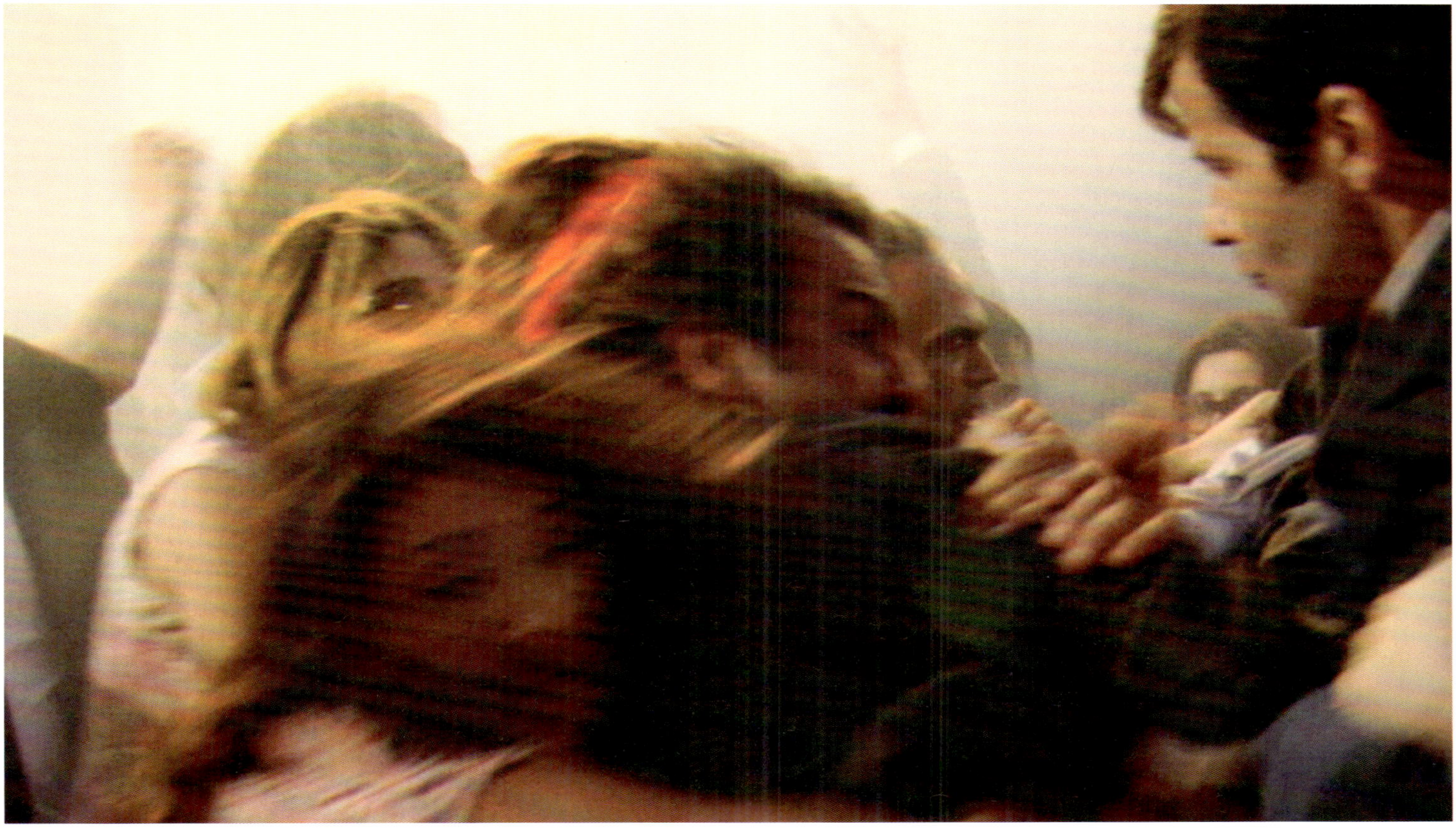

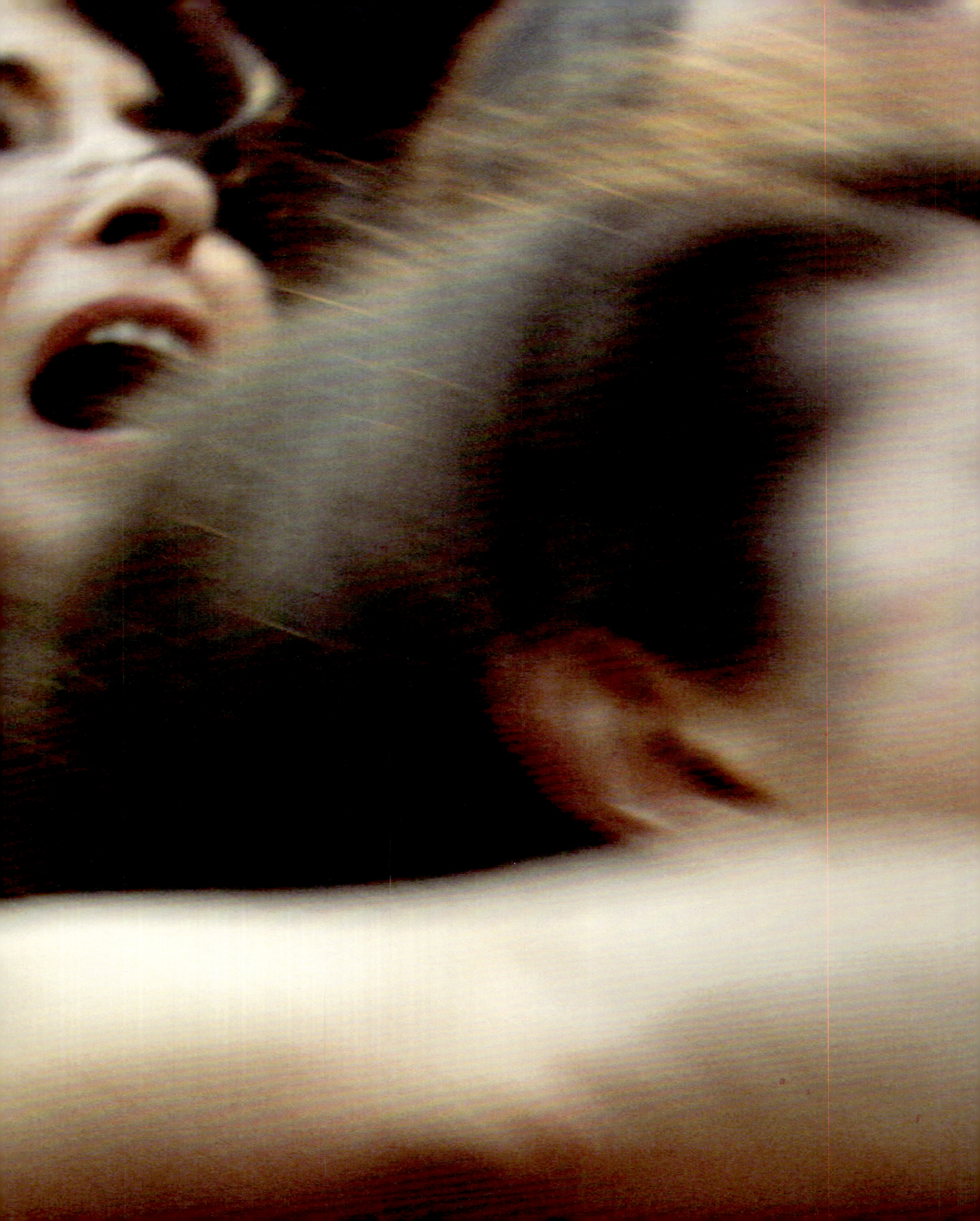

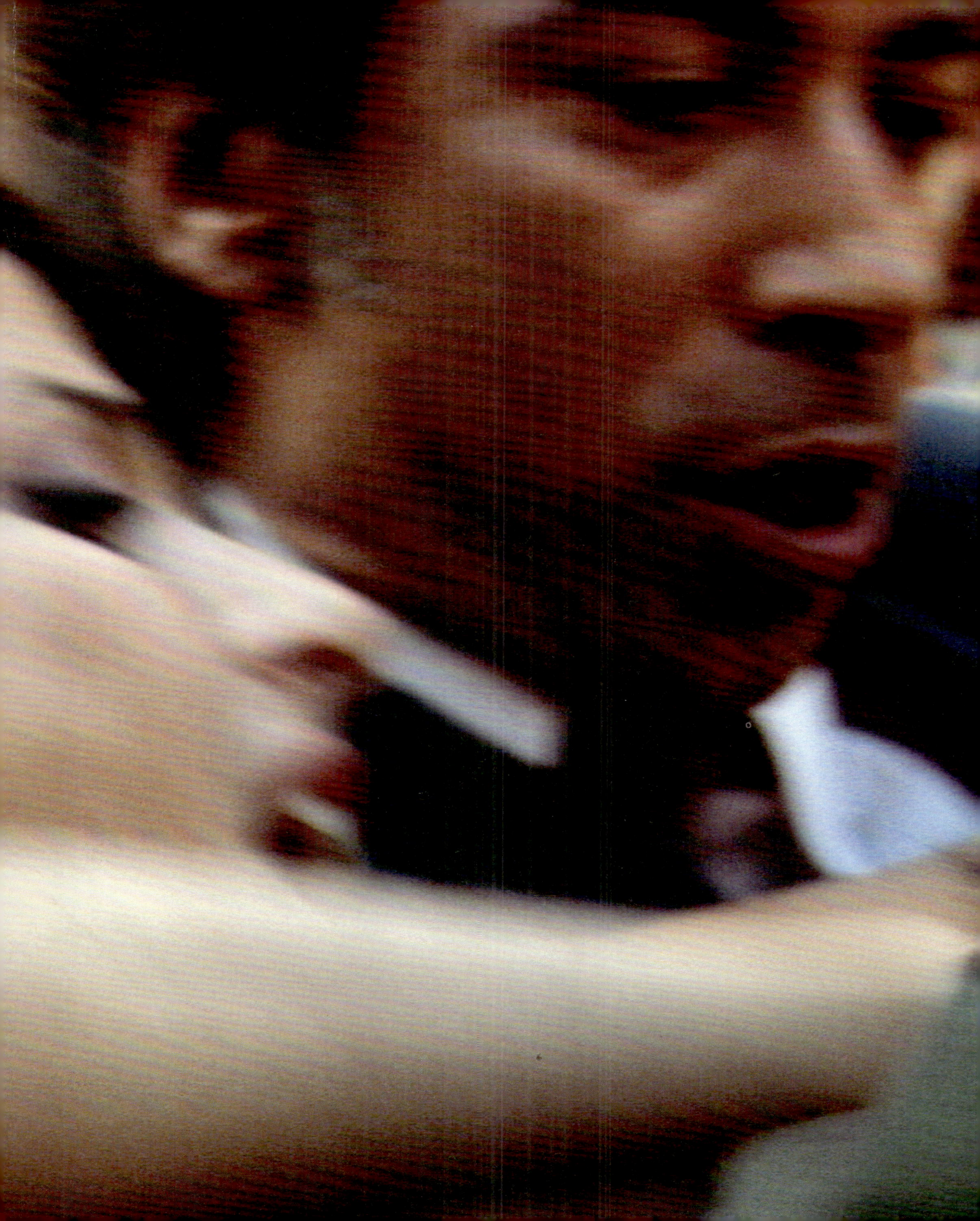

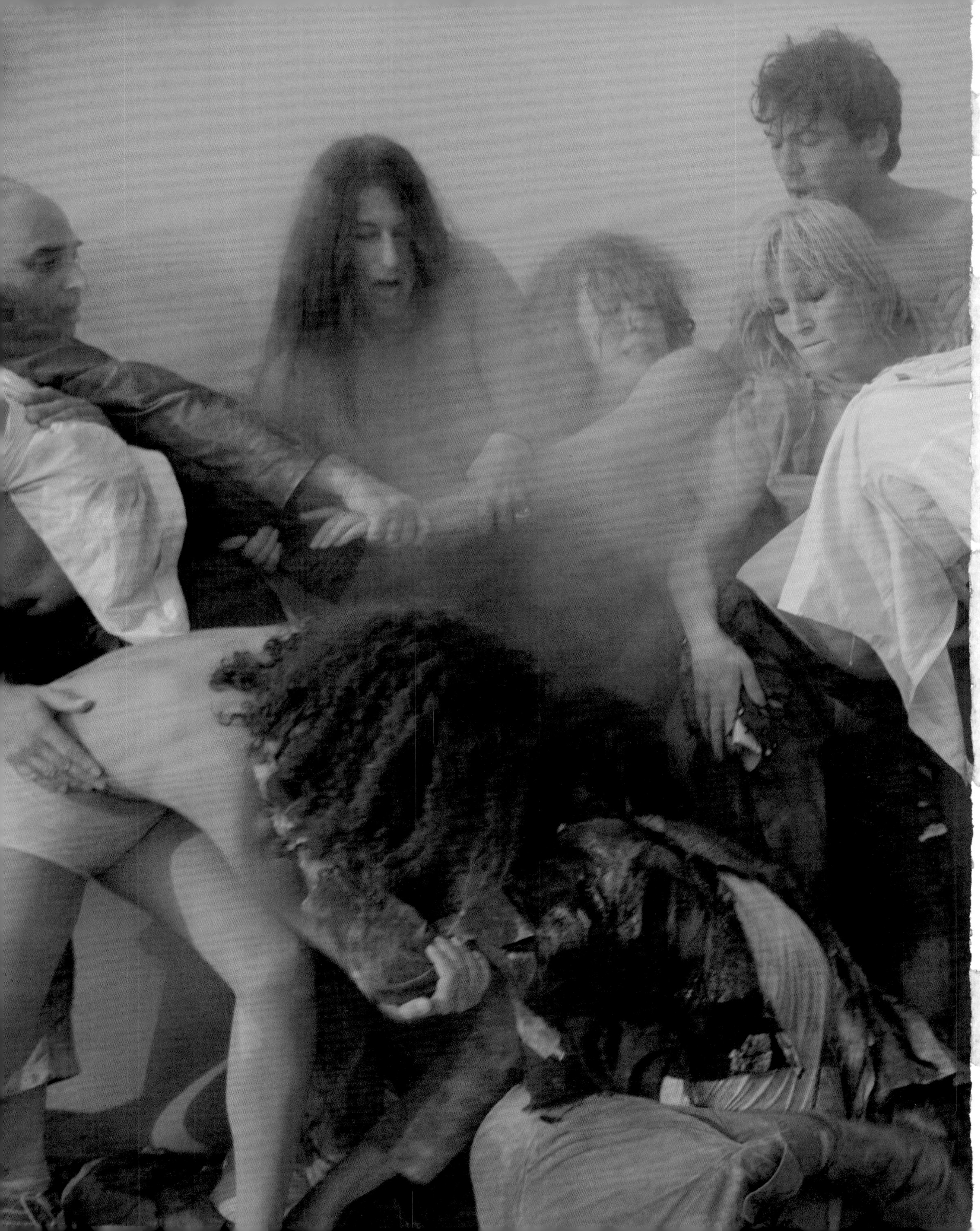

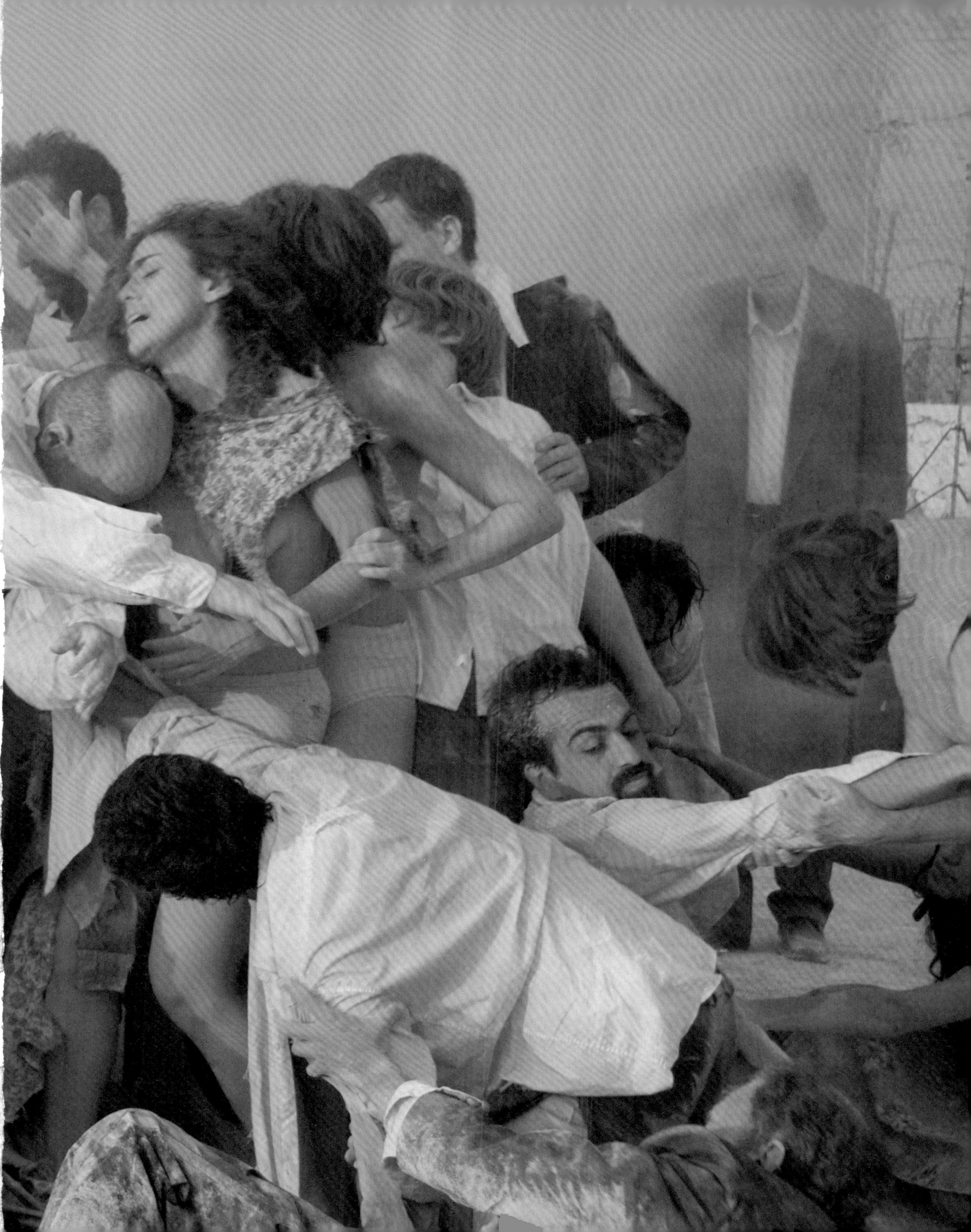

Jonathan

6 –

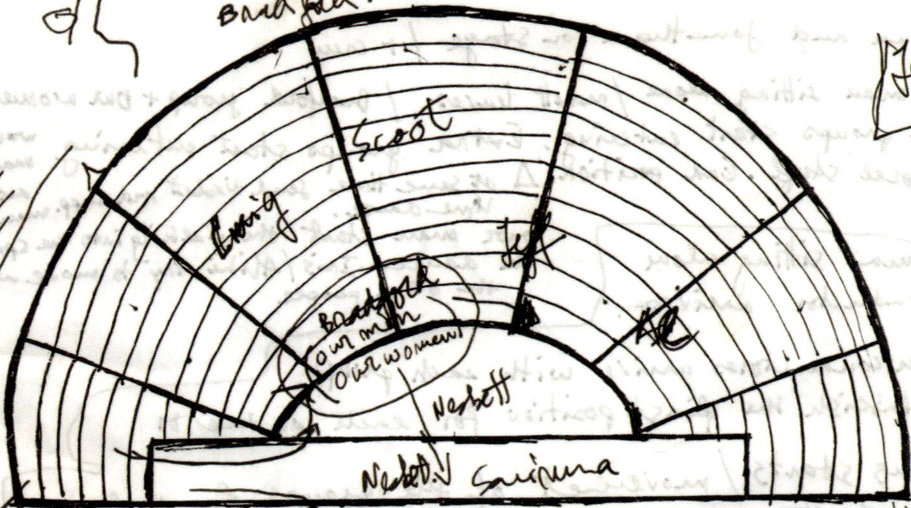

Bradford
our women
extramen

ERIC
& Greg

Scott
Greg

after Δ

Nesbett + Support.
man soft dance

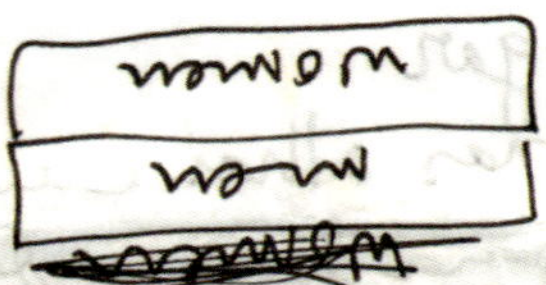

Bradford.
men don't
move
women walk
around.

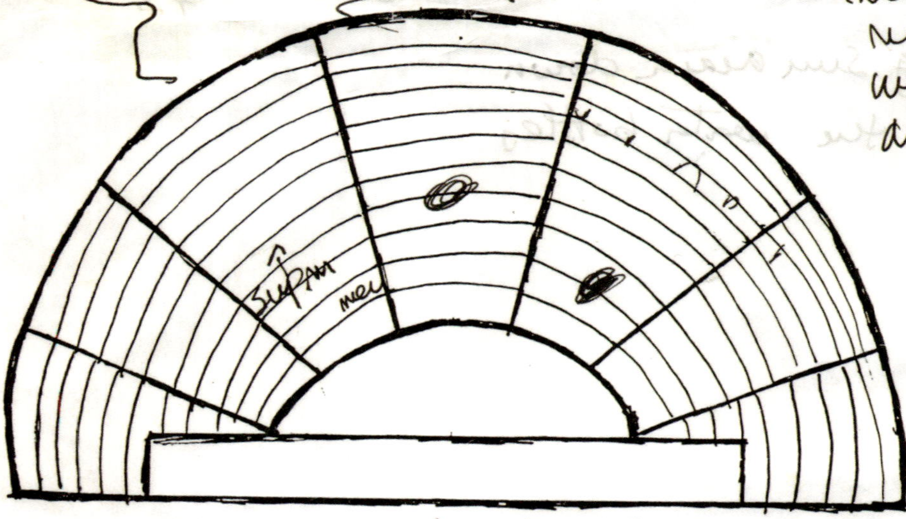

60 MAX

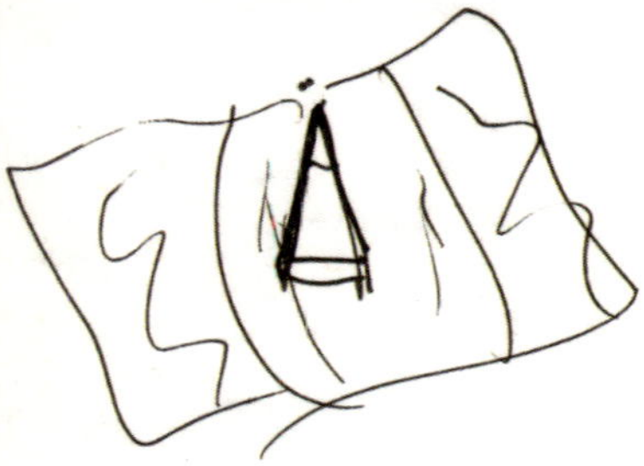

when V
– Some of our man
in front. Jeff
toni. + george → don't seat
in triangule
conducters
– Eve in seat

Supporting

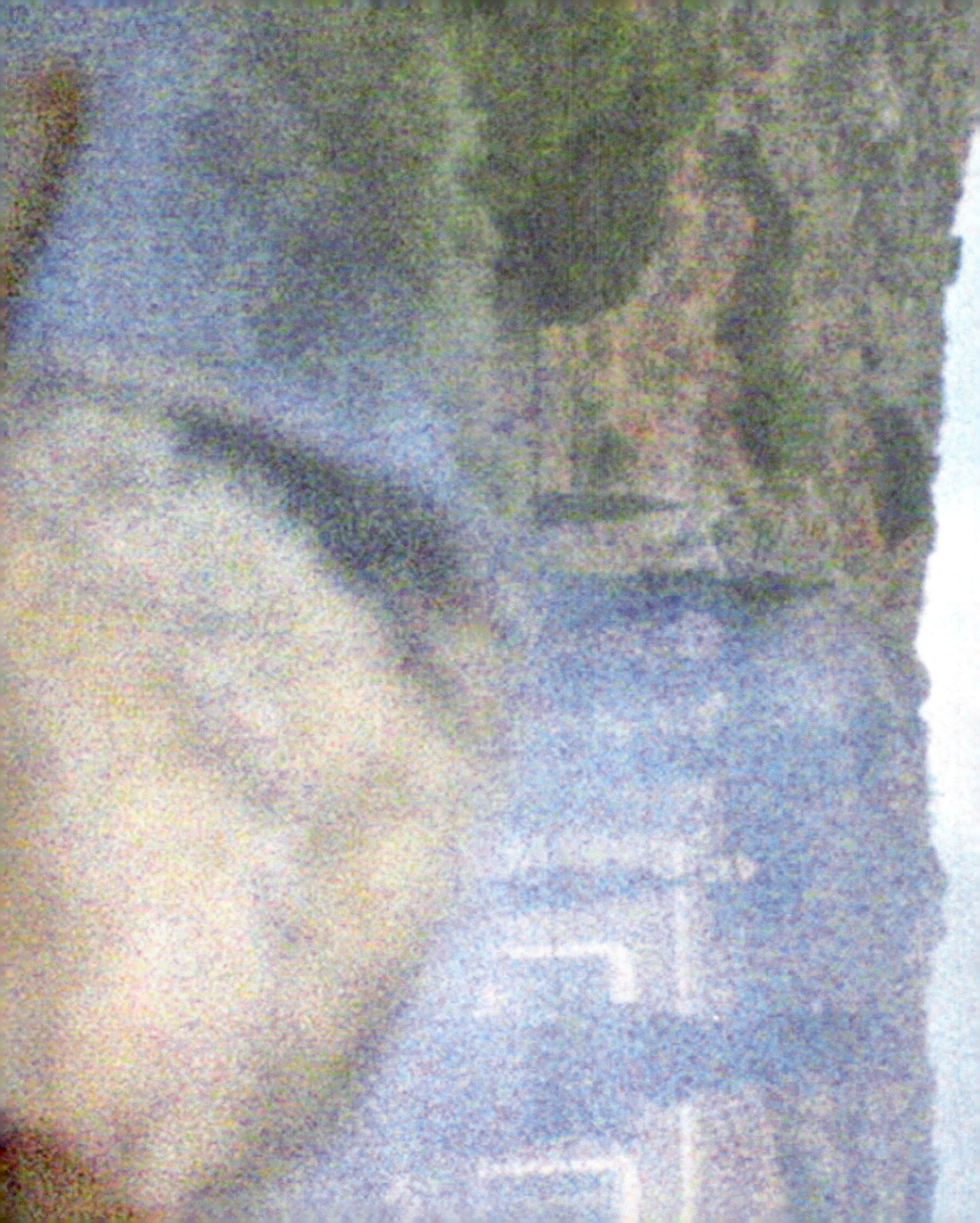

THE RAPE OF THE SABINE WOMEN
THE RUFUS CORPORATION

Eve Sussman
Jonathan Bepler
Claudia de Serpa Soares
Karen Young
Sergei Franklin
Evin Lowe
Ricoh Gerbl
Catherine Mahoney
Ioannis Savvidis
Wassili Zygouris
Angela Christlieb
Kevin Messman
Popi Alkouli-Troianou
Fergus Baumann
Themis Bazaka
Jolie Bepler
Kostas Beveratos
Nesbitt Blaisdell
Marilisa Chronea
Stergios Ioannou
Grayson Millwood
Katarina Oikonomopoulou
Helen Pickett
Annette Previti
Rosa Prodromou
Walter Sipser
Antonis Spinoulas
Christos Syrmakezis
Sotiris Tsakomidis
Jeff Wood
Sofie Zamchick
Zach Zamchick
Savina Yannatou
Geoff Gersh

Eric Hubel
Algis Antanas Kizys
Scott Moore
Bradford Reed
Cräg Rodriguez
Stavros Theodoropoulis
Christina Skokou
Nina Adamopoulou
Vasilia Rozana
Marina Anagnostopoulos
Minas Zois
Michalis Koukolomatis
Patrikios Kostis
Dimitris Beioglou
Alexandros Rapis
Eva Dimou
Michalis Georgiou
Aliki Dourmazeli
Kaliopi Ioannidou
Tassos Raptis
Iris Karajian
Michalis Gkinos
Evgenia Anagnostopoulou
Alessandro Figuerelli
Florian Günzel
Nicola Mascia
Matan Zamir
Sven Nagel
Jared Gradinger
Jago Salmon
Nuno Cera
Karsten Liske
Arthur Ställdi
Jan Ziegler

Markus Sabrowski
Felix Schlechtriem
Jaime Ortiz
Raphael
Michael Sonntag
Pierre Syna
Martin Wolf
Christofer Kohl
Andrés Castoldi
Pascal
David Fischer
Henning Küpper
Lorenz Huber
Marti Verges
Sebastian Louride
Simon Lee
Tony Ponti
Daniel Teige
Florian Kühnle
Markus Stemler
Chandi Lancaster
Jeff Blauvelt
Aliki Dourmazeli
Iris Karajian
Vassilis Panagiotakopoulos
Victoria King
Babis Kalntermitzis
Nektarios Souldakis
Kostas Levantis
Dimitris Prifitis
Georgios Metaxas
Vassiliki Kyriakou
Maria Voikou
Maria Kokkini

Stella Soulele
Ioanna Marmataki
Inessa Guenter
Manto Arvaniti
Zafiris Haitidis
Nikolas Miaoulis
Triandafylos Athanasopoulos
Michalis Christoforatos
Sotiris Terzis
Dimitris Kontaksis
Stelios Karaiskos
Vaggelis Kontodimas
Vaggelis Roussis
Kostas Tzelatis
K. Satolias
Vangelis Papadatos
Georg Bugiel
Maria Andromachi
Chatzinikolaou
Danny Burke
Kostas Kovatsos
Bobby Neel Adams
Benedikt Partenheimer
Steffen Seidel
Tonia Budelmann
Sven Klage
Jacob Wehrmann
Gaby Kislat
Isabelle Küster
Neda Sanai
Lars Kreuzmann
Heiko Matting
Tom Witt
Fabian Friedrich

Yvonne Miehlke
Moritz Jesch
Tobias Brand
Christiane Bucholz
Katharina Thieme
Martin Rink
Aylin Özbay
Tanja Schuh
Felicity Good
Daniel Doemer
Armin Ebert
Mario Nowak
Kira
Michal Krajczok
Judith Braeg
Shu Kaneko
Colleen Burke

Co-Producers
Richard Massey
Ninah & Michael Lynne
Hauptstadtkulturfonds-Berlin
Hamburger Bahnhof Museum
für Gegenwart-Berlin
The J.F. Costopoulos
Foundation-Athens
Roebling Hall Gallery-New York
Arario Gallery-Seoul
Sammlung Ackermans, London
The Zabludowicz Trust

Corporate Sponsorship
Panavision-London
HD Cinema
Microtek Gefell-Germany
Apple Computer Inc
DuArt Film & Video
LaCie-USA
Sony Professional Media
Dreamhire LLC
Tekserve
Final Frame-NYC
Coca-Cola Hellenic Bottling
Company-Greece
Ordino Casting
Services-Athens
Merc Clothing-London
Blackmagic Design
Marriott Hotels-Berlin
MAC Cosmetics
PastyFamily-Greece

Additional Co-Production
Support
The Nasher Museum of
Art at Duke University
The Smart Museum of Art at
The University of Chicago
New York State Council
on the Arts

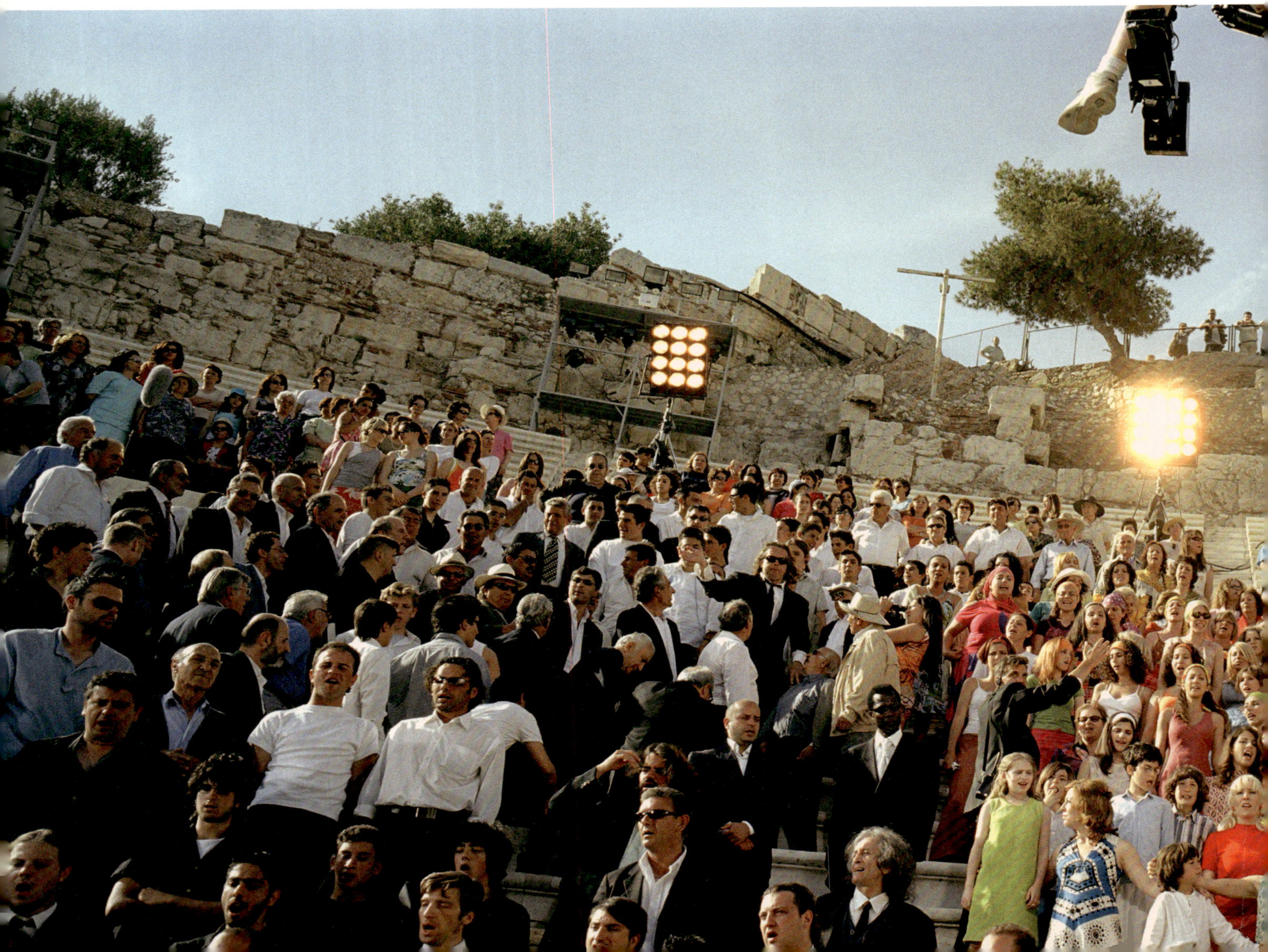

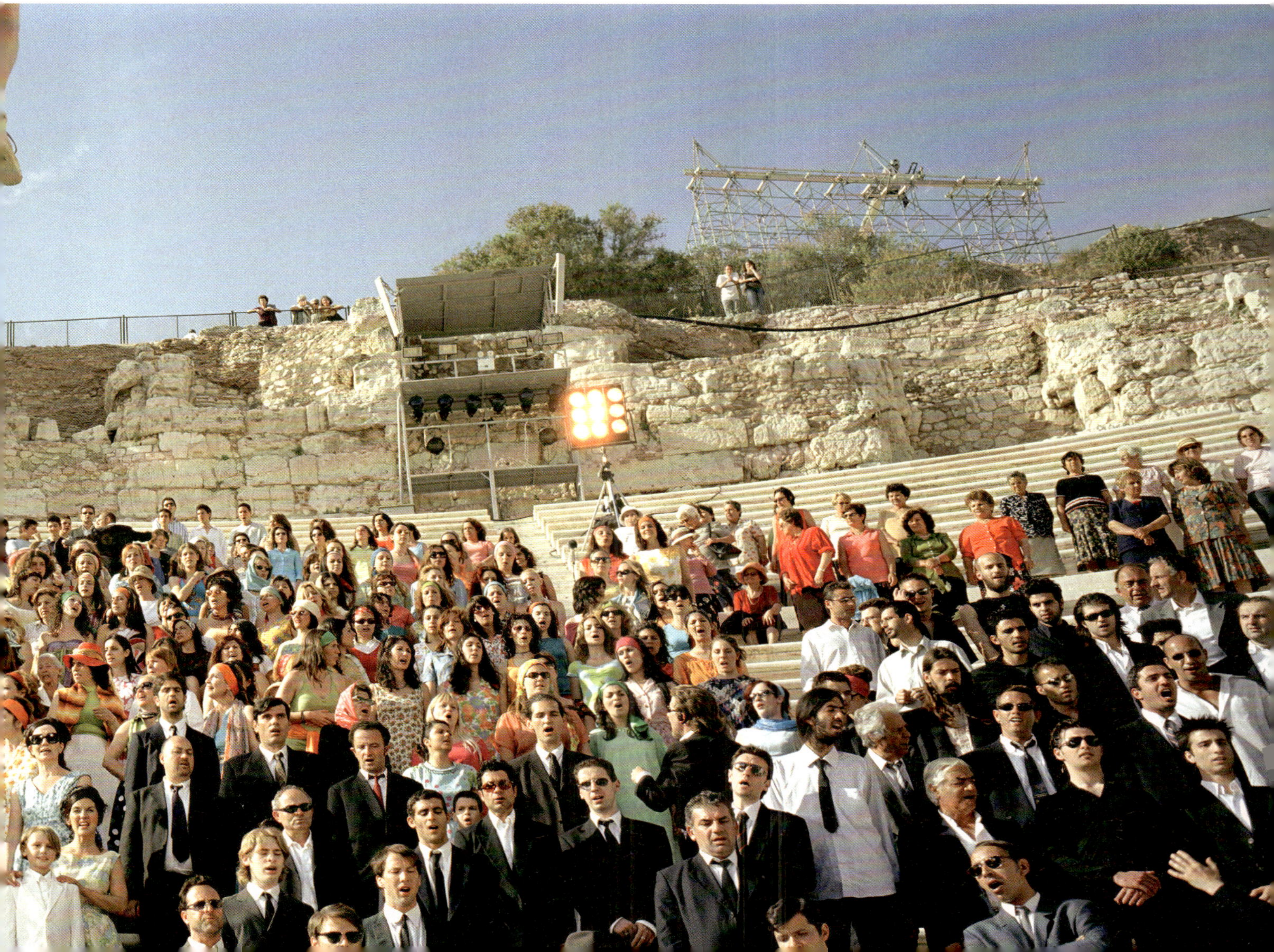

INDEX

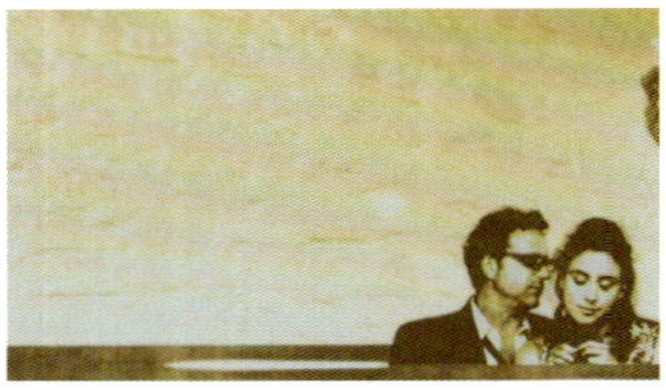

0

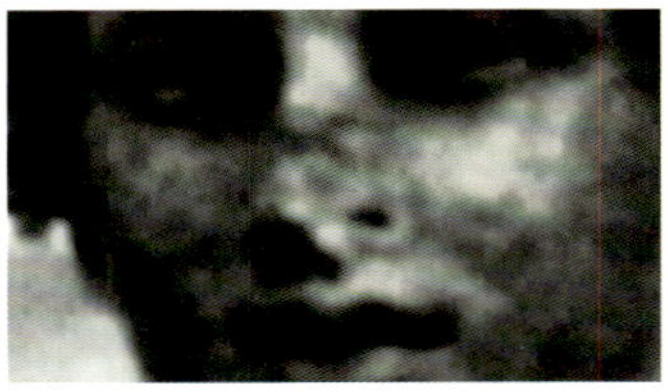

1

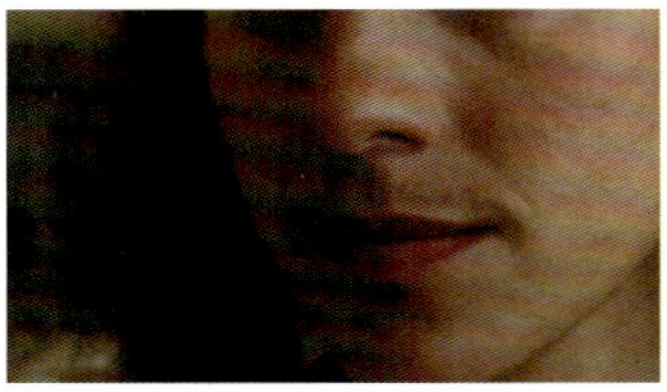

2

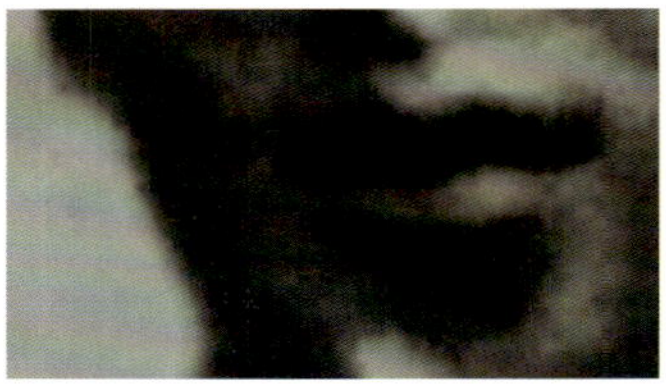

3

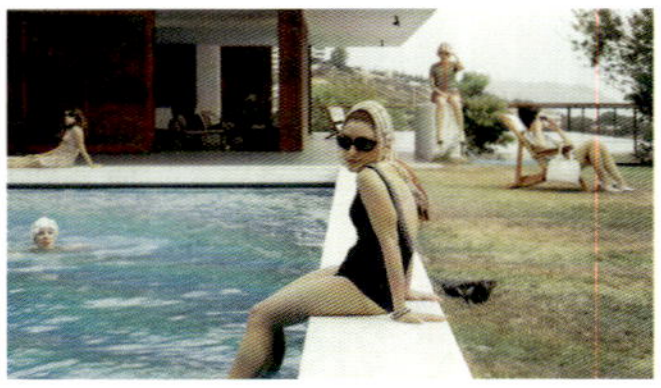

4

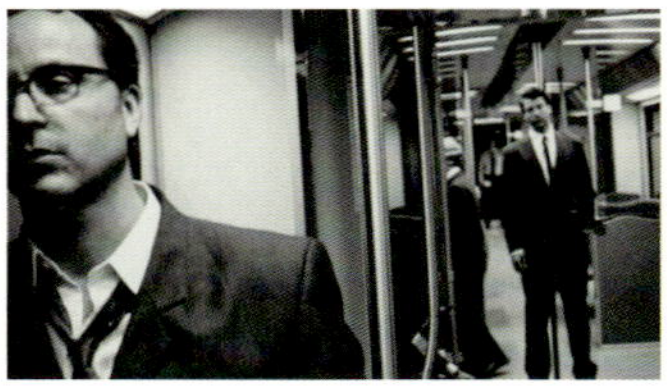

5

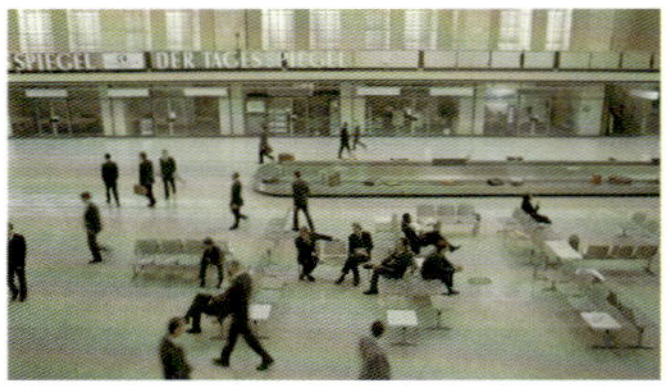

6

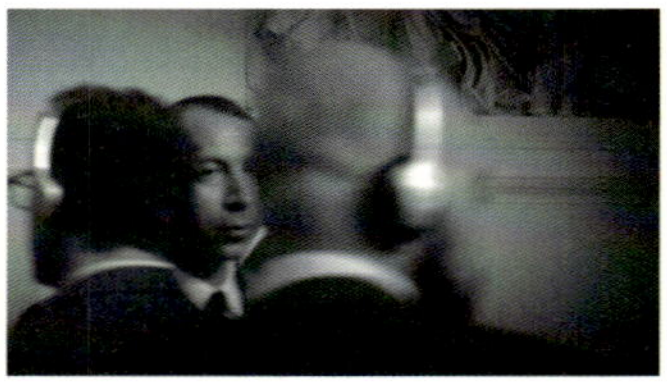

7

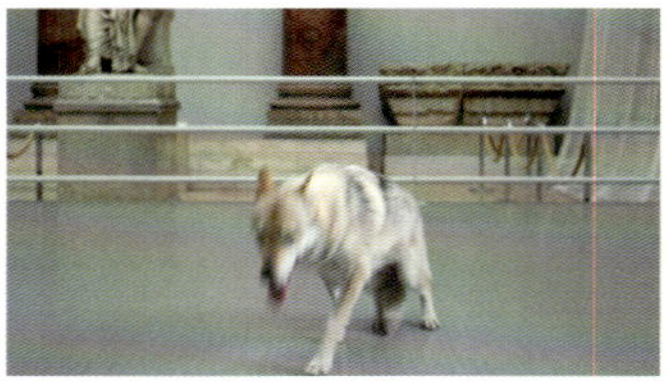

8

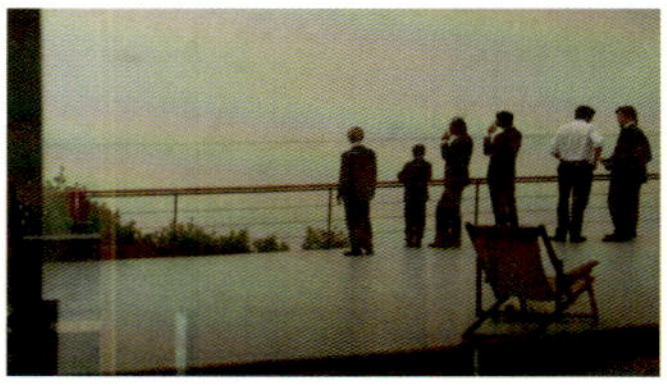

9

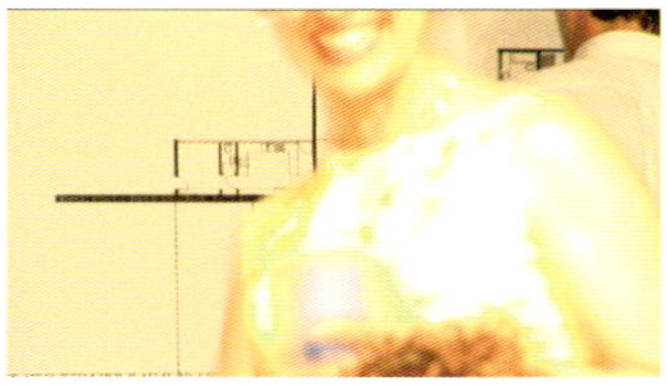

10

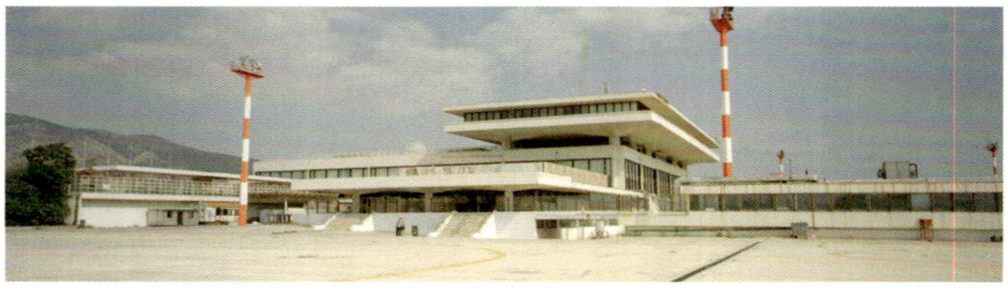

11

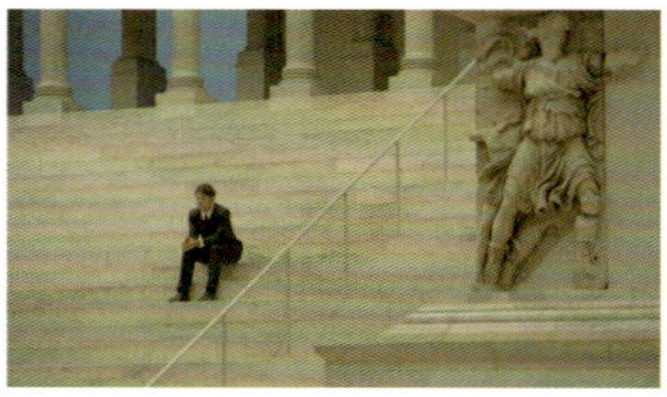

12

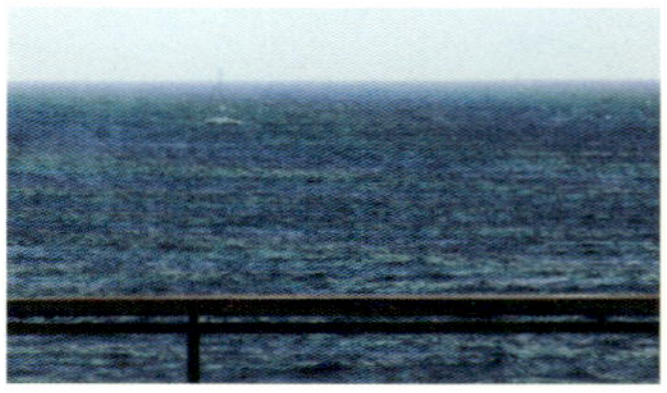

13

0 *Untitled*, video still

1 *Untitled*, video still

2 *Untitled*, video still

3 *Untitled*, video still

4 *Girls at the Pool*,
Photo: Benedikt Partenheimer

5 *Untitled*, video still

6 *Tempelhof at Dawn*,
Photo: Benedikt Partenheimer

7 *Untitled*, video still

8 *Pergamon Wolf*
Photo: Benedikt Partenheimer

9 *Agents at the Aegean*
Photo: Ricoh Gerbl

10 *Untitled*, video still

11 *Athena Airport (Abandoned)*
Photo: Bobby Neel Adams

12 *Romulus at Pergamon*
Photo: Ricoh Gerbl

13 *Untitled*, video still

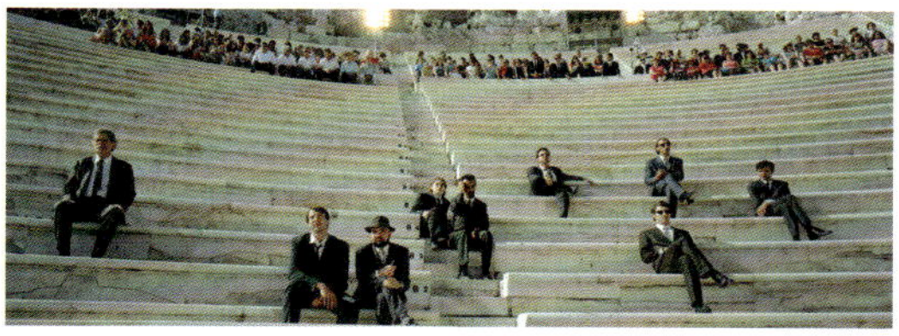

14

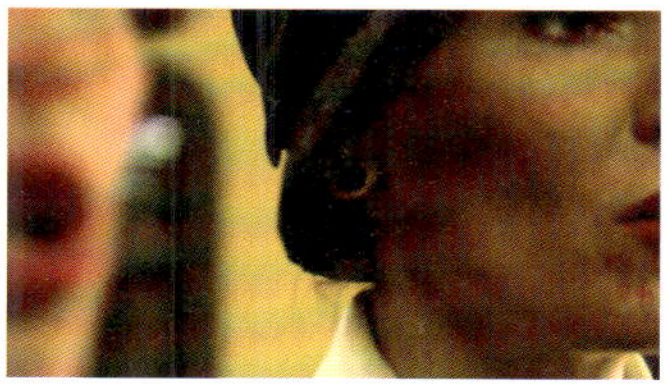

15

16

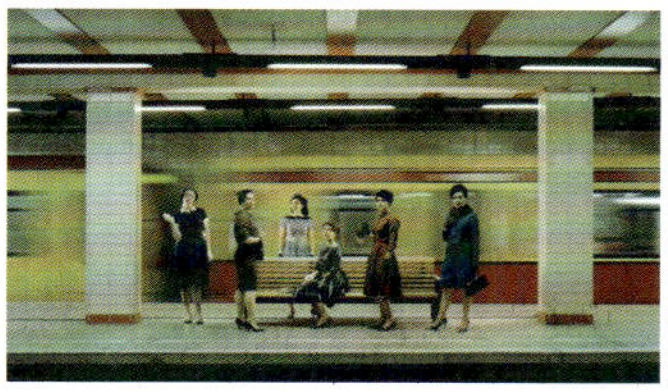

17

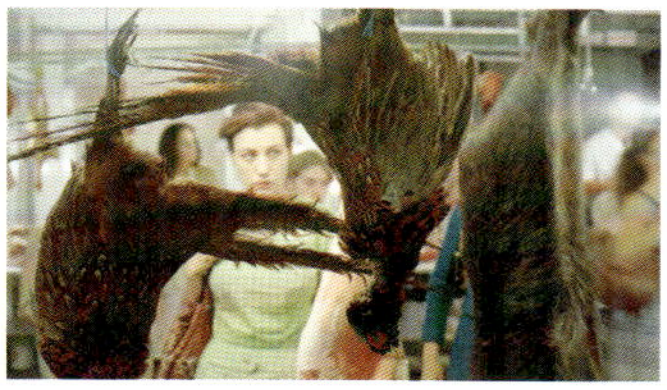

18

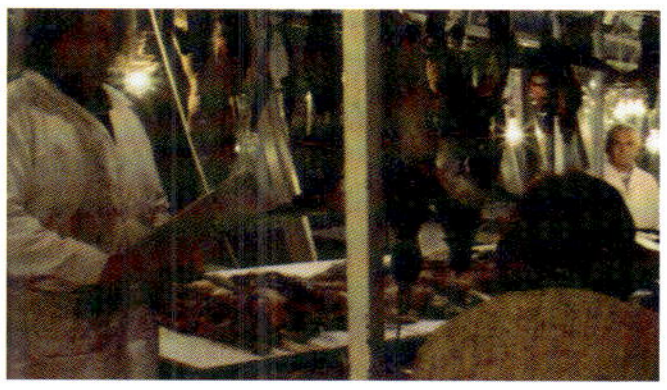

19

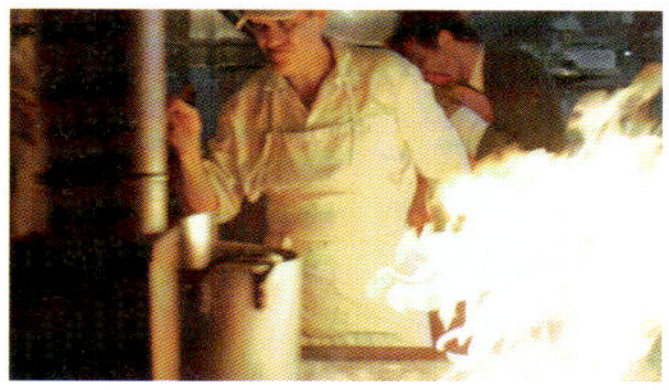

20

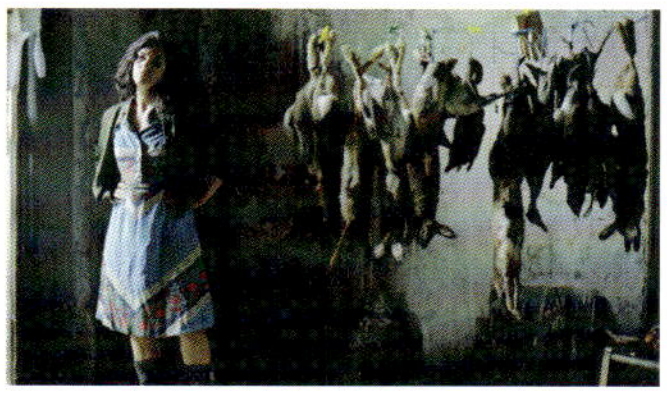

21

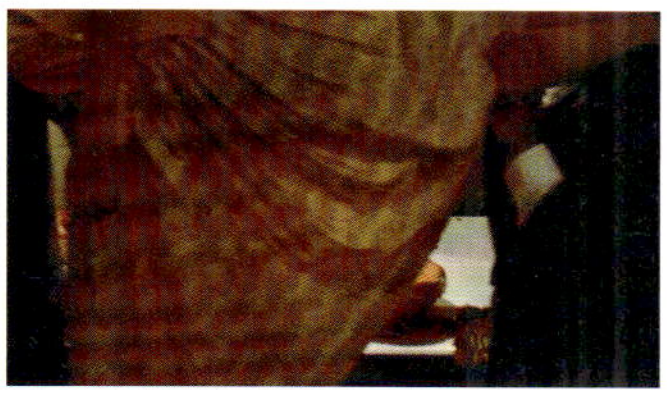

22

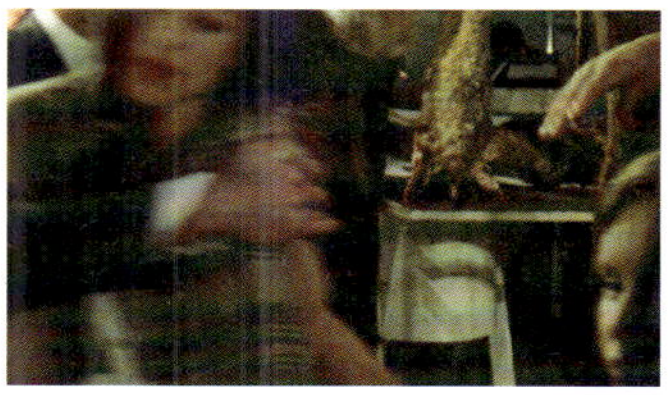

23

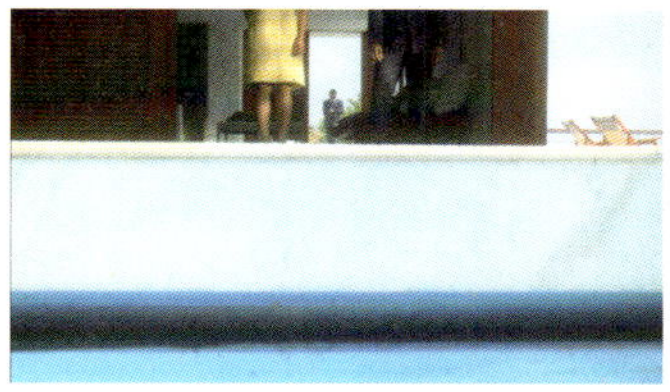

24

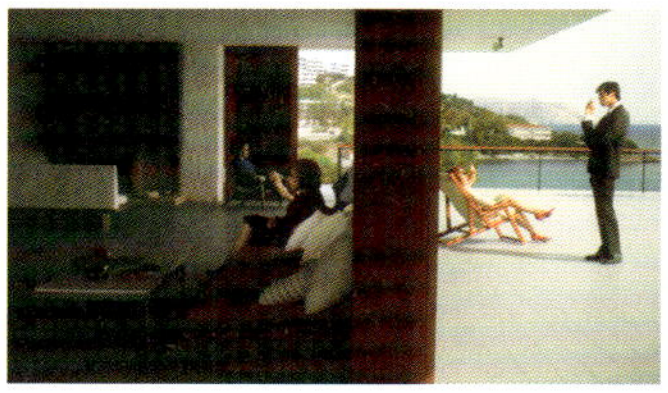

25

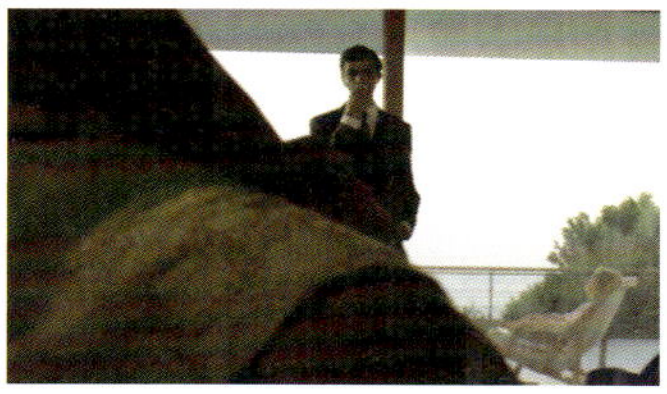

26

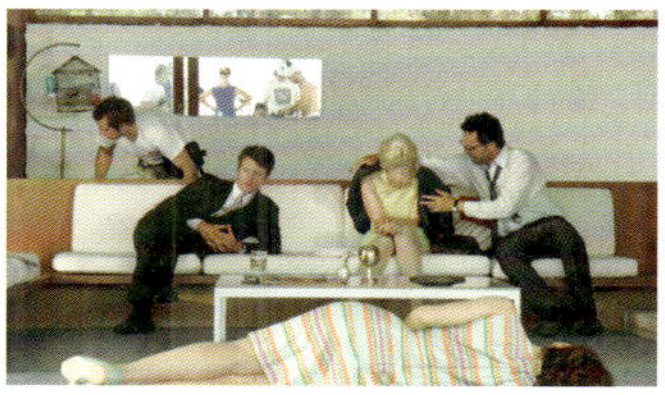

27

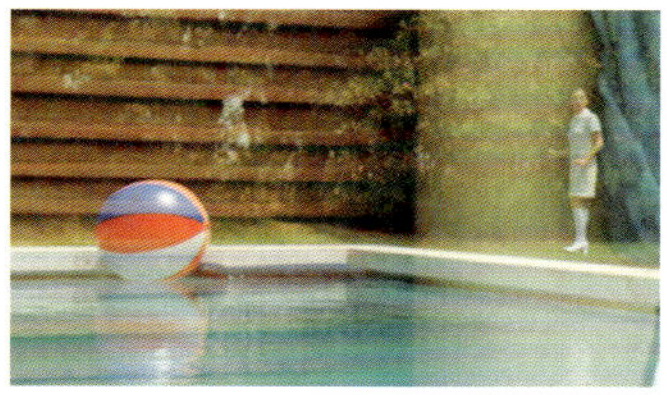

28

14 *The Patricians*
Photo: Bobby Neel Adams

15 *Untitled*, video still

16 *Untitled*, video still

17 *Women in the S-Bahn*
Photo: Benedikt Partenheimer

18 *Fowl*
Photo: Benedikt Partenheimer

19 *Untitled*, video still

20 *Untitled*, video still

21 *Annette with Rabbits*
Photo: Benedikt Partenheimer

22 *Untitled*, video still

23 *Untitled*, video still

24 *Untitled*, video still

25 *Untitled*, video still

26 *Untitled*, video still

27 *Marilisa on the Floor*
Photo: Sussman/Gerbl

28 *Hitchcock Beachball*
Photo: Ricoh Gerbl

INDEX

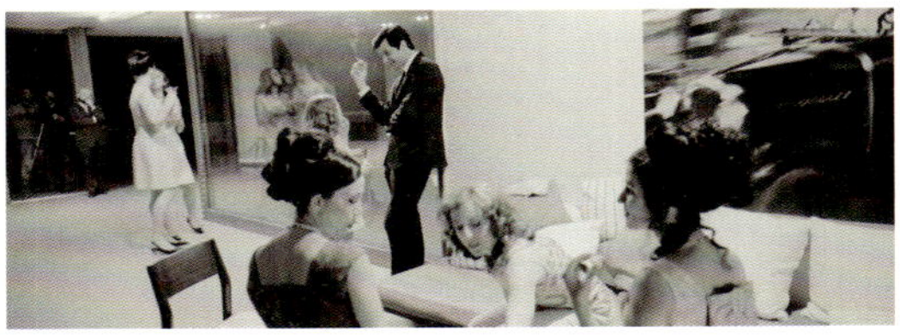

29

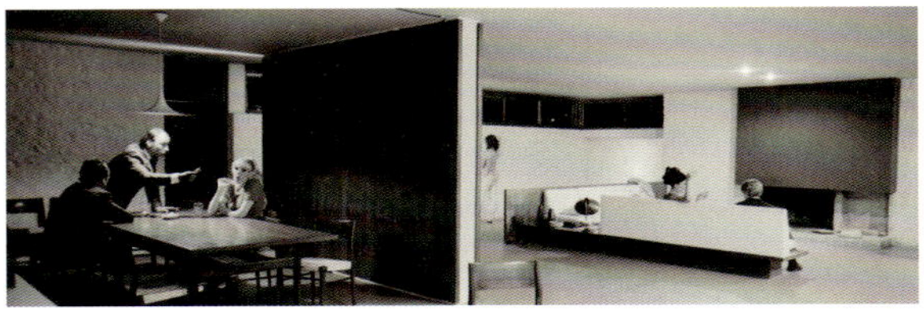

30

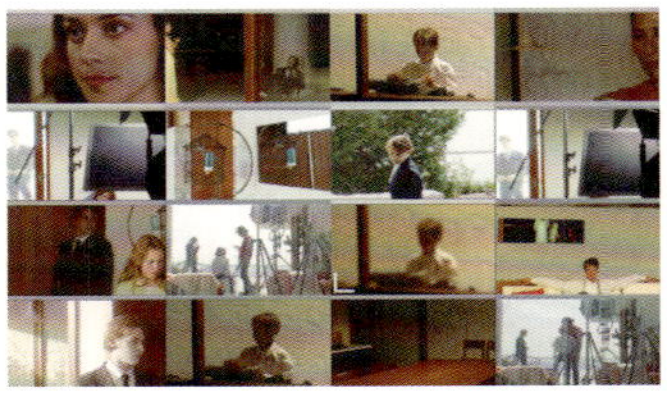

31

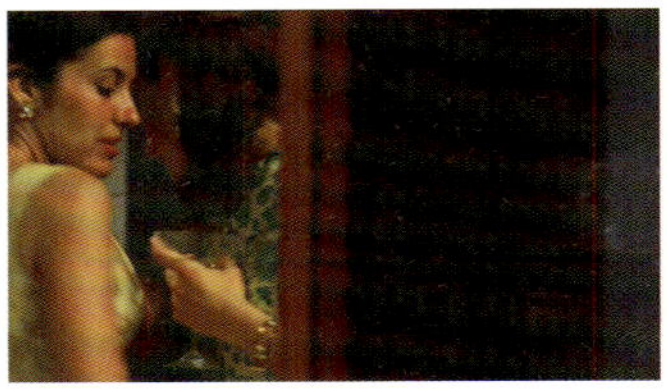

32

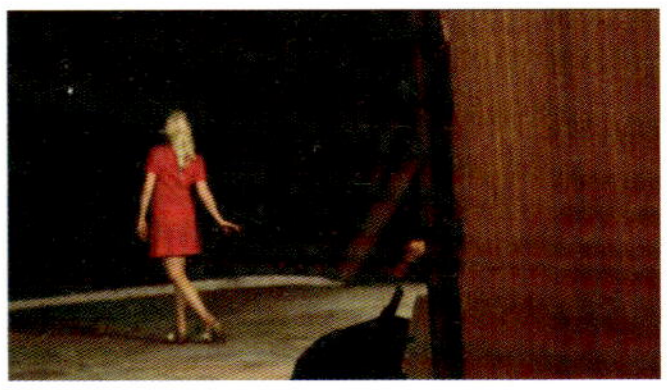

33

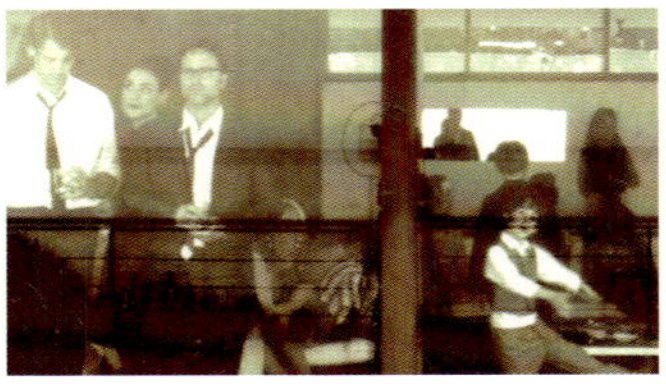

34

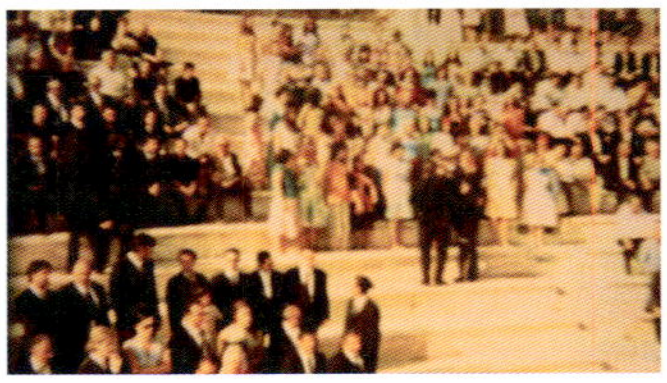

35

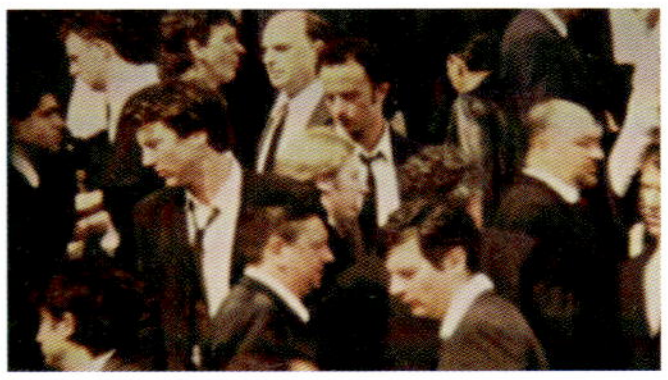

36

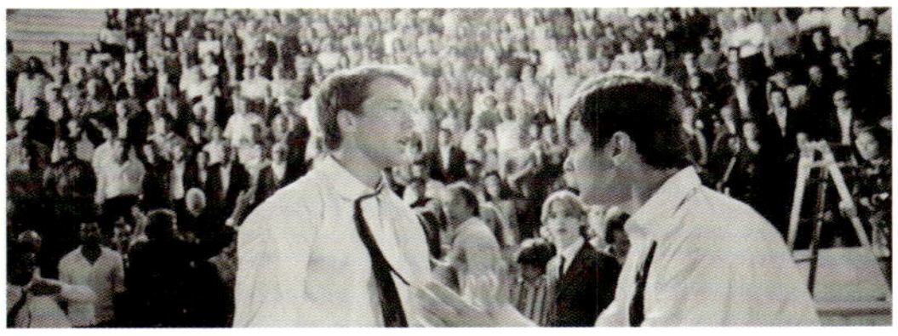

37

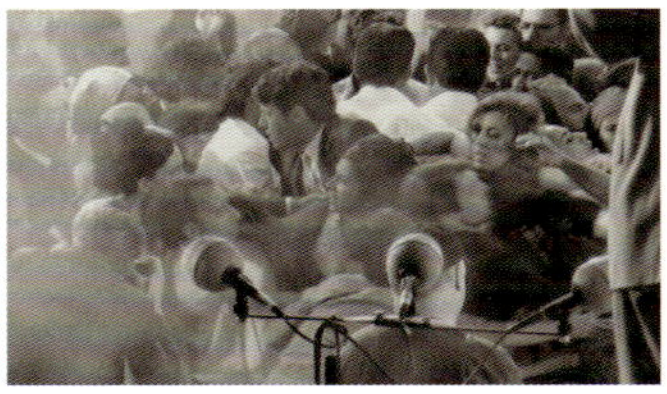

38

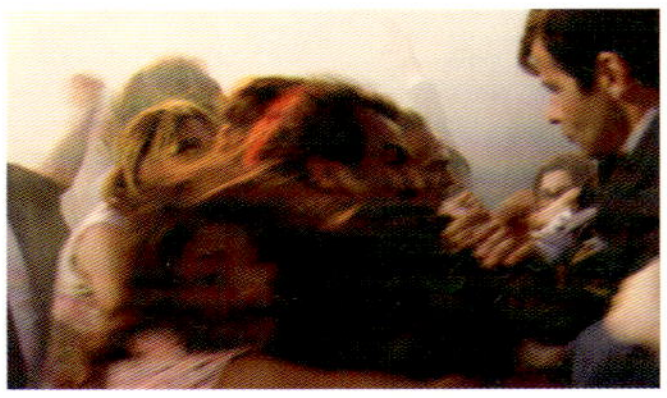

39

29 *Wives of Patricians*
Photo: Bobby Neel Adams

30 *Untitled (Katerina's Reluctance)*
Photo: Bobby Neel Adams

31 *Montage for House Edit,*
video stills

32 *Untitled,* video still

33 *Untitled,* video still

34 *Triangle,* video still

35 *Untitled,* video still

36 *Untitled,* video still

37 *Untitled*
Photo: Bobby Neel Adams

38 *Jeff's Kennedy Moment*
Photo: Daniel Teige

39 *Untitled,* video still

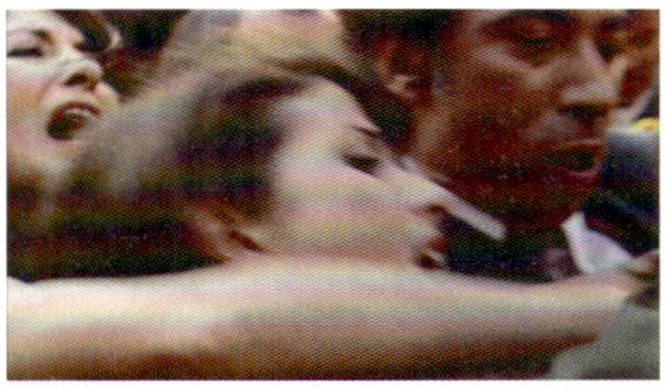

40

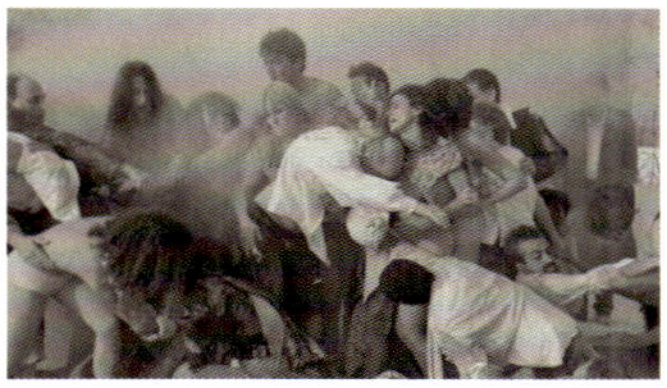

41

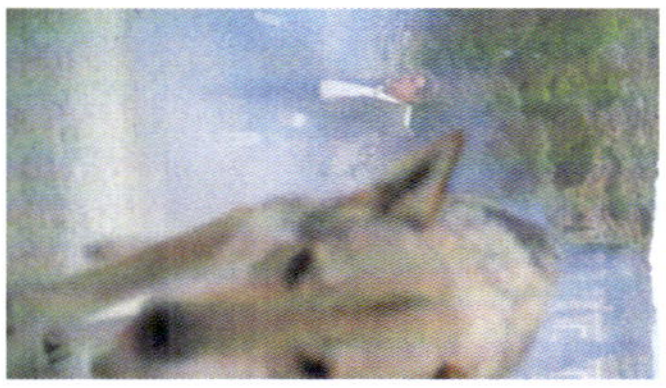

42

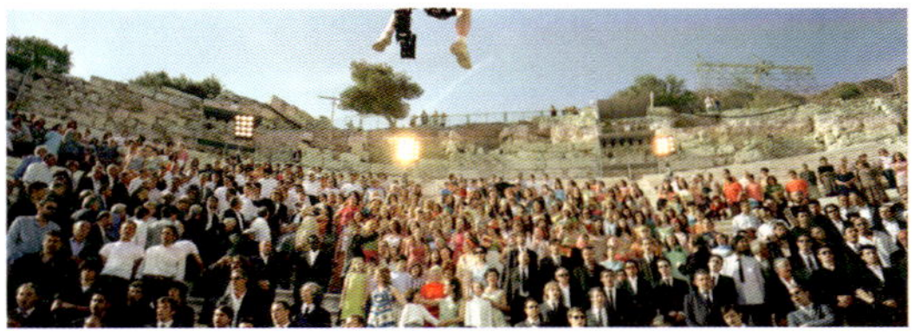

43

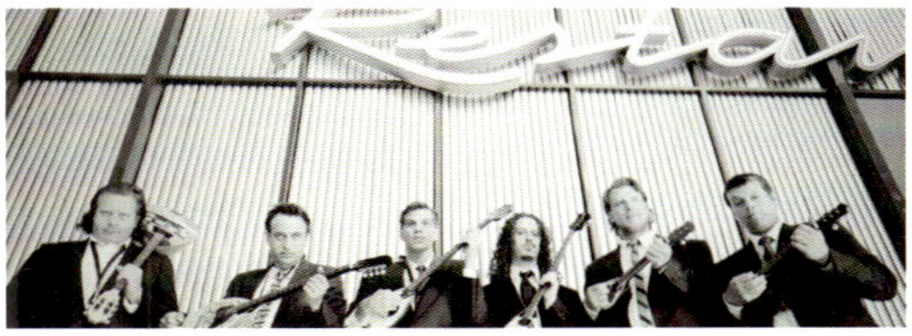

44

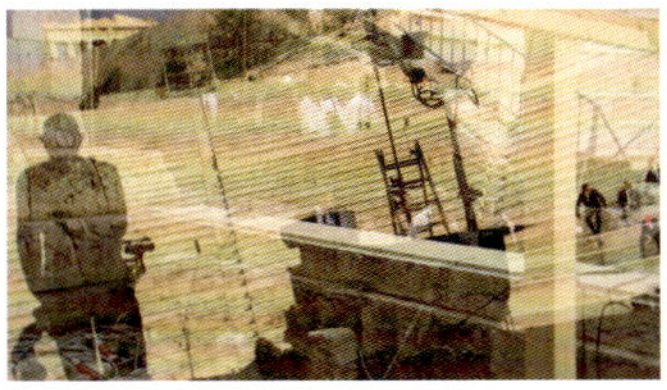

45

40 *Untitled,* video still

41 *Disintegration at Hydra*
Photo: Ricoh Gerbl

42 *Wolf at the End,*
video still

43 *Herodion Before the Fight*
Photo: Bobby Neel Adams

44 *The Musicians*
Photo: Bobby Neel Adams

45 *Untitled*
Photo: Ricoh Gerbl

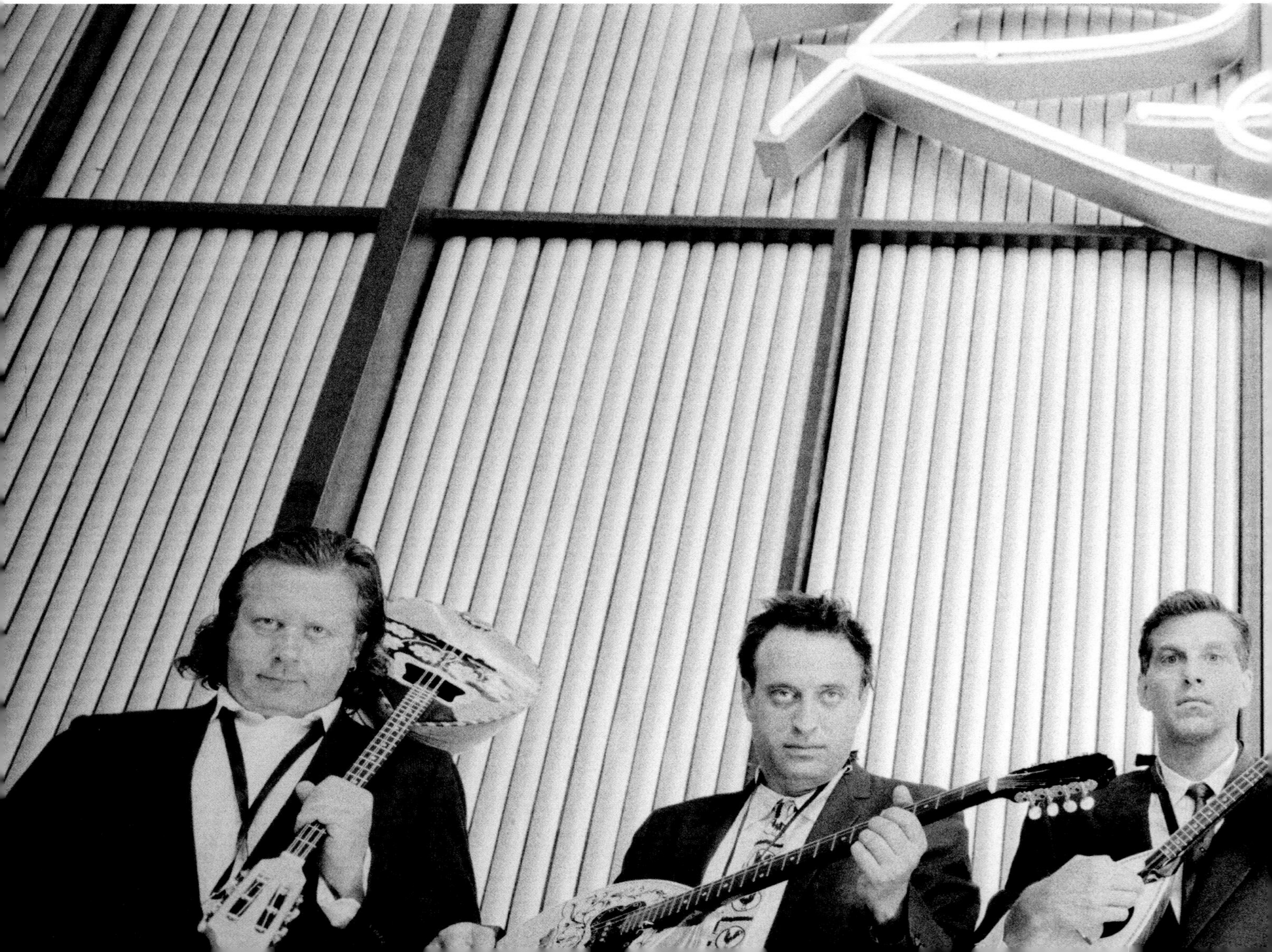

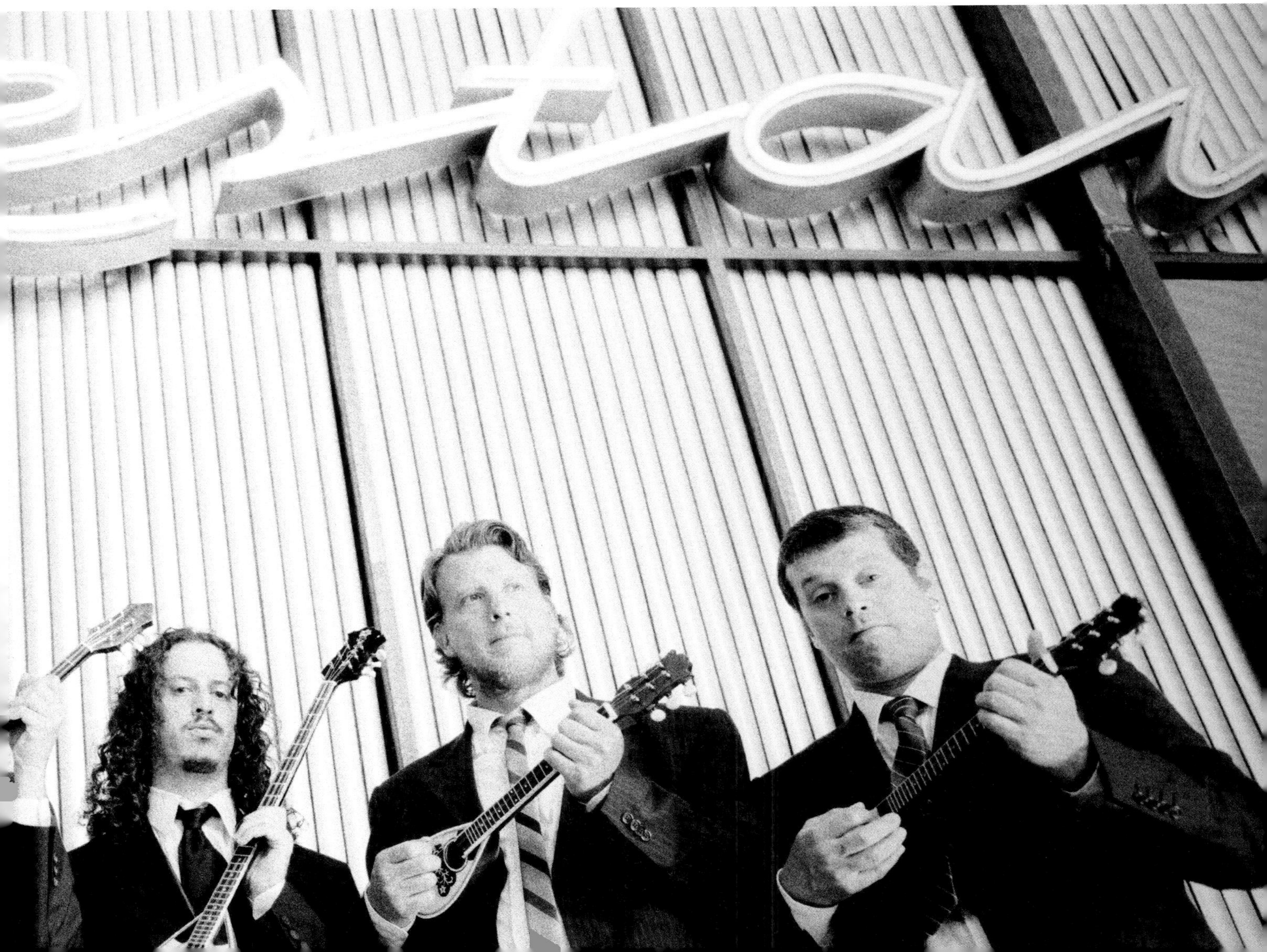

LIST OF WORKS

VIDEO INSTALLATIONS

89 Seconds at Alcázar, 2004
Single Channel High Definition Video; 5.1 Surround Sound.
Duration:10 minutes, looping
Eve Sussman & The Rufus Corporation

The Rape of the Sabine Women, 2005
Single Channel High Definition Video; 7.1 Surround Sound.
Duration: 83 minutes
Eve Sussman & The Rufus Corporation

PHOTOGRAPHIC WORKS
THE RAPE OF THE SABINE WOMEN

Girls at the Pool, 2005
Eve Sussman & The Rufus Corporation
Photographic Still from *The Rape of the Sabine Women*
125 x 146 cm
Photo: Benedikt Partenheimer
Richard J. Massey Collection

Marilisa Reflected, 2005
Eve Sussman & The Rufus Corporation
Photographic Still from *The Rape of the Sabine Women*
117 x 162 cm
Photo: Ricoh Gerbl
Galleri Bo Bjerggaard, Copenhagen
Courtesy Roebling Hall Gallery, New York

Helen & Toni & the Cook in the Kitchen, 2005
Eve Sussman & The Rufus Corporation
Helen Pickett and Antonis Spinoulas in a
Photographic Still from *The Rape of the Sabine Women*
101 x 219 cm
Photo: Bobby Neel Adams
Galleri Bo Bjerggaard, Copenhagen
Courtesy Roebling Hall Gallery, New York

Marilisa on the Floor, 2005
Eve Sussman & The Rufus Corporation
Production Still from *The Rape of the Sabine Women*
100 cm x 130 cm
Photo: Eve Sussman
Galleri Bo Bjerggaard, Copenhagen
Courtesy Roebling Hall Gallery, New York

The Wolf in Tempelhof, 2005
Eve Sussman & The Rufus Corporation
Production Still from *The Rape of the Sabine Women*
127 cm x 150 cm
Photo: Benedikt Partenheimer
Galleri Bo Bjerggaard, Copenhagen
Courtesy Roebling Hall Gallery, New York

Themis in the Birdcage, 2005
Eve Sussman & The Rufus Corporation
Photographic Still from *The Rape of the Sabine Women*
100 cm x 130 cm
Photo: Ricoh Gerbl
Torben Solgaard, Copenhagen

PHOTOGRAPHIC WORKS
89 SECONDS AT ALCÁZAR

De Espaldas, 2004
Eve Sussman & The Rufus Corporation
The Rufus Corporation in a
Video Still from *89 Seconds at Alcázar*
61 x 92 cm
Photo: Eve Sussman and The Rufus Corporation
Richard J. Massey Collection

Dog Rolls, 2004
Eve Sussman & The Rufus Corporation
The Rufus Corporation in a
Video Still from *89 Seconds at Alcázar*
61 x 92 cm
Photo: Eve Sussman and The Rufus Corporation
Richard J. Massey Collection

King Sleeps, 2004
Eve Sussman & The Rufus Corporation
Jeff Wood as Philip IV, King of Spain, in a
Photographic Still from *89 Seconds at Alcázar*
102 x 127 cm
Photo: Benedikt Partenheimer
Richard J. Massey Collection

The Meninas, 2004
Eve Sussman & The Rufus Corporation
Erin Kaleel and Andrea Huelse in a
Photographic Still from *89 Seconds at Alcázar*
102 x 76 cm
Photo: Bobby Neel Adams
Richard J. Massey Collection

Set with Red Curtain, 2004
Eve Sussman & The Rufus Corporation
Production Still from *89 Seconds at Alcázar*
108 x 133 cm
Photo: Benedikt Partenheimer
Galleri Bo Bjerggaard, Copenhagen
Courtesy Roebling Hall Gallery, New York

Philip and Mariana Reflected, 2004
Eve Sussman & The Rufus Corporation
Helen Pickett and Jeff Wood as Mariana of Austria,
Queen of Spain, and Philip IV, King of Spain, in a
Photographic Still from *89 Seconds at Alcázar*
127 x 102 cm
Photo: Benedikt Partenheimer
Galleri Bo Bjerggaard, Copenhagen
Courtesy Roebling Hall Gallery, New York

Widow on the Set, 2004
Eve Sussman & The Rufus Corporation
Annette Previti as the Doña Marcela in a
Photographic Still from *89 Seconds at Alcázar*
108 x 133 cm
Photo: Benedikt Partenheimer
Galleri Bo Bjerggaard, Copenhagen
Courtesy Roebling Hall Gallery, New York

Infanta Enters, 2004
Eve Sussman & The Rufus Corporation
The Rufus Corporation in a
Video Still from *89 Seconds at Alcázar*
61 x 91 cm
Photo: Eve Sussman and The Rufus Corporation
Galleri Bo Bjerggaard, Copenhagen
Courtesy Roebling Hall Gallery, New York

Annette as the Widow, 2004
Eve Sussman & The Rufus Corporation
Annette Previti as the Doña Marcela in a
Production Still from *89 Seconds at Alcázar*
Photo: Bobby Neel Adams
Galleri Bo Bjerggaard, Copenhagen
Courtesy Roebling Hall Gallery, New York

VARIOUS EPHEMERA FROM
THE RAPE OF THE SABINE WOMEN

Sketches, notes, snapshots and letters

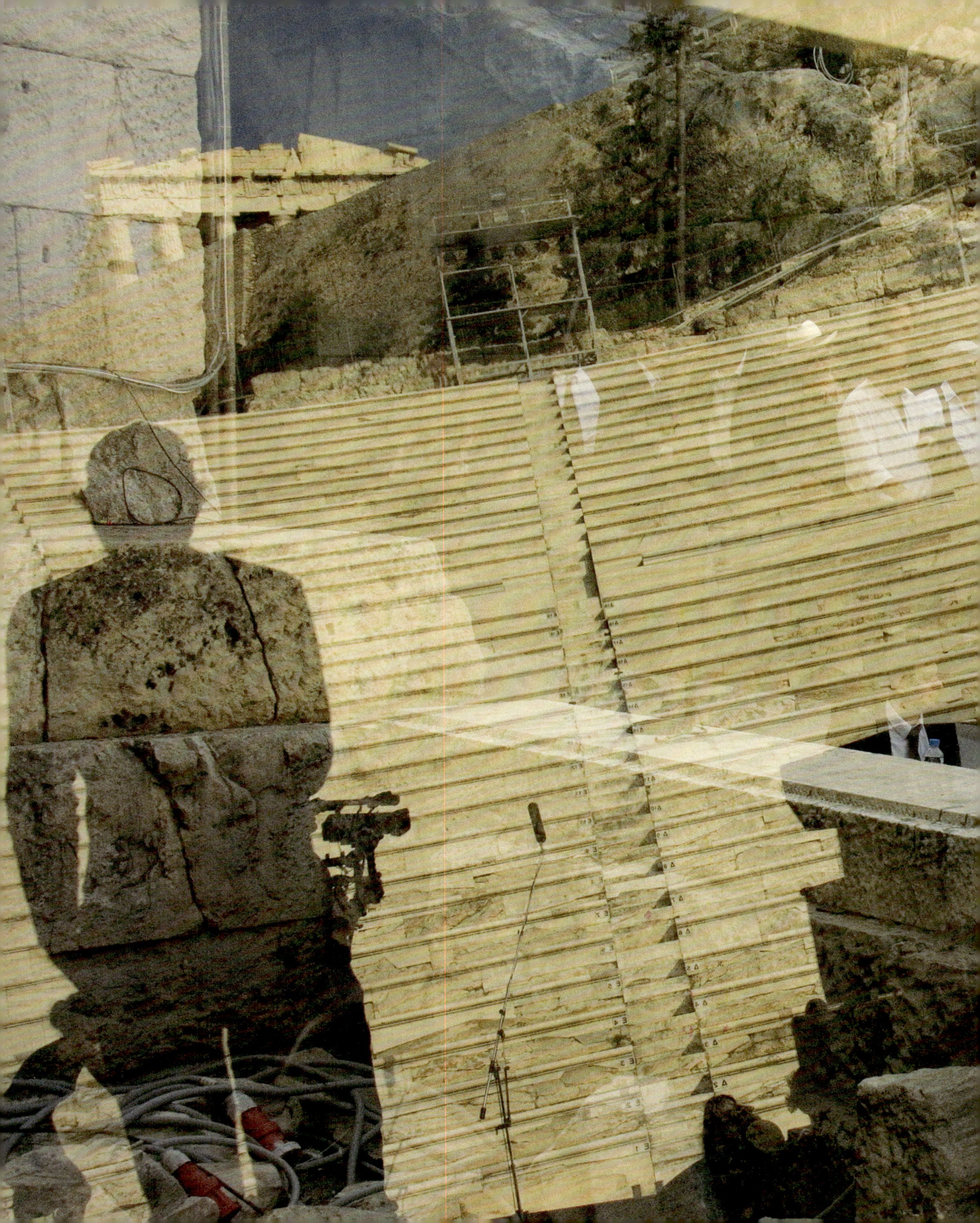

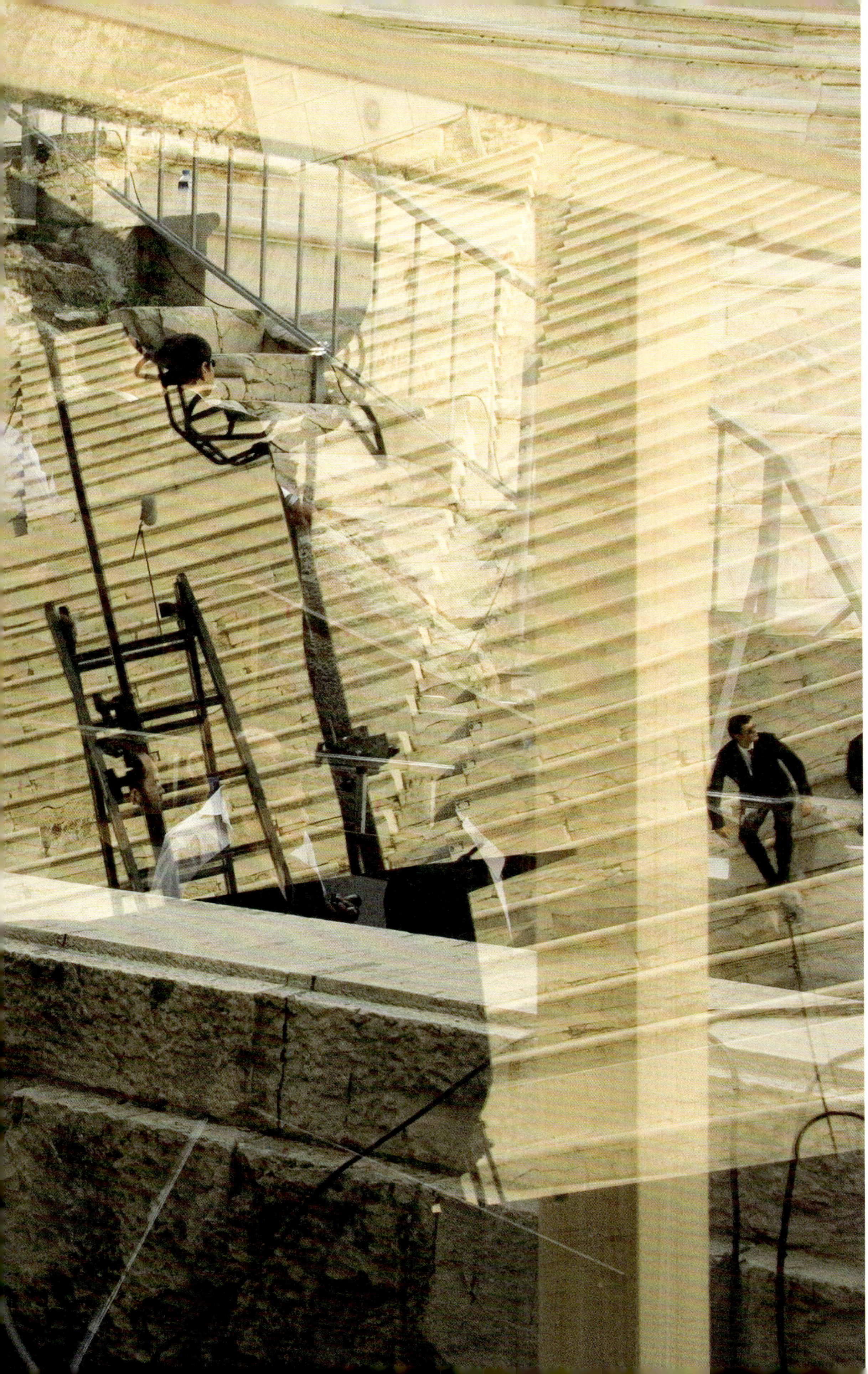